11 25

W9-BVA-962

MACCABEES, ZEALOTS, AND JOSEPHUS

MACCABEES, ZEALOTS, AND JOSEPHUS

An Inquiry into Jewish Nationalism
in the Greco-Roman Period

By WILLIAM REUBEN FARMER

DREW UNIVERSITY

GREENWOOD PRESS, PUBLISHERS
WESTPORT, CONNECTICUT

WINGATE COLLEGE LIBRARY
WINGATE, N. C.

Library of Congress Cataloging in Publication Data

Farmer, William Reuben.
  Maccabees, Zealots, and Josephus.

  Reprint of the ed. published by Columbia University
Press, New York.
  Bibliography: p.
  1. Jews--History--168 B. C. - 135 A. D. 2. Bible.
N. T.--History of contemporary events, etc. 3. Josephus
Flavius. 4. Nationalism--Jews. I. Title.
[DS109.912.F37 1974]   933   73-15052
ISBN 0-8371-7152-0

Copyright © 1956 Columbia University Press

Originally published in 1956 by Columbia University Press,
New York

Reprinted with the permission of Columbia University Press

Reprinted in 1973 by Greenwood Press,
a division of Williamhouse-Regency Inc.

Library of Congress Catalogue Card Number 73-15052

ISBN 0-8371-7152-0

Printed in the United States of America

TO C. H. DODD
AND
MEMBERS OF HIS
NEW TESTAMENT SEMINAR
CAMBRIDGE 1948–49

61087

PREFACE

This book is the result of an idea. That idea is that there is a positive relationship between the Maccabees and the Zealots. Josephus comes into the picture because he asserts the contrary, i.e., the Zealots began *de novo*, having no connection with the Maccabees.

How was the idea first conceived in the mind of the author and how did he come to write a book about it? It all began in one of Professor C. H. Dodd's New Testament seminars on the Fourth Gospel in Cambridge in 1949. The passage under discussion was the triumphal entry. Someone raised the question why John's account included a reference to palm branches. There flashed before my mind's eye the image of an oriental monarch seated in majestic splendor, being cooled by slaves waving huge fan-shaped palm branches. One train of thought led to another and I wondered whether the palm branches could have been symbols of royalty.

Later, as I was in the process of checking this possibility, I stumbled upon another. For in the course of looking up information on the use of palm branches in the ancient world, I noted that they were used in the triumphal processions into the temple by Judas and Simon Maccabeus. The parallels between these triumphal processions and the triumphal entry of Jesus seemed worthy of further attention, and so I read on. I was struck with the Maccabees' concern for cleansing the temple as a loose but significant parallel to Jesus cleansing the temple. When I found that these parallels were not cited in the New Testament commentaries, I was stimulated to dig deeper. I pored over I and II Maccabees to see what else I could learn. Finally, some one put me on to Josephus to find out what had happened between the time of the Maccabees and the New Testament period.

It was while I was reading Josephus that the light began to dawn and that the idea which has inspired this book was born. As I was reading his description of the events leading up to the outbreak of war between the Jews and the Romans, I found myself following the activities of Josephus' Fourth Philosophical Sect, his brigands, his seditious, his Sicarii, and his Zealots and thinking that these people were doing and saying the same kind of things that the Maccabees had done and said. Then I noticed how frequently the leaders of seditious activity against Rome bore the same names as the early Maccabees—Mattathias, Judas, John, Eleazar, Jonathan, and Simon. The inference was irresistible. There must have been some kind of positive connection between these patriots of the Roman period and the earlier Maccabees.

This thrilling first venture into the realm of biblical research culminated in a paper which was read before Professor Dodd's seminar and which after significant revision was subsequently published as a note in the April, 1952, issue of the *Journal of Theological Studies*.

For the next three years this one idea was to dominate my life, and those who knew me during that period must have often wondered whether I would ever recover from a severe case of what my wife affectionately termed "Maccabitis." In 1952 I submitted a doctoral dissertation on this subject to the Faculty of Union Theological Seminary. The substance of that piece of research is contained in this book, though the whole has been revised, some material having been added, some condensed, and some omitted.

Since 1952 the Dead Sea Scrolls have come to dominate the scene of biblical studies and have focused the attention of scholars upon the same period of Jewish history covered in this book. For this reason alone it seems timely to publish the results of my research. Moreover, there seems to be a growing willingness on the part of New Testament scholars to take a fresh look at the historical Jesus. I have been particularly impressed with the way in which scholars like Oscar Cullmann and Amos Wilder in recent works have shown a readiness to see Jesus against a realistic religiopolitical background.[1] If this marks a new trend in New Testament scholarship, then this book should prove very timely indeed. For in determining the relationship between Jesus and the Jewish patriots (or Zealots) of his day, it is a matter of the greatest importance to know whether those patriots were secularly motivated, as Josephus portrays them, or religiously motivated, like the Maccabees before them.

If the reader desires to taste some of the fruit of this study before he plows through the main sections of the book, let him turn directly to Chapter VIII, where he will find certain suggestions which have occurred to me concerning the implications of this work for New Testament studies. It must be emphasized that the views expressed in this chapter are in no sense final. They are intended to do no more than indicate the kind of new insight into old problems which may come once one begins to look at the Gospel records from the point of view that Jewish nationalism in the New Testament period was deeply motivated by Jewish piety. It should be added that the importance of this book does not depend upon the persuasiveness of the sug-

[1] Oscar Cullmann, *The State in the New Testament;* Amos Wilder, *Otherworldiness and the New Testament.*

gestions made in Chapter VIII (others may be prepared to
make better suggestions) but upon the persuasiveness of
Chapters IV, V, and VI.

Chapters I, II, and III state the case and prepare the
reader to hear the evidence. Chapters IV, V, and VI argue
the case. Chapter VII deals with the bearing of the Dead
Sea Scrolls upon the subject under discussion, and Chapter
VIII seeks to open up some of the possible implications of
the book for New Testament studies.

While this book has been written with New Testament
scholars in mind, I have not been unmindful of the fact
that it will be of general interest to Jewish scholars as well,
and I sincerely hope that it will be received by them as a
labor of love in the Lord's vineyard inspired only by a concern for truth and motivated by no conscious bias other
than that which may grow out of a sympathetic identification of the author with the Jewish nation in its struggle for
survival against great world empires. One would have to be
callous indeed not to respond to the heroic dimensions of
this struggle whatever his ultimate judgment upon its
meaning might be. I have not sought to make any ultimate judgment in this book. One day I hope to write an
account of the struggle in which I may venture to do this
from the perspective of my own tradition. Meanwhile, I
should be very pleased if my work were to stir interest in
a reexamination of the origins, basic causes, and significance of the war with Rome. Such a reexamination could
conceivably provide a basis for new conversations between
Christians and Jews, since scholars are becoming increas-
ingly aware of the decisive effect which this war had upon
both the Church and the Synagogue.

In Cambridge, in addition to Professor C. H. Dodd other
members of his seminar to whom I am especially indebted
for helpful suggestions are the late Wilfred Knox, the late
S. A. Cook, Peter Katz, W. F. Flemington, J. Y. Campbell,

and David Daube. I also remember gratefully a student friend, Ernest Goodrich, who gave freely of his time and talent as a New Testament scholar.

At Union Theological Seminary, during a period of three years, Professors Fredrick C. Grant, John Knox, and James Muilenburg gave generously of their time and learning in helping me to formulate the idea I had brought from Cambridge into a convincing thesis. Each in his own way made an invaluable contribution. Whatever scholarly merit this book may have is in no small part due to their unsparing efforts in my behalf. Certainly, whatever defects it has cannot be laid to any failure of theirs to hold before me at all times the highest standards of critical achievement.

The courteous assistance of the staff of Union Theological Seminary library I gratefully acknowledge.

I especially wish to thank Mr. and Mrs. Carl Cochran, without whose kindly cooperation the publishing of this book would not have been possible.

Also I am deeply grateful to the Administration of Drew University and to my colleagues in the Bible Department of Drew Theological Seminary for the encouragement I have derived from the interest they have shown in the publication of my work.

Above all, the patience, understanding, and helpfulness of my wife has been indispensable to the successful completion of my task.

WILLIAM R. FARMER

Drew University
Madison, New Jersey
May, 1956

CONTENTS

PART ONE

THE PROBLEM

I: INTRODUCTION

Josephus opens the preface to his *Bellum Judaicum* with a reference to the war of the Jews against the Romans as "the greatest not only of the wars of our own time, but so far as accounts have reached us, well nigh of all that ever broke out between cities or nations."[1]

According to Dionysius of Halicarnassus one of the essential first principles of historical writing was to choose a good subject of a lofty character which would be profitable to the reader.[2] Even without the explicit words of Josephus, quoted above, no more than a cursory reading of *Bellum Judaicum* is needed to see that its author abided by this principle.

Another of Dionysius' principles was that an historian was under obligation to devote the utmost care and industry to the task of providing himself with proper sources for his compositions.[3] James T. Shotwell, referring to the eighteenth and nineteenth books of the *Antiquitates Judaicae,* has written: "Especially valuable are the many documents dealing with the legal position of the Jews in the Empire. This represents the nearest approach to systematic archival research which the ancient world af-

---

[1] *B.J.* 1.1 (1), translation by H. St. John Thackeray in the Loeb Classical Library edition of Josephus, II, 3.
[2] *Ancient History of Rome,* Book I, Chap. i.
[3] *Ibid.*

fords."[4] Josephus not only took care and showed industry in providing himself with proper sources for the history of his own times; he also preserved in his writings many important fragments, which otherwise would be lost to us, from the works of earlier historians.[5]

Furthermore, in his *Bellum Judaicum* Josephus fulfilled that ancient requirement of historiography preserved for us in the writings of Diodorus of Sicily, viz., that historians should aim at embracing in their histories such series of events as are self-contained from beginning to end.[6] Why Josephus took the trouble to go back two and one half centuries to start his history of the Judaeo-Roman war with an account of the Judaeo-Seleucid war and yet failed to draw explicit attention to the connection between these two wars we shall consider in some detail as the argument of this book unfolds. At this point we need only note that there is real continuity of action between these two wars and that, with the intervening events, they do provide us with a self-contained unity.

The evidence that Josephus was acquainted with and sensitive to the highest standards of ancient historiography is sufficient to convince any serious reader of the importance of this historian's work. In the judgment of Shotwell, "he was one of the eight or ten great historians of the ancient world."[7]

For over fifteen centuries the works of Josephus enjoyed immense popularity among Christians, to whom in fact goes the credit for having preserved his writings. However, Josephus began to fall into disfavor when, with the rise of critical studies, doubt was cast upon the authenticity of

[4] *A History of History*, p. 150.
[5] E.g., Ephoros, Polybius, Nicolaus of Damascus, Strabo.
[6] Book XVI, Chap. i.
[7] *A History of History*, p. 153. Toynbee lists Josephus along with Herodotus, Thucydides, Xenophon, and Polybius among the five greatest figures in Hellenic historical writing. *Greek Historical Thought*, p. xi.

the passages referring to Jesus Christ. It has been over sixty years since Professor Emil Schürer observed that modern criticism of the works of Josephus had run from the naive appreciation of the precritical period "to the precisely opposite extreme of depreciation." Schürer predicted that scholarship would probably recognize "that the truth lies midway between these extremes."[8] This prediction has come true at least to the extent that it is no longer fashionable for writers to indulge in the negative criticism which finds its primary motivation in personal dislike for Josephus or in theological animosity toward his works. Yet on the whole the balance has not been redressed. The very neglect of the works of this great historian in our day is a silent witness to the fact that his works still suffer from the unjustified stigma placed upon them by nineteenth-century critics.

Yet however much one may deprecate the indiscriminate disparagement of Josephus, and however sympathetic one may be with the kind of passionate defense of him offered by Leon Bernstein,[9] the need for careful analysis of certain aspects of Josephus' account of the Judaeo-Roman war remains. Even the most objective critics have noted a certain distortion in Josephus' picture of the leaders of the revolt.[10] He himself indirectly acknowledged a lack of objectivity in his attitude toward the seditious elements in his preface to *Bellum Judaicum*:

Should, however, any critic censure me for my strictures upon the tyrants or their bands of marauders or for my lamentations over my country's misfortunes, I ask his indulgence for a compassion which is contrary to the law of history. For of all the cities under Roman rule it was the lot of ours to attain to the

8 E. Schürer, *Geschichte des jüdischen Volkes*, I, 93 (English translation, *A History of the Jewish People in the Time of Jesus Christ*, Part I, I, 97).

9 *Flavius Josephus, His Time and His Critics* (New York, 1938).

10 E.g., Schürer, *Geschichte des jüdischen Volkes*, I, 94 (English tr., Part I, I, 98).

highest felicity and to fall to the lowest depths of calamity. Indeed, in my opinion, the misfortunes of all the nations since the world began fall short of those of the Jews; and since the blame lay with no foreign nation, it was impossible to restrain one's grief. Should, however, any critic be too austere for pity, let him credit the history with the facts, and the historian with the lamentations.[11]

One way of stating the thesis of this book would be to say that those Jews who led the revolt against Rome were probably neither simply the "children of darkness," as Josephus and writers like Bernstein have made them out to be, nor unambiguously the "children of light," as many critics of Josephus would have us believe. Their nearest counterparts were, as we shall seek to establish, the early Maccabees. More specifically it is our purpose to establish the view that on the whole the same fundamental motives operative in the religio-nationalistic uprising of the Jews against the Seleucids in the second century B.C. also lay behind the revolt against the Romans in the first century A.D.

The importance of this thesis for New Testament studies is evident once it is realized that, with the exception of *Megillath Taanith* and possibly the *Assumption of Moses*, we have no literary remains from the hands of those who fought and died in their desperate struggle against the legions of the Roman Empire.[12] It is the victors who write histories. These Jews lost their fight; therefore we should not be surprised that we have no picture of it from their point of view. If we had such a picture, it would certainly be different in important respects from the account given

---

11 *B.J.* Preface 1.4 (11–12).

12 Solomon Zeitlin, *Megillat Taanit, as a Source for Jewish Chronology and History in the Hellenistic and Roman Periods,* pp. viii, 3–4. As to the question of whether or not the *Assumption of Moses* is of Zealot authorship, such authorship was at first affirmed by Schürer and later denied. His earlier view is conveniently found in the English translation of the second edition of his *Geschichte,* Part II, II, 80. His later view is to be found in the untranslated fourth edition, III, 300. R. H. Charles denied Zealot authorship: *Apocrypha and Pseudepigrapha of the Old Testament,* II, 411.

us by Josephus.[13] Allowing for distortions in both pictures, we might then draw one of our own which at least in some respects would be more true to the facts. A more reliable picture than we now have of those extreme religio-nationalistic elements, were such a one possible, would be of tremendous value to the student who seeks to understand most fully the background of the New Testament period.

The importance of a proper understanding of the war and of the Jewish nationalism of the prewar period for New Testament studies is threefold. In the first place, the events leading up to and culminating in the ministry of Jesus belong to that stream of Jewish history which flows turbulently between the momentous victory over the Seleucids and the catastrophic defeat at the hands of the Romans. That ministry must have been relevant to the collective needs and hopes of the Jewish people; a people who, while living under the wings (and talons) of the Roman eagle, would be reminded of their glorious victories over the Seleucids and would look to the future with both hope and fear for a time of redemption.

Secondly, the gospel tradition in large part reached its final form after the cataclysmic events of A.D. 66–70. The gradual formation of the gospel tradition was to some extent the result of a process of selection and interpretation of those events in the ministry of Jesus which were remembered by those who believed in him. This continuous proc-

[13] Elias Bickermann has made a similar observation with reference to the defeated Jewish party of Menelaus in the Maccabean period: "Weder die seleukidische noch die jüdische Überlieferung lässt die verhasste und besiegte Partei des Menelaos zu Wort kommen" ("Neither the Seleucid nor the Jewish tradition allowed the hated and defeated party of Menelaus to speak for itself"). *Der Gott der Makkabäer*, p. 127. Our thesis, therefore, is not only of importance for N.T. studies; it is also of significance for the Maccabean period. Bickermann has gone to the Jewish reform movement of the nineteenth century to find parallels to the hellenizing party in the Maccabean period. *Ibid.*, p. 132. But the writings of Josephus give us insights into the motives and mind of a hellenistic Jewish leader who stands temporally, geographically, culturally, and personally much closer to the Maccabean period.

ess inevitably involved some omission and reinterpretation according to the changing needs and hopes of the primitive church. These needs and hopes could not have been unrelated to the turbulent and catastrophic events in Palestine during the third quarter of the first century A.D.

Finally, a proper understanding of the war in all its ramifications can hardly help but throw some light on the earliest history of the church, not only in Palestine but also in the rest of the Greco-Roman world. This is true because the geographical expansion of the early church, as it is reflected in the New Testament, was largely coextensive with the Jewish dispersion in the West. And the writings of Josephus provide indisputable evidence that the significance and repercussions of the Judaeo-Roman war were not confined to the limits of Palestine but that, on the contrary, the question of Jewish nationalism was critical throughout the Greek-speaking part of the Empire and indeed in Rome itself.[14]

At present the discussion concerning the character and motivation of this Jewish nationalism of the first century A.D. has reached a stalemate; for we have only one picture at which to look, the one painted by Josephus. Since, aside from this picture, there seems to be no other criterion, we are reduced to private interpretation in which personal predilections tend to influence us either for or against Josephus. But the discussion can be resumed if our thesis is sound, viz., that the continuity of Jewish history between the time of Antiochus Epiphanes and that of Titus includes a positive relationship between the national religious forces operative within these two great uprisings. For the Jews won their war against the Seleucids, and like so many victors, they produced histories of the conflict; these have been

---

14 Furthermore, it continued to be critical for over half a century. The last religio-nationalistic uprising of the Jews occurred in A.D. 135, during the reign of Hadrian.

preserved to us, at least in part, in I and II Maccabees.[15] In these records we are provided with a sympathetic and favorable, if not highly glorified, portrait of those "by whose hands salvation was given to Israel."[16] This is just the kind of picture we need of the leaders of Israel's fight against the Romans—a self-portrait, so to say—in order to balance the hypercritical realism of Josephus.

If in both wars the same kind of forces were at work in forming the character of the national resistance, then the eyewitness accounts from the earlier period of national resistance (those drawn upon by the authors or by sources used by the authors of I and II Maccabees) should be set alongside the firsthand report from the later period (that found in the writings of Josephus). The earlier accounts, dominated by the Deuteronomic theodicy, favor the national resistance and regard it as a "holy war."[17] But the account of Josephus, strikingly congenial in important respects to the outlook of Isaiah of Jerusalem and more especially to that of Jeremiah,[18] is unsympathetic to nationalistic aspirations and regards the leaders of the Jewish forces as sinners, disobedient to the will of God.

We need both the earlier and later accounts if we are to form a truer picture than is given to us by either alone. The fact that the actual events which are reflected in these two pictures are separated in time by over two centuries need not present an insuperable obstacle to the historian who is careful to make every necessary allowance. It is the

---

[15] Some fragments from those histories may also have been preserved by Josephus in his *Bellum Judaicum*. See M. Abel, *Les Livres des Maccabées*, pp. xi-xv, where the problem is discussed and the relevant literature cited.

[16] I Macc. 5:62.

[17] See Gerhard von Rad, *Deuteronomium-Studien*, Part A, Section 4, on Deuteronomy and the Holy War, where he outlines the concept of the "holy war." There is hardly a single point there mentioned that cannot be duplicated from the accounts of the battles against the Seleucids given in I and II Maccabees.

[18] Cf. *B.J.* 4.9.4 (392); 6.2.1 (109-10).

same Israel, inspired by the same scriptures, worshiping the same jealous God. It is, on the whole, the same Hellenistic culture, syncretistic, polytheistic, universal and cosmopolitan, ever alluring yet ever threatening the pious Jew.[19] The idolatrous character of heathenism appeared much the same both to the author of Daniel and to the author of Fourth Ezra.[20]

One purpose of this book is to prepare the way for a further attempt to paint that truer picture of Jewish nationalism in the first century A.D. We are not justified in taking up our brushes until we have examined carefully all the evidence and know with reasonable certainty that there *is* some positive resemblance between the religious nationalism of the two wars.

We shall seek to show in the next chapter how Josephus may have obscured the otherwise obvious connection between the Jewish nationalism of the earlier and later periods.

[19] By the first century A.D., having destroyed the Hellenistic state system, Rome was "compelled to take its place as the standard-bearer of Greek culture." W. W. Tarn, *Hellenistic Civilization*, p. 2.

[20] F. C. Porter in *The Messages of the Apocalyptical Writers,* Introduction, p. 3, has observed that apocalypse began and ended the period of Jewish nationalism. He also noted the similarity between the role played by the Romans and that played by the Seleucids in the eyes of the apocalyptists. *Ibid.*, p. 10. Cf. James Stevenson Riggs, *History of the Jewish People during the Maccabean and Roman Periods*, p. 179; C. C. Torrey, *Documents of the Primitive Church*, pp. 22ff.; Robert H. Pfeiffer, *History of New Testament Times with an Introduction to the Apocrypha*, p. 56.

II: JOSEPHUS

We had occasion to say at the end of the preceding chapter that we would seek to show that Josephus may have obscured the obvious continuity between the Jewish nationalism of the second century B.C. and that of the first century A.D. But why, one might ask, is it thought that there is an obvious continuity between these two periods, when, after all, they are separated by more than a century? There are several reasons, which will be considered later, but most important of all is that the continuity is suggested by Josephus' own writings.

The histories of Josephus constitute for us the main source for our understanding of the Jewish nationalism of the first century A.D. If one reads Josephus' account of the Jewish uprising against the Seleucids in the time of Antiochus Epiphanes[1] and then turns to his record of the Jewish revolt against Rome in the first century A.D., one gains the impression that the two rebellions had much in common. The Jews in both periods seem to have been doing and saying the same kind of thing.

Nevertheless, in spite of this apparent kinship between the two periods of nationalistic upsurge, Josephus explicitly tells that the Jewish revolt against Rome began *de novo* after the banishment of Archelaus and during the procuratorship of Coponius (A.D. c.6–9).

[1] Which account corresponds essentially with that found in I and II Maccabees.

This apparent discrepancy in the writings of Josephus constitutes a major problem and raises two important questions. The first and more important question may be formulated as follows: Did the Jewish revolt against Rome have its primary source in the teachings of some new sect at the beginning of the first century A.D., or did it gain its fundamental impetus from age-old Jewish nationalism, a nationalism which in the Maccabean period reached heights never attained before or since by the Jews? A carefully documented answer to this question is the main purpose of this book.

A second and really subsidiary question is this: How can we best account for the discrepancy to which we have called attention? We shall attempt to account for it through our understanding of the circumstances under which Josephus wrote his histories. This second question is preliminary to the first because it is necessary to have some conception of the circumstances under which Josephus wrote before we can properly evaluate his conflicting evidence concerning the relationship between the two periods of nationalism under consideration.

The crucial passage in which Josephus deals with the question concerning the origin of the war of the Jews against Rome is found in *Ant.* 18.1.1 (1–10). There he writes that when Cyrenius was sent by Caesar to take a fiscal census of Syria and Judaea, the Jews were persuaded by the high priest Joazar to cease their initial opposition to the census. But a certain Judas and Zadok, a Pharisee, exhorted the Jews to oppose this as a further effort to enslave the nation. These men went further and encouraged active sedition. The nation, according to Josephus, became infected with the seditious madness which sprang from this source. One violent war followed another. The sedition at last increased to such a point that the Romans took the extreme measure of burning down the very temple of God.

Such were the consequences of this sedition, that the traditions of our fathers were altered in a new way, and so great a change was made, as added a mighty weight toward bringing all to destruction, which these men occasioned by their thus conspiring together, for Judas and Zadok, who excited a fourth philosophical sect among us, and had a great many followers therein, filled our civil government with tumults at present, and laid the foundations of our future miseries by this system of philosophy, which was previously unknown (τῷ ἀσυνήθει πρότερον φιλοσοφίας τοιᾶσδε . . . .), concerning which I will discourse a little and this the rather, because the younger sort, who were zealous for it, brought the public to destruction.[2]

Referring to this incident in the parallel passage in his *Bellum Judaicum*,[3] Josephus did not mention Zadok the Pharisee and wrote concerning Judas: "This man was a sophist who founded a sect of his own, having nothing in common with the others" (ἦν δ᾽ οὗτος σοφιστὴς ἰδίας αἱρέσεως οὐδὲν τοῖς ἄλλοις προσεοικώς).

Taken by themselves, the intent of these passages seems to be quite unambiguous. Josephus seems to say that the war of the Jews against the Romans had its beginning in the activities and teachings of a sect which had little or nothing in common either with what the Jews knew to be traditional doctrine or with the teachings of any contemporary party. Of course, Josephus, a page or so after this crucial passage in his *Antiquitates Judaicae*, makes certain conflicting statements. He tells his readers that this "fourth philosophical sect" held all things in common with the Pharisees, except that they had an inviolable attachment to liberty (ἐλευθέρου), and taught that God was to be their only ruler and lord. They also made light of dying, by whatsoever manner, and even refused to be influenced by the

---

[2] *Ant.* 18.1.1 (9–10). Cf. *B.J.* Preface 1.4 (10) where Josephus says that it was the Jewish tyrants who caused the unwilling Romans to burn down the temple.

[3] *B.J.* 2.8.1 (117–18).

WINGATE COLLEGE LIBRARY
WINGATE, N. C.

torture of their relations and friends to call any man lord.[4]
These exceptions, however, set forth attitudes which were
neither new nor strange for the Jews. The distinctive features of the sect, said to have originated with Judas of
Galilee, are precisely those for which the Maccabees were
remembered, as the Maccabean literature, and even Josephus himself, indicates.[5]

What we want to do is to find some kind of answer to the
question: How could Josephus make such apparently conflicting statements? We shall at this point confine ourselves
to the interpretation that Josephus gives of the origin of
the war of the Jews with Rome, since it is in the interpretation of facts, more than in their recording, that an historian
reveals his motives.

Josephus admits that there were other causes for the war
besides the influence of this "fourth philosophical sect."
For example, there was abuse of authority by the Roman
procurator Gessius Florus. This caused the Jews to go wild
with seditious madness.[6] But whatever the Romans did to
help bring on the war, Josephus is careful to make clear
that the responsibility rests ultimately upon the shoulders
of the seditious elements among the Jews.[7] According to his
account in the Preface to his *Bellum Judaicum,* it was internal sedition that destroyed the nation, and it was the

---

[4] *Ant.* 18.1.6 (23–24).

[5] "Judas Maccabaeus had been a man of valour and a great warrior . . .
and had undergone all difficulties, both in doing and suffering, for the
liberty (ἐλευθερίας) of his countrymen. And because his character was so
excellent, he left behind him a glorious reputation and memorial, by gaining freedom (ἐλευθερώσας) for his nation, and delivering them from
slavery under the Macedonians." *Ant.* 12.11.2 (433–34).

[6] *Ant.* 18.1.6 (25).

[7] *B.J.* Preface 1.4 (12). In his autobiography written later in life, Josephus
tends to qualify this position somewhat, for there he points out that circumstances were such "that the Jews' war with the Romans was not voluntary,
but in the main, they were forced by necessity to enter into it" (*Vita* 6 [27]).
But here he only wishes to draw attention to the relative innocence of the
Jews as a whole. He still regards the seditious innovators as chiefly to blame
for the war. *Vita* 4–6 (17–24).

tyrannical Jewish brigand element which brought the Roman arms against the people. Moreover, the Romans attacked the Jews quite unwillingly. Titus pitied the populace which was tyrannized by the seditious and several times voluntarily delayed taking Jerusalem in order to allow time for the authors of the revolt to repent.[8]

This interpretation of the war and its causes conforms closely to what we would expect from Josephus, a former Jewish rebel who, after his capture, had come over to the side of the Romans. He had also been personally befriended by Vespasian and Titus.[9] When Josephus came to Rome with Titus, Vespasian went so far as to honor him with the privileges of Roman citizenship and to give him an annual pension[10] which provided him with the necessary leisure and resources to write his histories.[11] Thus we can see that Josephus was heavily indebted to his Roman protectors and benefactors. His very name Flavius came to him by virtue of his close relationship to the Flavian imperial household. After the death of Vespasian and Titus the emperor Domitian and his wife Domitia continued to do kindnesses for the great Jewish historian.[12]

One way in which Josephus could show his gratitude toward his Roman friends and at the same time place his going over to the side of the Romans in the most favorable light, was so to write his history of the war as to make it clear that Rome had had a just cause in fighting the Jews, whose very defeat was in accord with the judgment of God.[13]

The question of who started a war was as important to the literate ancients as it is to us today.[14] Rome was just as

[8] *B.J.* Preface 1.4 (10–12). Cf. *B.J.* 5.9.3–4 (362–419).
[9] *B.J.* 4.10.7 (626–9); *Vita* 75 (414), 76 (424).
[10] *Vita* 76 (423).
[11] *Contra Apionem* 1.9 (50).
[12] *Vita* 76 (428–29).
[13] Cf. *B.J.* 5.9.4 (395, 412).
[14] Cf. *Vita* 5 (22).

anxious to avoid being charged with aggression as are the
great powers of the twentieth century. In some ways the
continuous battle to win the approval of public opinion
was as important for the securing of world dominion as
was any campaign carried out by the Roman legions.

Any one who looks into Josephus without seeking to
read between the lines gains the impression that Rome was
not responsible for starting the war. Under the influence
of the author the reader might even conclude that the destruction of the nation's temple was necessitated by the
perverse resistance of the people, though by Hellenistic
standards the violation of a sacred place, especially a temple, was a most shameful act. Whatever his intentions may
have been, Josephus was a very effective apologist for the
Romans.

Josephus, however, was not only pro-Roman but also in
his own way a strong apologist for the Jewish people. This
dual role might seem to be contradictory. But Josephus
was not the first great Hellenistic historian who, entering
the arena of public opinion, sought to serve his defeated
nation by defending and glorifying Rome and by interpreting Rome's victory over his native land as providential.
The illustrious Polybius, with whom Josephus had many
striking affinities, had set the example long before.

The war of the Jews against Rome may not have been
the greatest of which the public of the Empire had ever
heard, as Josephus claimed,[15] but it had been a terribly
costly war both in lives and in resources, and the victory
was not one taken lightly by Rome. Josephus' graphic account of the triumphal celebrations in the capital are evidence of this.[16] Moreover, we have the Arch of Titus, which
is a mute but eloquent witness to the same effect.[17]

15 *B.J.* Preface 1.1 (1).
16 *B.J.* 7.5.3–6 (116–157).
17 Cf. the two illustrations of the Arch of Titus in *The Legacy of Israel,*
edited by Edwyn R. Bevan and Charles Singer (Oxford, 1927), pp. 28, 432.

What was to happen to the defeated people? We know something about the conditions of the Jews in Palestine after the war.[18] Theirs was a terrible fate; that of the vanquished usually is. But what about the millions of Jews outside Palestine who were scattered all over the Empire? How was the defeat of the fatherland going to affect them? They were the beneficiaries of important privileges granted or sanctioned by the head of the Roman state. However, their claims to these privileges depended on their being faithful adherents of the Jewish religion, a religion which recognized one temple only, and that in Jerusalem. Jerusalem, however, was the very city known throughout the Empire as the center of the Jewish rebellion and the occasion of heavy casualties among the Roman legions. Were the Jews of the western *diaspora* to be held in any sense responsible for the rebellion in Palestine? Must they suffer on account of the revolt of their coreligionists?

These were no idle questions! We know that after the Roman victory in Palestine the people of Antioch and Alexandria urged Vespasian and Titus to deprive the Jews in their cities of certain ancient privileges. According to Josephus, it was the judgment of these Roman leaders that those who had borne arms against them had suffered punishment already, and that it was not just to deprive non-offenders of the privileges they enjoyed. But Josephus goes on to admit that this judgment was astonishingly generous and showed great moderation in view of all of the trouble to which the Jews had put the Romans.[19] We may be confident that if this were the policy of Vespasian and Titus, it was a policy which could well be opposed by the native populations of cities in which there were large Jewish com-

---

The latter illustration is reproduced from the engraving made by the artist Pietro Santo Bartoli in the seventeenth century and gives details which are now obliterated by ill usage.

[18] *B.J.* 7.5.2 (109, 112–13).
[19] *Ant.* 12.3.1–2 (121–24).

munities. Some of these cities had no doubt provided troops for the Roman legions fighting in Palestine,[20] and the heavy casualties which had been suffered in the fighting would have added to whatever resentments they might have already felt because of the special privileges granted to the Jews.

Among those who wrote about this great war for the reading public of the Empire, some flattered the Romans; others went further and gave free rein to the expression of their hatred toward the Jews.[21] Apparently no one dared to defend the Jews. The dangerous and difficult task of defending the Jews was undertaken, we suggest, by Josephus. In order to defend these Jews, however, he had to write his history of the war against Rome so as to show that the leaders of the revolt were not true Jews. He had to show that they were rebels not only against the Roman Empire but also against their own God and his holy religion.[22]

By contrast the true Jews had a long and respectable history.[23] Their national and religious origins went back earlier than those of the Greeks.[24] Alexander the Great had honored the Jewish religion while on a friendly visit to the temple in Jerusalem by offering sacrifice according to the directions of the high priest.[25] More important, when Rome first appeared in the East, the Jews allied themselves with her.[26] Julius Caesar had paid high honors to the Jewish nation,[27] and after his death the Romans continued to

[20] There is no doubt that Rome sometimes recruited troops from her eastern provinces and used these troops to put down rebellions in adjoining countries. Cf. *Ant.* 14.15.10 (449) and *B.J.* 1.17.1 (324), where Josephus says that the Roman regiments sent against Antigonus were in great part collected out of Syria.

[21] *B.J.* Preface 1.1 (2).

[22] *B.J.* 5.9.4 (424).

[23] *Ant.* 16.2.3 (44).

[24] *Contra Apionem* 1.1–5 (1–27).

[25] *Ant.* 11.8.5 (336).

[26] *B.J.* 1.1.4 (38); 1.2.1 (48); *Ant.* 13.7.3 (227). Cf. I Macc. 8:17–32; 12:1–4; 14:16–24, 40; 15:15–22.

[27] *Ant.* 14.10.1–8 (185–216).

treat the Jews with great respect.[28] Later, under Roman rule, Jerusalem, the chief city of the Jews, arrived at a higher degree of felicity than any other city in the Empire.[29] Then catastrophe struck. The Jewish nation became infected by a mad seditiousness which spread till full-scale war with Rome was inevitable. But apparently, according to Josephus, this seditiousness was so perverse that it had nothing in common with any past tradition of national independence, nor was it based on the scriptures of the Jews.[30] In the beginning, implies Josephus, this seditiousness had no contact with the temple in Jerusalem, though later the "robbers" dared to secure themselves in it and defile it by their presence.[31] The founder of the sect which started the sedition did not come from Jerusalem, the chief city of the Jews, but from Galilee.[32]

The defeat of the rebellious Jews of Palestine is represented by Josephus as both the judgment of God upon the seditious sinners and the divine approval of Roman dominion.[33] By placing this kind of interpretation upon the war, Josephus was able to serve his Roman masters and at the same time make a distinction between the great majority of his Greek-speaking brethren and their sinfully rebellious coreligionists in Palestine, a distinction that would serve to justify the continuation of imperial privileges to nonbelligerent Jews throughout the Empire.

We shall consider in a moment other reasons why Jose-

[28] *Ant.* 14.10.9–26 (217–67). Cf. *Ant.* 16.6.1 (160–78), where Josephus demonstrates that when the Jews of Asia and Africa were ill-treated by the local populations, the Romans responded by issuing decrees which guaranteed to the Jews those special privileges previously granted to them.

[29] *B.J.* Preface 1.4 (11).

[30] Cf. *B.J.* 5.9.4 (375–419), where Josephus, for the benefit of his readers, uses scripture to confute the rebellious Jews. For the average reader, unacquainted with the whole of the Jewish scriptures, this must have been quite convincing evidence that the revolt was not a true expression of the Jewish religion.

[31] *B.J.* 5.9.4 (402).

[32] *B.J.* 2.8.1 (118).

[33] *B.J.* 5.9.3 (367).

phus may have been led to obscure any possible connection between the national resistance against Rome and the tradition of national independence which had been stimulated by the achievements of the Maccabees. At this point it is sufficient for us to observe that his dual role as apologist for both the Romans and the Jews would have encouraged him to praise the Maccabees, who had been allies of Rome, while simultaneously blaming those Jews who had brought catastrophe upon his people by their revolt against Rome. To admit that there was any kind of positive relationship between the two periods of Jewish nationalism would have increased his difficulty in persuading the Roman public that the revolt was not a true expression of the Jewish religion. We suggest that in part it was for this reason that Josephus purposively obscured the connection between the fourth philosophical sect (so called) and earlier Jewish nationalism.

Aside from these considerations of politics and apologetics there were theological grounds on which Josephus with good reason could conclude that all the similarities between the Maccabees and the seditious elements in his own day were purely superficial compared with the fundamental differences between the two groups. The victory of the Maccabees over the Seleucids, in the view of Josephus, was proof that in those days the Jews were led by pious men,[34] but the defeat of the Jews by the Roman legions apparently was regarded by him as evidence that God did not approve of the nation's rebellion against Rome,[35] and consequently that the seditious were sinners.[36] If the

[34] Cf. *Ant.* 12.7.1 (290), where Josephus, apparently with approval, quotes Judas Maccabaeus as having said in effect that victory comes in the exercise of piety toward God. See also *Ant.* 12.6.1-2 (267-71), where Josephus points out that the Maccabean revolt had its origin in zeal for God's law.

[35] In fact, Josephus was able to see in the elevation of Vespasian, who was appointed emperor while he was in Judea, the fulfillment of a scriptural oracle foretelling the coming of one from Judea who would govern the whole of the inhabited earth. *B.J.* 6.5.4 (312-13).

[36] Cf. *B.J.* 4.6.3 (386-88), where Josephus describes the seditious as holding

Maccabees were praiseworthy, pious Jews while the leaders
of the revolt against Rome were blameworthy sinners, obviously there could be no fundamental similarity between
them. The former were no doubt motivated by their zeal
for the traditions of their country and the worship of God,[37]
while the latter were mainly influenced by their own selfish
desire for gain.[38] Thus we see that for theological reasons
Josephus might have been influenced to obscure any apparent connection between the two groups.

Finally, there were important personal considerations
which might have blinded Josephus to a possible identity
of spirit between the Maccabees and the leaders of the
Jews' revolt against Rome. Josephus was of noble parentage
and evidently quite proud of his blood kinship with the
royal Hasmonean house.[39] In his description of the feats of
the early Maccabean heroes, his accounts are no less generous than those of I and II Maccabees. As he records the
history during the period when the Hasmoneans gradually
lost power, he notes that it was civil strife which gave occasion for Roman intervention. Yet he seems to be genuinely
concerned to paint a fair and even favorable picture of
these last reigning descendants of the heroic Maccabees.
According to his account, even after control of the state
had passed over into the hands of the Roman-supported
Herodians, the reappearance on the Jewish political scene
of one with royal Hasmonean blood in his veins was the
occasion for a wild and spontaneous manifestation of popular support.[40]

It was only natural that Josephus would be extremely
proud of the marvelous achievements of his illustrious

God's law in ridicule, and their sins as the occasion for the fulfillment of a
prophetic oracle to the effect that Jerusalem would be taken and the sanctuary burned.

[37] Cf. *Ant.* 12.6.2 (271).
[38] Cf. *Ant.* 18.1.1 (7).
[39] *B.J.* 5.9.4 (419); *Vita* 1 (1–6).
[40] Cf. *Ant.* 15.3.3 (51–52); 17.12.1 (330).

forefathers, the early Maccabees. For that very reason it would have been difficult for him to admit that there was any positive resemblance between the Maccabees and the leaders of the revolt against Rome. To have done so would have been tantamount to the admission that not he, but his most bitter enemies, were the true spiritual heirs of the Maccabean heroes.

We noted at the beginning of this chapter that there was a certain discrepancy in the writings of Josephus. On the one hand, the Jewish revolt against Rome as described by Josephus seems to have had much in common with the Maccabean uprising against the Seleucids. Yet, on the other hand, Josephus quite explicitly informs his readers that the revolt against Rome originated in a new party which had no connection with earlier Jewish nationalism. It would seem that the most plausible way in which to account for this discrepancy in the writings of Josephus is to say that above all he was concerned with writing true history,[41] and in so doing he set down in the best tradition of ancient historiography what was said and what was done by the respective parties in the conflict. Thus he has given us a reliable account of the teaching and actions of the seditious elements. But when it came to his interpretation of the origin, meaning, and consequences of events leading up to the war, then certain political, theological, and personal factors led him to obscure the true nature and origins of Jewish nationalism in the first century A.D. Thus we may account for the discrepancy noted if we recognize that Josephus wrote in two capacities. First and foremost he functioned as an historian for the ages. But at many points he functioned also as a propagandist for his own times. This, we suggest, is the reason the facts as he sets them down often dispute the interpretation he places upon them. Perhaps we may put it this way: Josephus was too honest as an historian to be completely consistent as a propagandist.

[41] *B.J.* Preface 1.12 (30); *Ant.* Preface 1 (4); *Contra Apionem* 1.9 (47).

But we need to realize that in any analysis of motivation we are necessarily involved in dealing with the mysterious and intangible forces of a human soul. Therefore all conclusions based upon such an analysis as this must be held to be highly tentative. None the less, the purpose of this chapter has been served if the reader has gained some insight into the circumstances under which Josephus wrote his histories and if he is now prepared to go on to consider the more fundamental question: Was there any positive connection between the Jewish nationalism of the first century A.D. and that of the second century B.C.?

But before we undertake the major task of answering this question it will be profitable to survey briefly some of the literature dealing with the history of the Jews in the Greco-Roman period, in order to ascertain the extent to which previous authors have recognized and dealt with the problem which concerns us.

III: MODERN LITERATURE

As we might expect, those who wrote during the eighteenth century about the ancient history of the Jews tended to follow the accounts of Josephus uncritically.[1] This tendency continued among some historians even into the nineteenth century.[2] Josephus exalted the Maccabees and condemned the Zealots.[3] These writers do the same.

But by the middle of the nineteenth century the attitude toward the histories of Josephus began to change radically. The work of Jost, Salvadore, and Kitto, who attacked the reliability of Josephus' accounts as well as his character,[4] served to emancipate authors from a literal dependence

[1] E.g., Laurence Echard, *A General Ecclesiastical History from the Nativity of our Blessed Saviour to the First Establishment of Christianity by Human Laws under the Emperour Constantine the Great . . . With so much of the Jewish and Roman History as Is Necessary and Convenient to Illustrate the Work* (London, 1702), pp. 41ff.; Ludwig Holberg, *Jüdische Geschichte* (Flensburg, 1747; trans. from the Danish into German by Auguste Detharding), Part II, pp. 185–86; James Home, *The Scripture History of the Jews and Their Republick* (London, 1737), pp. 251ff.

[2] E.g., John Jahn, *A History of the Hebrew Commonwealth* (Andover, 1828; trans. from the German into English by Calvin E. Stowe), pp. 421ff.; Archibald Alexander, *A History of the Israelitish Nation* (Philadelphia, 1853), pp. 588ff.; Joseph Henry Allen, *Hebrew Men and Times* (Boston, 1861), p. 383.

[3] I am aware that the name *Zealot* was used by Josephus to refer to only one of the revolutionary parties participating in the war against Rome in A.D. 66–70. However, the name *Zealot* is used in a much wider sense to refer to those who actively resisted Rome, and more especially to the party of Judas of Galilee, by all writers until quite recent times. Therefore, in this chapter, the name shall be used more loosely than it was by Josephus.

[4] Cf. Leon Bernstein, *Josephus, His Time and His Critics*, pp. 288–95.

upon his writings. Both Ewald[5] and Graetz[6] are remarkably free in their use of Josephus as a source for their histories. These historians see clearly that the nationalism of the first century A.D. had its roots in the earlier political and religious history of Israel. They reverse the portrait which Josephus has painted of the Zealots. Instead of "brigands," the Zealots are portrayed as "patriots." As Jewish patriots they are religiously motivated, and their opposition to Rome is grounded in their zeal for the Law.

This view has prevailed among a large number of scholars until the present day. Many writers have noted the close resemblance between the Maccabees and the Zealots— particularly Judas of Galilee, the founder of the "fourth philosophical sect."[7]

Some authors have noted a close resemblance between the Seleucids and the Romans and have pointed out that they played a similar if not identical role in the conflict between Judaism and Hellenism.[8]

Sometimes, though the resemblances between the Maccabees and the Zealots is acknowledged, certain alleged differences are pointed out. So it has been said that in the Roman period the national character of the Jews was changed for the worse; Rome's power was much greater

[5] Heinrich Ewald, Geschichte des Volkes Israel (Göttingen, 1847). See 3d ed. (1867), V, 69 (Eng. trans., The History of Israel, VI, 51).

[6] Heinrich Graetz, Geschichte der Juden (Leipzig, 1856). See 2d ed. (1863), III, 208 (Eng. trans., History of the Jews, II, 133).

[7] Morris J. Raphall, Post-Biblical History of the Jews (Philadelphia, 1855), pp. 364–65; E. H. Palmer, A History of the Jewish Nation (London, 1874), p. 170; Elizabeth Latimer, Judea From Cyrus to Titus, 2d ed. (Chicago, 1900), p. 257; A. Hausrath, Neutestamentliche Zeitgeschichte, 2d ed., (Heidelberg, 1873), I, 297; Lady Katie Magnus, Outlines of Jewish History, 2d revised ed. (Philadelphia, 1890), p. 49; Oskar Holtzmann, Geschichte des Volkes Israel (Berlin, 1888), Vol. II, Part 2, pp. 511–12, published under name of Bernhard Stade; Arthur Penrhyn Stanley, Lectures on the History of the Jewish Church, new ed. (New York, 1893), III, 411; James Stevenson Riggs, History of the Jewish People during the Maccabean and Roman Periods (New York, 1900), pp. 248–49.

[8] See references in footnote 20 of Chap. 1.

than that of the Seleucids; the God who had given the Jews
victory over the Seleucids was about to abandon them in
their war against the Romans.[9]

Of these so-called differences the extreme nationalists
of the first century A.D. would have been inclined to acknowledge only one. That concerned the greater power of
the Romans as compared with the Seleucids. But precisely
here the example of the Maccabees would have given them
courage. After all, the difference between the Seleucids and
the Romans was relatively small compared to the tremendous difference between the tiny hosts of Israel and the
armies of either of the great world empires. Because of their
zeal for the Law, God had given his people victory over the
armies of Antiochus Epiphanes. If they were zealous for his
Law now, surely he would give his people victory over the
armies of Caesar also! Later writers saw quite clearly this
relevance of the Maccabees for the Jews of the Roman
period.

For example, in 1884 the German author, L. Seinecke,
was able to see the vast difference between the power of
Rome and that of the Seleucids. Yet he observes: "The
Zealots often enough might have pointed to the small host
of the Maccabees, which, nevertheless, accomplished a reso-
lute resistance against a world power."[10] Seinecke, like
Hausrath before him, identifies the sect founded by Judas
and Zadok as the "neo-Maccabean" party.[11]

The year before Seinecke published the above-mentioned
work, Alfred Edersheim produced the first edition of his
Life and Times of Jesus the Messiah, which proved to be
so popular as to run through eight editions during the next
twenty years. For him the so-called "fourth philosophical
sect" was made up of "Nationalists." This party "was in

[9] See Henry Hart Milman, The History of the Jews, reprinted from the
newly revised and corrected London edition (New York, 1875), II, 125.
[10] Geschichte des Volkes Israel (Göttingen, 1884), Part 2, p. 220.
[11] Ibid.

fact a revival of the Maccabean movement, perhaps more fully in its national than its religious aspect, although the two could scarcely be separated in Israel."[12] It is doubtful if a more categorical repudiation of Josephus' account could be made, yet Edersheim says not a word about the witness of his primary source at this point. If "in fact" the party of Judas the Galilean was "a revival of the Maccabean movement," why did not Josephus bring this point out? Edersheim is the last great figure to stand in the tradition of Ewald and Graetz, a tradition in which authors seldom assumed the responsibility of justifying even the most radical divergencies between their own reconstructions and the witness of their primary source, especially if that source happened to be the discredited historian, Josephus. However, at the same time that Edersheim's popular work was going through its several new editions, Emil Schürer's published works were gaining a firm and respected reputation within scholarly circles. Schürer's magnum opus is still considered by many scholars as the definitive work in the field. We shall have occasion to say more about Schürer later in our survey. At this point it is necessary only to note that with him a new day was beginning to dawn for the writing of Jewish history, a day in which scholars began more and more to take Josephus' accounts seriously, and therefore, a day in which writers were both more cautious in affirming a connection between the Maccabees and the Jewish nationalism of the first century A.D., and at the same time concerned, to some degree, with the discrepancies in the writings of Josephus.

In 1893 Arthur Penrhyn Stanley, distinguished Dean of Westminster and influential friend of Queen Victoria, published his famous *Lectures on the History of the Jewish Church*. Taken as a whole, this history is long since dated. But for the period with which we are concerned, it still

[12] 8th ed., revised (New York, 1903), I, 237.

makes very rewarding reading—provided, that is, one does not mind looking at Galilee through the eyes of a romantic lover of the British highlands.

[Galilee] . . . that border-land of Jew and Gentile, where the hardy and secluded habits of the peasants and foresters kept them pure from the influence of the controversies and corruptions of the capital, where the precipitous and cavernous glens furnished inaccessible retreats, where the crowded population of artisans and fishermen along the shores of the Lake of Gennesareth teems with concentrated energy. There were born and bred Hezekiah and his gallant band whom Herod treated as robbers. . . . There was nurtured his son Judas, of Galilee . . . who, in the same cause, "calling none master save God alone," died a death of torture, and was believed to be enrolled amongst "the just men made perfect." There were, still continuing the same heroic cause, his sons, James and Simon, who suffered for their revolt on the cross. In the craggy sides of the romantic dell of Arbela . . . took refuge the band, whom Herod extirpated by letting down his soldiers in baskets over the cliff-side and kindling fires at the entrance of the caverns. Robbers, it may be, but, like the Maccabean patriots who had occupied the same hiding places before, and the troops of the insurgents later, they numbered amongst them that fine old man who, like the mother of the Maccabean martyrs, stood at the mouth of the cave . . . rather than submit to Herod . . . slew one by one his seven sons and their mother, and then flung himself over the precipice. . . .[13]

One of the most startling assertions that will be found in this survey comes from the pen of Stanley. In connection with an observation he has made relative to the Herodian period, he writes: "The famous apostolic names of the coming history were inherited from the enduring interest in the Maccabean family—John, and Judas, and Simon, and Matthias or Mattathias."[14] When we realize that among the disciples of Jesus, there were at least two Simons

---

[13] New ed. (New York, 1893), III, 411.
[14] *Ibid.*, p. 378.

and two Judases, the significance of the assertion that these names witnessed to an enduring interest in the Maccabean family becomes apparent at once.

About the same time that Stanley was publishing his lectures, across the Channel the renowned German scholar Julius Wellhausen referred to the party founded by Judas and Zadok as "die theokratische Actionspartei." Wellhausen adds significantly, "They esteemed patriotism more highly than the Law."[15]

Wellhausen's judgment that this "theocratic action party," which like the Maccabees orientated its piety politically, put patriotism before the Law, is very interesting. It suggests that there was a note of secular patriotism that had entered into the aims and program of this otherwise religious party. From whom are the Zealots more likely to have obtained the example for this secular patriotism than from the Maccabees? Whatever may have been in the mind of Wellhausen, we find later writers who draw exactly this conclusion. Thus, Herbert L. Willett, in a popular history, wrote thirty-odd years later with reference to the Zealots: "Led on by such men as Zadok the Pharisee and Judas the Galilean they joined the sanctions of religion to the practical aims of the early Maccabees in a combination of apocalyptic hope and patriotic passion."[16] Here we see the complete reversal of the value judgments of Josephus, for whom the early Maccabees were exemplars of piety whose patriotism was not pragmatically grounded but wholly motivated by zeal for the Law.

Some authors have seen the Maccabean war and the war of the Jews against Rome as two coequal episodes in the same dramatic struggle between Hebraism and paganism. Thus Norman Bentwich at the outbreak of the First World War wrote: "The war against the Romans was then not

[15] *Israelitische und jüdische Geschichte,* 3d ed. (Berlin, 1897), p. 346.
[16] *The Jew through the Centuries* (Chicago, 1932), p. 263-64.

merely a struggle for national liberty, but, equally with the wars of the Maccabees against the Seleucids, an episode in the more vital conflict between Hebraism and paganism."[17] To make this equation between the two great wars is tantamount to the assertion that the nationalism of both periods had much in common. Strange as it may seem, even in a book devoted to the study of Josephus, the author never mentions the fact that the great Jewish historian makes some very explicit statements diametrically opposed to the view he is putting forth.

Other authors have made the connection between the Maccabees and the Zealots so explicit as to leave no doubt that in their view there was some positive relationship between the nationalistic uprisings in the two periods. Hausrath and Seinecke had identified the sect founded by Judas and Zadok as the "Neo-Maccabean" party. Another German scholar, C. F. Lehmann-Haupt, in 1911 wrote: "Judas [the Galilean] became the progenitor of the new 'Maccabees,' his sons and grandson the leaders of the later resistance against Roman rule.[18]

The Italian scholar, Giuseppe Ricciotti, writing in 1941, has made the most categorical statement of all: "Now the Zealots revived in full the program of the father of the Maccabees."[19] However, Ricciotti fails to give any evidence to support this statement, except to point out that both the Zealots and the Maccabees were nationalists with religious motivation. Where does Ricciotti turn to find his evidence that the Zealots were motivated by religion? He turns directly to the man responsible for the view that they were secularly motivated. He turns to Josephus. In so doing he deals with that basic discrepancy in the writings of Jose-

---

[17] *Josephus* (Philadelphia, 1914), p. 36. Cf. J. Angus, "History of Israel," in Hastings' *Encyclopedia of Religion and Ethics*, XII, 849b.

[18] *Israel, seine Entwicklung im Rahmen der Weltgeschichte*, p. 227.

[19] *Vita di Gesu Cristo*, 9th ed. (Milan, 1946), p. 57 (Eng. trans. by Alba I. Zissamia, *The Life of Christ* [Milwaukee, 1947], p. 40).

phus which we brought out in the previous chapter. We shall quote the passage in full:

> Josephus, who is a little too prone to find similarities between the Jewish and the Graeco-Roman world, presents the Zealot tendency as a "fourth philosophy." . . . But in reality the Zealots not only did not represent a "philosophy," they did not even constitute a fourth current of Jewish thought because substantially they were Pharisees. The same Flavius Josephus states shortly afterward that the Zealots "in all other things are in agreement with the opinion of the Pharisees, except that they have a most ardent love of liberty and admit no head or lord but God alone; they pay no heed whatever to suffering the most extraordinary deaths and the punishment of relatives and friends in order not to recognize any man as their lord." Evident in their attitude was a fidelity to the national-theocratic principle, which was a fundamental one in Pharisaic teaching. The difference lay in the fact that most Pharisees did not apply this principle to political matters while the Zealots did so with complete rigor, carrying it right out to its ultimate consequences.[20]

Ricciotti is not the first to note this apparent contradiction on the part of Josephus, nor is he the first to trace the origin of the Zealots back to the Pharisees. Riggs, as early as 1900, wrote: ". . . Josephus calls them 'a new school.' . . . They were rather the extreme exponents of the old school of the Pharisees." In 1906 O. Holtzmann, in his *Neutestamentliche Zeitgeschichte,* expressed himself as follows:

> Josephus tries at first to separate the party of the Zealots from the party of the Pharisees completely. The Galilean Judas is for him a "sophist" who follows his own line and has nothing in common with the others. . . . He ascribes the responsibility of the Roman war to the Zealots, from which responsibility he would like to keep his own party free. But this is effort spent in vain.[21]

20 *Ibid.*
21 Tübingen, 1906, p. 206.

M. J. Lagrange, in his *Le Judaïsme avant Jésus-Christ,*
makes very much the same point. He observes that Josephus, by his own testimony, has shown that it is a mistake
to qualify Judas the Galilean as a clever sophist and the
leader of a fourth philosophical school. Lagrange goes on
to say in effect that when it comes to defining this sect Josephus contradicts himself. "Josephus at times states that it
has nothing in common with others. And at other times
that it agrees in general with the doctrine of the Pharisees."[22]

All of these scholars, Riggs, Holtzmann, Lagrange, and
Ricciotti have detected the contradictory statements in
Josephus relative to the origin of the party of Judas of
Galilee. They all agree in tracing the origin of this party
back to the Pharisees. However, none of them has supplied
an adequate explanation for these contradictions. Holtzmann has made a bold attempt to explain this phenomenon
by suggesting that when Josephus wrote his *Bellum Judaicum* he wanted to obscure the connection between the
Zealots and the Pharisees in order to free his own party,
namely the Pharisees, from any responsibility for the war,
which responsibility he had decided to put upon the Zealot
party. This part of Holtzmann's hypothesis appears to be
sound enough, for it does on the surface seem to offer an
adequate explanation for the phenomenon we find in Josephus' *Bellum Judaicum.* If we had only his account in his
Bellum Judaicum, we would look in vain for some positive
contact between the sect of Judas the Galilean and the
other Jewish parties. However, when we turn our attention
to the *Antiquitates,* Holtzmann's hypothesis explains only
part of the phenomenon. There Josephus makes explicit
statements which link the party of Judas of Galilee with
the Pharisees. Holtzmann says that Josephus "admits in a
round about manner" the connection between the "fourth

[22] *Le Judaïsme avant Jésus-Christ,* 3d ed. (Paris, 1931), pp. 213–14.

philosophy" and the Pharisees. This kind of language begs the question. If one looks at Josephus' account in the *Antiquitates* without expecting him to hide any connection between this new sect and the Pharisees, he sees first of all that the cofounder of this new party was a Pharisee, and later on that with some notable exceptions this new party held a great deal in common with the Pharisees. Josephus does not seem to be "admitting" anything, nor does there seem to be anything "round about" in his manner of presenting this connection. What Holtzmann had in mind, perhaps, is that since the *Antiquitates* was written some time after the *Bellum Judaicum,* the pressure on him to free his party from responsibility for the war was not so great, and so he could afford to be more truthful in his later account. This is a sound working hypothesis. The recognition of the lapse of time between the two histories no doubt could account for their contradictions. However, the most important discrepancies do not occur between the earlier and later histories of Josephus. The greatest contradiction is found within the *Antiquitates* itself. In fact, it occurs within the same book and chapter. If by the time Josephus wrote his *Antiquitates* he was prepared to draw attention to the connection between the "fourth philosophy" and the Pharisees, as he certainly was, why did he allow to stand in the same account a statement which categorically asserts that this "philosophy" was one with which the Jews were previously unacquainted?

As has been pointed out previously, the only features which are said to distinguish this sect from the Pharisees are precisely those for which the Maccabees were remembered, as Josephus himself indicates.[23]

---

[23] See p. 14 above. Our own conjecture on this is that in an earlier draft of his *Ant.* Josephus included only the statement about the fourth sect being one with which the Jews were previously unacquainted. This statement corresponds closely to his account in *B.J.,* where he refers to this sect as one having nothing in common with the other sects. Then, in our view, some

Emil Schürer

Among the many historians who wrote prior to the First World War and who did not make any explicit connection between the Maccabees and the Jewish nationalism of the first century A.D. (e.g., Hitzig, Ledrain, Morrison, Bertholet, Thomas, Guthe, *et al.*), the name of Emil Schürer stands out from all the others. No survey, however brief, would be complete without some reference to the way in which he has dealt with the questions which concern us. We have already had occasion to mention the important role he has played in the development of the writing of Jewish history since the last decade of the nineteenth century. At this time we shall explicate his importance.

---

time later while preparing a new draft of his *Ant.*, he inserted the passage in which he describes the fourth sect as being most like the Pharisees except for its inordinate concern for liberty, etc. We conjecture that he made this insertion without altering the former statement about the "newness" of the sect. In our view the qualification of this "newness," implied in the description of the sect as most like the Pharisees, was partially explained by inserting into the text the name of Zadok the Pharisee as a cofounder of the fourth sect. A fact which somewhat confirms our conjecture is that the description of the fourth sect is not found where we might logically expect it, i.e., immediately following the reference to the very serious effect of its teachings on the course of ensuing events, but rather separated from this initial reference by the passages describing the sects of the Pharisees, Saducees, and Essenes. A further fact which tends to confirm our conjecture concerning when and for what purpose the name of Zadok the Pharisee was introduced into the text is that in the passage which describes the teachings of the fourth sect, Judas alone is mentioned as its author. This is natural enough if we assume that when this passage was inserted—perhaps in response to the request that he give a description of this fourth sect as he had for the other three—Josephus did not at first notice the apparent contradiction that was being created. Once it was called to his attention, the most effective way in which to smooth over the contradiction without radical revision was to insert the name of Zadok the Pharisee as a cofounder of the sect, along with Judas, in those earlier passages.

We do not mean to suggest that Josephus has invented the figure of Zadok the Pharisee. On the contrary, we believe that such a person probably did play a leading part in founding the so-called fourth sect. However, Josephus' desire to clear his party from war guilt would have been reason enough for him not to mention Zadok in his *B.J.* And it could also explain why he would not at first introduce his name into the account of the

Emil Schürer completed his *Lehrbuch der Neutestament-liche Zeitgeschichte*[24] in 1873, the same year that Hausrath published the second edition of the first volume of his *Neutestamentliche Zeitgeschichte*. A comparison of these two works, which cover much the same ground, shows that with the appearance of Schürer's volume an important change was to take place in the writing of Jewish history. We have noted above that in the precritical period there was a slavish adherence to the accounts of Josephus. However, by the time of Ewald and Graetz scholars had swung to the opposite extreme and tended to use the writings of Josephus in an irresponsible manner. This irresponsibility continued among some scholars on into the twentieth century. The pendulum was bound to swing back to some

founding of the sect given in his *Ant.* nor even in the passage inserted later in which the teachings of the sect are described. But once Josephus was called upon to explain the apparent discrepancy he had created by this last insertion, he might well have recorded for the first time a fact he had known from the first but had never before mentioned—viz., that a Pharisee had helped found the fourth sect. After all, by the time the last edition of his *Ant.* was ready for publication, the whole question of war guilt had changed its complexion in the mind of Josephus, as will be indicated in the next chapter.

However, granting the plausibility of the above conjectures, we still have a partial contradiction on our hands in that the only thing "new" about the fourth sect seems not to be "new" at all. As we have seen, these were precisely the things for which the Maccabees were said by Josephus to have been remembered. We recognize this partial contradiction as somewhat of an indigestible problem which confronts every student of Josephus who seeks to understand how best to interpret his histories. We have suggested in our second chapter that Josephus has deliberately obscured the connection between the Maccabees and Jewish nationalism in the first century A.D. Perhaps the "indigestible problem" has been created for us by the attempt of Josephus to cover up a connection which was really impossible to obscure completely once an honest description of the teachings of the sect had been provided. By the time this description was provided, quite possibly Josephus' desire to produce a new version of the war was already with him. He refers to this desire in the paragraph added to his last edition of his *Ant.* We hold that had he been able to produce such a new version it might well have given us a different picture of the Jewish nationalists in the Roman period than is given to us in our version of his *B.J.*

24 This was an earlier form of his *Geschichte des jüdischen Volkes*, the first edition of which was published in 1886–90.

middle position in which the works of Josephus would be dealt with critically and responsibly. The advent of the writings of Schürer mark clearly and unmistakably the beginning of that swing. Those writings are marked by a wealth of documentation and a paucity of speculation. Hausrath, like Ewald and Graetz before him, was loath to be brief. These men write from an interior point of view in which the reader is made to feel the living historical situation being described. Schürer's writing by comparison is cold with objectivity. His material is condensed as much as possible. Hardly a phrase or word is unessential. Every sentence on every page is packed full of relevant information, carefully organized so as to prevent the slightest repetition and yet give complete coverage of all details. Naturally, in historiography of this character there is no place for interesting but irrelevant observations. It *is* interesting to note that Judas the Galilean and his party paralleled in certain respects the early Maccabees. But what is the significance of such an observation? Is there any evidence that the Maccabees *did* exert a formative influence upon Judas the Galilean? What is the evidence that the party of Judas of Galilee used a war cry dating from the Maccabean period? Did the Maccabees ever oppose a census made by the Seleucids? Did the Romans ever force the Jews to eat the flesh of swine? These are among the questions that may have gone through the mind of the great Schürer. Here was a scholar who seldom made a point he was not able to document fully. To connect the Maccabees with the Jewish nationalism of the first century A.D. would require more than documentation by footnote. Even if Schürer believed that there was some connection, he would have been reluctant to state this in print, until all the evidence had been carefully analyzed.

Once historians were freed from a literal dependence upon Josephus' works, they could survey the whole period and see the connection between the war against the Seleucids and the war against the Romans. These wars had much in common. The Jews in both periods were doing and saying the same kind of thing. It is this over-all kinship which provides the logical ground out of which grows the willingness to see behind the literal account that Josephus gives of some of these crucial events into the inner core of what in all probability actually took place. All great historians need at times to rely on this historical intuition in making their reconstructions. However, this is precisely what a historian like Schürer is loath to do. Take care lest you go beyond the evidence! This is the watchword for the historiographer who would emulate Schürer. If there is evidence that Josephus is wrong in his account, then by all means attempt to reconstruct the events on the basis of the best evidence available. But unless there is evidence that the account Josephus gives is wrong, then abide by his description of what happened. No other path is safe! There is no way in which a scholar can curb his fancy once he abandons the best evidence he has and indulges in speculation! There was no denying the strength of Schürer's methodology. He was to dominate the writing of Jewish history in the Greco-Roman period long after his death in 1910. The final volume of the fourth and last edition of his monumental *Geschichte des jüdischen Volkes im Zeitalter Jesu Christi* was published posthumously in 1911. Popular histories of the Jews were yet to be written in the free spirit of Ewald, Graetz, Hausrath, Edersheim, and Stanley, but henceforth scholarly works would be produced in the more reliable and restrictive manner of Schürer.

Joseph Klausner

We can see the extremes to which the restrictive objectivity of Schürer can be carried when we consider a book

written by Joseph Klausner. For many years this Jewish
scholar has been an ardent Zionist. The Maccabees stand
as heroes for modern Zionists.[25] Klausner's *Jesus of
Nazareth* was composed in modern Hebrew and first published in Jerusalem in 1922. Therefore it should not surprise
us that in this book Klausner, when giving an account of the
history of the Jews during the Herodian period, never
fails to mention how popular the Maccabees were with the
Jewish people. Thus he states that the Herodians first "tried
to free themselves from the danger which threatened them
from the mass of the people who longed for Maccabean
rule."[26] Later, with reference to Antigonus II, he, unlike
most writers, calls attention to the Maccabean blood in
Antigonus' royal veins, by giving his full name *Mattathias
Antigonus.*[27] With reference to this descendant of the early
Maccabean heroes, Klausner states that he "endeavoured
to regain the throne of his fathers," and that he "immediately found himself surrounded by Jewish supporters."
Herod defeated him amid considerable bloodshed, and
"this defeat of a member of the Maccabean family did not
greatly please the people."[28] The next year Antigonus
made an agreement with the Parthians whereby they would
help restore him to his ancestral throne. "But before this
army arrived, Mattathias Antigonus found, as did all the
Maccabeans, supporters from among the Jews."[29] Of an
aged Galilean who preferred death to capture by Herod,
Klausner observes: "So great was the hatred of the zealots
against the Edomite slave, and so great their faith in the

[25] In the words of Elias Bickerman, "Today the Maccabees are patron
saints of Zionist athletic clubs." *The Maccabees* (New York, 1947), p. 13.
[26] *Jesus of Nazareth, His Life, Times, and Teaching,* Eng. trans. by Herbert Danby (New York, 1949), p. 140.
[27] That Antigonus was also named Mattathias is a conjecture based
upon evidence drawn from the study of Jewish coinage.
[28] *Jesus of Nazareth,* p. 142.
[29] *Ibid.,* p. 143.

Maccabean house!"[30] At one point he is moved to reflect: "So very strong was the widespread popularity of the Maccabeans that, according to the spontaneous evidence of Strabo 'the Jews would not recognize Herod as king because of their esteem for Antigonus.' "[31] Finally, in reference to the case of the pseudo-Alexander who posed as being of Hasmonean descent and heir to the throne, and who found ready support from various Jewish sources, Klausner exclaims: "To such a degree could even a doubtful descendant of the Maccabeans inspire the Nation!"[32]

From his description of the history of the Jews in this period, in which the widespread popularity of the Maccabees is emphasized again and again, until with the effect of a crescendo, the reader is prepared for some great climax, one would expect that in the ensuing period there would be some further disclosure of the outcome of all this mass enthusiasm for the Maccabees. Such a natural expectation is not fulfilled. Never again in his book does Klausner refer to the Maccabees. However, the reasons for Klausner's action are clear enough. In the first place, Klausner's condensed history involved a selection of the material included by Josephus in his histories. As a Zionist, writing in a language known to few outside Jewish circles, and writing for a public interested in the Maccabees, he never failed to include in his selections from Josephus those passages which actually point to the continued popularity of the Maccabees during the Herodian period. But this selection was possible only so long as his original source made reference to the Maccabees. By the time the Roman procurators took over from the Herodian puppet princes, Josephus had discreetly stopped connecting popular uprisings with the Mac-

30 *Ibid.*, p. 143–44.
31 *Ibid.*, p. 145.
32 *Ibid.*, p. 157.

cabees and was ready to describe the seditiousness of the Jews under direct Roman rule as inspired by a new school of thought, beginning with the party of Judas the Galilean which arose in the time of the census of Quirinius. At this point the long shadow of Schürer is cast over the pages of Klausner's book, and for no other conceivable reason than that his primary source never mentions the Maccabees, neither does Klausner. That the tremendous popularity of the Maccabees should have died out suddenly seems strange indeed. The silence of Josephus concerning the Maccabees is not so strange if his assertion that most of the later opposition to the Romans had its source in a "fourth philosophy" is taken seriously. However, Klausner takes great pains to show that this "new sect" in fact was a union of "all the more extreme nationalists, who . . . had existed since the time of Pompey."[33] These were the very nationalists with whom, as both Klausner and Josephus agree, the Maccabees were so popular! Whereas Josephus is at least consistent in isolating the nationalism of the Jews under the Romans from its historic roots, Klausner, in connecting the so-called "fourth philosophy" with the earlier nationalism, is without excuse for not even mentioning the name of the heretofore popular Maccabees in his discussion of the fourth philosophical sect. The best way in which to explain the omission by Klausner of any reference to the Maccabees in his account of the nationalists' response to the census of Quirinius is to credit it to the restraining effect of the sober and unspeculative methodology employed in the writing of Jewish history by Emil Schürer.

However, as we have already pointed out, there have been first-rate scholars who, while maintaining the same high standards of objectivity as did Schürer, have, none the less, found occasion to refer to the Maccabees in their accounts

[33] *Ibid.,* p. 162.

of Josephus' "fourth philosophy." The names of Eduard Meyer and Martin Noth need to be added to those already mentioned.[34]

In 1949 Robert H. Pfeiffer made the following comparison: "As the Pharisees are the heirs of the Hasidim so the Zealots are the heirs of the Maccabees."[35] Later on, when referring to the Jewish elements which resisted Rome in A.D. 70, Pfeiffer has this to say: "In all probability, like the Maccabees before them, these various patriotic parties and their leaders advocated a war to the finish against foreign domination."[36]

In referring to Herod Agrippa who ruled the Jews as a puppet prince in A.D. 37-44, Pfeiffer notes that "Agrippa was beloved of the patriotic Jews as the heir of the Hasmoneans (through his grandmother Mariamne I)."[37] If this be true, it would mean quite definitely that the memory of the Maccabees was still alive and influential among the patriots even after the time of the earthly ministry of Jesus.

The noteworthy fact about these statements Pfeiffer has made is not that they are very different from those we have cited from authors writing previously but rather that they occur in the book of a scholar who is as careful and objective as Emil Schürer in dealing with the sources. It is quite possible that the writing of Jewish history is entering a new period, in which the cold objectivity of a Schürer is being combined with the warm insight of scholars like Hausrath and Stanley.

We shall close this survey of modern literature on the connection between the Maccabees and the nationalism of

[34] Meyer, *Ursprung und Anfänge des Christentums* (Stuttgart, 1921), II, 402-4; Noth, *Geschichte Israels* (Göttingen, 1950), p. 365.

[35] *History of New Testament Times with an Introduction to the Apocrypha* (New York, 1949), p. 36.

[36] *Ibid.*, p. 59.

[37] *Ibid.*, p. 37.

the Jews in the first century A.D. with a reference to a book written by S. G. F. Brandon, published in 1951 under the title *The Fall of Jerusalem and the Christian Church*. Brandon goes so far as to make an important argument for his thesis depend upon the assumption that the memory of the example and teaching of the early Maccabees was influential in the New Testament period.[38] Yet Brandon seems not to be concerned with the possibility that the memories of which he speaks were no longer alive in the New Testament period. This is really the crucial question: Were these memories of the glorious Maccabean resistance still alive in the New Testament period? If they were, this fact would be of the greatest interest to students concerned with the New Testament and its Palestinian background during the first century A.D.

Summary

It was stated at the beginning of this chapter that the question to be dealt with herein was: To what extent have modern critics indicated some kind of connection between the early Maccabees and the religious nationalists of the Roman period? We have shown in the preceding survey of the relevant literature that ever since the middle of the nineteenth century there have been scholars, including such notable figures as Hausrath, Holtzmann, Wellhausen, Meyer, Pfeiffer, and North, who have affirmed some kind of positive connection between the Maccabees and the Jewish nationalism of the Roman period. Sometimes the authors in referring to the Maccabees seem only to be marking some illuminating parallel between the two periods. At other times we find authors who make statements implying a definite and formative influence of the Maccabees upon

[38] London, 1951, p. 108. Cf. R. Travers Herford, *Judaism in the New Testament Period* (London, 1928), pp. 66ff.

the Jewish resistance to Rome. However, neither the significance of the parallels nor the character of the influence is ever clearly defined, nor is adequate evidence ever cited to support the many sweeping assertions that have been made.

The fact that so many scholars have shown some awareness of this positive connection needs to be set over against the fact that other scholars, equally eminent, show no awareness of this connection in their histories of the Jews.[39] None of these authors denies that there was some signifi-

[39] E.g., Ferdinand Hitzig, *Geschichte des Volkes Israel* (Leipzig, 1869); Eugène Ledrain, *Histoire d'Israël*, Part 2 (Paris 1882); W. D. Morrison, *The Jews under Roman Rule* (New York, 1902; written 1890); Alfred Bertholet, *Die Stellung der Israeliten* (Leipzig, 1896); C. Thomas, *Geschichte des alten Bundes* (Magdeburg, 1897); Hermann Guthe, *Geschichte des Volkes Israel*, Vol. III, 3d ed. (Tübingen, 1914); Joseph Klausner, *Jesus of Nazareth, His Life Time and Teaching*, tr. into Eng. from original Hebrew by Herbert Danby (New York, 1949; Hebrew original first published in Jerusalem, 1922); Simon Dubnow, *Die alte Geschichte des jüdischen Volkes*, Vol. II, tr. into German from original Russian by A. Steinberg (Berlin, 1925); Max L. Margolis and Alexander Marx, *A History of the Jewish People* (Philadelphia, 1927; this work contains a faint parallel between the Roman and Seleucid periods, but it is so obscure it would hardly be noticed if one were not looking for such parallels, pp. 179–80); George A. Barton, *A History of the Hebrew People* (New York, 1930); M.-J. Lagrange, *Le Judaïsme avant Jésus-Christ*, 3d ed (Paris, 1931); W. O. E. Oesterley, *A History of Israel*, Vol. II (Oxford, 1932; this work marks a parallel between the military tactics of the Maccabees and the Jewish rebels against Rome but does not suggest any influence of the earlier combatants over the later Jews); Shailer Mathews, *New Testament Times in Palestine*, new and rev. ed. (New York, 1933); A. Momigliano, *The Cambridge Ancient History*, Vol. X (New York, 1934), Chap. 25, Sect. iv-vii (Momigliano sees a parallel between the cosmopolitanism of the rich in the Roman and that in the Seleucid period but does not parallel the resistance movements in the respective periods); Salo Wittmayer Baron, *A Social and Religious History of the Jews* (New York, 1937); H. Wheeler Robinson, *The History of Israel* (London, 1938); C. Guignebert, *The Jewish World in the Time of Jesus*, tr. from original French by S. H. Hooke (London, 1939). With reference to Josephus' account of the origin of the philosophy, Guignebert observes, "I have no great faith in this account," but he notes no connection of this party with the Maccabees.

This list is by no means complete, but it serves the purpose of showing the widespread omission of any reference to the Maccabees in well-known works in which such references might be expected if their authors thought that there was any significant connection between the nationalism of the Seleucid and that of the Roman period.

cant relationship between the Maccabees and the first century A.D., but their very silence witnesses to the fact that for them the case for asserting such a relationship has never been proved. No thorough study of the relationship between the Maccabean uprising and the first century A.D. has ever been made. It is, therefore, with some sense of the need for such an examination that we now turn to a consideration of the evidence bearing on the question: Was there any positive connection between the Maccabees and the Jewish nationalism of the first century A.D.?

PART TWO

ANALYSIS OF EVIDENCE

IV: JEWISH NATIONALISM
AND THE TORAH

Our thesis is that there was a positive connection between the Jewish nationalism of the second century B.C. and that of the first century A.D. We are now ready to consider the evidence which sustains this thesis. This evidence falls into two categories. First, there is the evidence which supports the view that both periods of Jewish nationalism are positively connected through their common character. This evidence will be presented in the form of resemblances between what the Jews were doing and saying in the earlier and in the later periods of nationalism. Resemblances in themselves do not necessarily indicate positive connection between two periods. But when they occur in historical periods temporally contiguous and culturally continuous, then they take on more than ordinary significance and do indicate some kind of positive connection. Second, we have the evidence which supports the view that the example and teaching of the Maccabees was actually influential in the first century A.D.

However justified we may be on theological grounds for dividing history into B.C. and A.D., such a division serves no constructive purpose in the consideration of our subject. For our purposes it is better to regard the period of Jewish history which is the object of our study as one continuous whole, properly designated as the Greco-Roman period. This we shall refer to as the Hellenistic period, since it is Hellenistic culture which characterizes both Seleucid and Roman rule in Palestine. The extreme limits of this period, beginning with the coming of Alexander the Great and ending with the destruction of Jerusalem by Hadrian, are shrouded in obscurity. In between, however, is the best-illumined of all periods, viz., from Antiochus Epiphanes to Vespasian and Titus.

The beginning of this period is marked by the rise of an independent Jewish nation, while the end is marked by the fall of Jerusalem. This is really one story, that of the rise and fall of Jewish nationalism. It is not our purpose to delineate the place of the Jewish nation relative to the great world powers in the Hellenistic period. Rather we seek to demonstrate that throughout the Hellenistic period the dynamic of this nationalism was rooted in Jewish piety and that its motivation was theological. Jewish nationalism in the Roman period, in our view, was not secular. Nor was it, properly speaking, ethnocentric. Rather, as in the Maccabean period, it was theocentric. And if we may coin a word, we can be more explicit and say that it was *Torahcentric*. That is why, once the danger to orthodox Judaism was averted and freedom to worship and live according to the Torah was guaranteed by the establishment of national independence, the religious dynamic, which had been the main support of the Jews in their war against the Seleucids, was turned inward and sometimes ran counter to what may be regarded as the more or less secular national aims of some of the Hasmonean princes.[1] Thus, strictly speaking, Jewish nationalism largely subsided under the royal high-priestly Hasmoneans and did not strongly reassert itself again until that national independence won by the Maccabees was lost, in

[1] This is, we believe, the proper interpretation to be placed upon the mass revolt of the Jews against Alexander Janneus.

the time of Pompey, to the pagan Romans and their puppets, the Herodians. The second upsurge of Jewish nationalism, which finally culminated in the destruction of the national sanctuary by Titus, actually began 133 years earlier with the Jewish resistance to Pompey. Josephus witnesses to this fact when he gives voice to the official Roman view in a speech placed in the mouth of Titus who addresses the defeated Jews in these words, "You who from the first, ever since Pompey reduced you by force, never ceased from revolution, and have now ended by declaring open war with the Romans. . . ."[2]

This never-ceasing resistance to Rome can be only artificially divided into B.C. and A.D., and for our purposes we will speak henceforth only of Jewish nationalism in the Roman period, meaning in the period from Pompey to Titus. And instead of speaking of Jewish nationalism of the second century B.C., we shall speak only of the Seleucid period or the time of the Maccabees, meaning the period from Mattathias to the death of his son Simon.

Jewish nationalism throughout the Hellenistic period is characterized by "zeal for the Torah." Behind this zeal for the Law lay the more fundamental and original zeal for the covenant God of Israel known to Elijah—a God who had chosen a peculiar people and who was, in his love for his people, exceedingly jealous of all other gods. All the decalogues of the Pentateuch agree in beginning with a divine prohibition against idolatry.

A cardinal tenet of the postexilic community was that the promises of the covenant were conditional upon strict obedience on the part of Israel to every detail of the Law as it is written down in the Five Books of Moses. To abandon the Torah was for postexilic Judaism to break the covenant. Thus Law and covenant became inseparable. For

---

[2] *B.J.* 6.6.2 (329). Cf. Plutarch's *Parallel Lives,* "Pompey" xlv. 2, where Judea is listed along with others as a country conquered by Pompey.

example, to submit to "uncircumcision" was to abandon the covenant.[3] To eat what the Law forbade was to profane the covenant.[4] Conversely to stand by the Law was to stand by the covenant[5]—the covenant of promise made with Abraham, Isaac, and Jacob;[6] the covenant made between Israel and the redeeming and saving God who had delivered his people from the hands of Pharaoh.[7]

As long as the Torah remained the unchallenged ruling factor in the postexilic life of Israel, just so long did aggressive Jewish nationalism lie dormant. However, inherent in Hellenism was an inexorable challenge to the particularity of the Torah. The supreme test came in the time of Antiochus Epiphanes, as the apocalypse of Daniel makes very clear. It has been Elias Bickerman more than any other who, through his brilliant researches into the causes of the Maccabean uprising, has shown that this challenge to the Torah did not come wholly from outside in the form of heathen opposition or persecution, but rather had its deeper origins in the internal conflicts within the Jewish community over the question of how Israel, the chosen people of the one God, was to relate itself to the cultural and commercial life of its Hellenistic environment—with its cosmopolitanism, polytheism, and syncretistic tendencies.[8]

Of course the Maccabean victory had a decisive effect upon the history of Israel. The Hellenizing party's attempt to break down the barriers of the Law which separated Israel from the heathen and to incorporate Yahweh into the pantheon of syncretistic Asiatic Hellenism was de-

[3] I Macc. 1:15. For the practice of "uncircumcision," see Note 25 below.
[4] I Macc. 1:63.
[5] I Macc. 2:27.
[6] II Macc. 1:2.
[7] I Macc. 4:9-10.
[8] *Der Gott der Makkabäer: Untersuchungen über Sinn und Ursprung der makkabäischen Erhebung* (Berlin, 1937). Cf. J. C. Dancy, who follows Bickerman in his excellent *Commentary on I Macc.* (Oxford, 1954).

feated.[9] However, this victory was mainly an internal victory over the radical Hellenizing tendency within Judaism. The triumph over the heathen, though it was truly marvelous, was only temporary. The Maccabean victory accomplished no perceptible change in the Hellenistic character of the outer environment in which Israel still had to live and breath.[10] Nor was that environment significantly changed with the advent of Rome, which became in the East the standard bearer of Hellenistic culture.[11] The fundamental problem of how the nation Israel was to relate itself to the Hellenistic world remained unsolved. It was precisely for this reason that, when in the time of Pompey Israel once again came under the "yoke of the heathen," the old "zeal for the Torah" began to manifest itself again in "nationalistic" forms which closely resemble the religio-nationalistic phenomena of the Maccabean period.

The attitude of Hellenistic powers toward the religious customs and beliefs of particular ethnic groups was usually one of tolerance. Hellenism triumphed over national religions by infiltration and assimilation rather than by frontal attack or persecution. Were it not for the fact that Judaism was preeminently a religion of the book, the process of Hellenization within Judaism would undoubtedly have gone on unchecked. This is true because the powerful aristocratic priestly class, which otherwise would have had

[9] *Ibid.* Cf. W. W. Tarn, *Hellenistic Civilization*, Chap. 6, especially pp. 194–96.

[10] This is not to say that the policies of later Hellenistic powers toward the Jews were uninfluenced by the political fact that the Jewish nation had demonstrated that it would fight rather than participate in polytheism. When the Romans conceded to the Jew the privilege of abstaining from sacrifice to the emperor, they may well have been influenced by knowledge of this fact so well established by the successful Maccabean revolt. It would still be true to say that the character of the Hellenistic world remained largely unchanged by the Jewish victory, and that consequently the threat of Hellenism to Judaism remained.

[11] Tarn, *Hellenistic Civilization*, p. 2. This fact was recognized even in ancient times. Cf. Philo *Legatio ad Gaium* 21 (147).

a monopoly on the interpretation of the religious tradition, actually favored the policy of gradual Hellenization. However, the cultic life of Israel was inseparably related to the Torah, and that lay open for all who could to read. It was the Torah which served as the focal point around which the conservative religious forces within Israel rallied. Mattathias cried out in Modin, "Whoever is zealous for the law, and maintaineth the covenant, let him come forth after me."[12] It is to the Law, therefore, that we turn first in our consideration of the phenomena which characterize both the Seleucid and Roman periods of Jewish nationalism.

Burning of Torah Scrolls

We shall begin our study of the resemblances between the phenomena of the earlier and later phases of Jewish nationalism in the Hellenistic period by noting two of the extreme forms which pagan opposition to the Jewish Law sometimes took. The first is that of burning, defacing, or otherwise profaning the actual Torah scrolls. We read in I Maccabees with reference to the persecution: "And they rent in pieces the books of the law which they found, and set them on fire. And wherever was found any with a book of the covenant, and if any consented to the law, the king's sentence delivered him to death."[13]

In the Roman period, under the procuratorship of Comanus, soldiers were sent out into the country to round up some of the villagers who were protecting Jewish rebels. We read that "On this occasion a soldier, finding in one village a copy of the sacred law, tore the book in pieces

[12] I Macc. 2:27.
[13] I Macc. 1:56-57. Cf. I Macc. 3:48, which may refer to the heathen's practice of defacing the Torah scrolls. The manuscript evidence is not uniform. See the discussions of this question by Fairweather and Black, *The First Book of the Maccabees* (Cambridge Bible for Schools and Colleges, Cambridge, 1936), and M. Abel, *Les Livres des Maccabees*, 2d ed., (Paris, 1949).

and flung it into the fire. At that the Jews were aroused as
though it were their whole country which had been consumed in the flames."[14]

In the earlier period the act is represented by the pro-
Jewish source as having occurred in accordance with the
king's decree, whereas in the later period it is recorded as
if it were an isolated incident. In fact, the pro-Roman
Josephus goes on to tell us that the soldier was ordered executed by his Roman superior. We may certainly say that
official Roman policy was not congenial to such acts of
barbarity. However, neither was that of the Seleucids.[15]
To damage a sacred book was universally regarded with
abhorrence by the ancients. The very crudeness of the act
witnesses to the desperation to which both Romans and
Greeks were sometimes driven in their attempt to oppose
the religious fanaticism of the zealous Jews. According to
Rabbinic tradition even Titus, whom Josephus pictures as
a model of Roman patience, is said to have desecrated a
scroll of the Torah.[16] Whether this be a trustworthy tradition or not, an even more significant report is that given
by Josephus when he relates that Titus took a copy of the
Jewish Law with him to Rome. This was carried in the
triumphal procession along with the trophies from the
temple and was immediately followed by many men carry-

[14] *B.J.* 2.12.2 (229). The parallel account in *Ant.* 20.5.4 (115) reads, "Now,
as this devastation was making, one of the soldiers seized the laws of Moses
that lay in one of those villages, and brought them out before the eyes of
all present and tore them to pieces; and this was done with reproachful
language and much scurrility."

[15] Evidence of the conciliatory attitude of the Seleucids toward the Jewish
Law can be seen in such passages as, I Macc. 10:25, 30, 31, 34, 37; 11:34 ff.;
15:21; II Macc. 13:23. For a similar attitude on the part of the Romans cf.
B.J. 1.7.6 (153), 2.9.3 (174), 2.11.6 (220), 2.12.2 (231), 2.12.7–8 (245–47), 5.9.4
(402), 6.2.1 (101), 6.2.3 (120), 6.6.2 (333ff.); *Ant.* 14.4.4 (73), 14.10.12–25 (225–
64), 14.5.10 (488), 15.5.4 (147), 16.2.1 (14), 16.2.3 (27ff.), 160.6.1–8 (160–78),
18.3.1 (56), 18.8.5 (279–83), 18.8.9 (306), 19.5.2–3 (285ff.), 19.6.3–4 (301ff.),
20.5.4 (117). See also Philo, *Legatio ad Gaium*, where it is argued quite
persuasively that the usual attitude of the Roman emperors was conciliatory toward the peculiarities of the Jewish law.

[16] Gittin 56b.

ing images of Niké, the Hellenic goddess of victory.[17] The suggested symbolism was, we may assume, the conquest by the champions of Hellenism of the last great vestige of barbarous particularism.

Enforced Eating of Swine's Flesh

The second extreme form which pagan opposition to the Jewish Law sometimes took was that of forcing the Jews to eat food forbidden to them by the Torah. According to I Maccabees, at the height of the persecution under Antiochus Epiphanes, "many in Israel were fully resolved and confirmed in themselves not to eat unclean things. And they chose to die, that they might not be defiled with the meats, and that they might not profane the holy covenant."[18]

We read in II Maccabees that Eleazar, one of the leading scribes, "was compelled to open his mouth to eat swine's flesh."[19] We read also of the mother and her seven sons, all of whom "were at the king's command taken and shamefully handled with scourges and cords, to compel them to taste of the abominable swine's flesh."[20]

In the Roman period, according to Philo, similar measures were taken during the persecution of the Jews in Alexandria in the time of Caius Caligula. Philo writes:

If they [certain captive Jewish women] were shown to be of our people, these spectators turned tyrants and masters would order swine's flesh to be brought and offered them . . . the more stubborn were handed over to torturers for intolerable acts of maltreatment.[21]

---

[17] *B.J.* 7.5.5 (150–51).
[18] I Macc. 1:62–63.
[19] II Macc. 6:18.
[20] II Macc. 7:1.
[21] *In Flaccum* 11 (96). Translation by Herbert Box, *Philonis Alexandrini: In Flaccum* (Oxford, 1939), p. 35.

Josephus suggests that this same practice was carried out in Palestine during the war of the Jews against Rome. In writing about the Essenes he says:

The war with the Romans tried their souls through and through by every variety of test. Racked and twisted, burnt and broken, and made to pass through every instrument of torture, in order to induce them to blaspheme their lawgiver or to eat some forbidden thing, they refused to yield to either demand, nor even once did they cringe to their persecutors or shed a tear.[22]

It cannot be emphasized too strongly that such extreme forms of opposition to the Jewish Torah on the part of the heathen are only found to characterize the final stage of the conflict between Hellenism and Judaism. These phenomena are not representative of the true Hellenistic spirit, which was irenic rather than polemical. Hellenism usually operated on the principle of religious toleration. This principle of toleration was based on the presupposition that different peoples really worshiped the same god under different names, which presupposition also provided the basis for Hellenistic syncretism—the practice of uniting names and cults.[23]

In so far as the Jew held to the belief that Yahweh was the universal creator God, he could give a varying degree of affirmation to this basic presupposition of Hellenistic syncretism. However, in so far as he held to the belief that Yahweh was the jealous, covenant God of Israel who absolutely forbade the making of any graven image, he stood diametrically opposed to the practical application of this principle to the cult life of Israel.

From the cosmopolitan commercial classes and from the aristocratic priestly class in Jerusalem in the Seleucid period there grew up a party which favored the introduction

[22] B.J. 2.8.10 (152).
[23] Cf. Tarn, *Hellenistic Civilization*, p. 196.

of Hellenistic institutions and practices into the life of
Israel. In response to this Hellenizing tendency there arose
a party zealous for the Torah. This party found leadership
from among the village priests and mass support from the
agrarian population. As readers of the histories of Josephus
know, the same was true in the Roman period. We return
now to our documentation of the similarity between the
earlier and later phases of Jewish nationalism relative to
the Torah.

Cultural Hellenization of Palestine

The phenomenon to which we wish to draw attention
next is the erection by Hellenizing Jews of buildings necessary to the practice of Greek customs—which customs were
recognized as being in conflict with the Torah. In II Maccabees we read with reference to the high priest Jason:

He brought in new customs forbidden by the law: for he
eagerly established a *Greek* place of exercise under the citadel
itself. . . . And thus there was an extreme of Greek fashions, and
an advance of an alien religion . . . so that the priests had no
more any zeal for the services of the altar: but despising the
sanctuary, and neglecting the sacrifices, they hastened to enjoy
that which was unlawfully provided in the palaestra [wrestling
school], after the summons of the discus; making of no account
the honours of their fathers, and thinking the glories of the
Greeks best of all. By reason whereof sore calamity beset them;
and the men whose ways of living they earnestly followed, and
unto whom they desired to be made like in all things, these
they had to be their enemies and to punish them. For it is not
a light thing to do impiously against the laws of God. . . . When
certain games that came every fifth year were kept at Tyre . . .
the vile Jason sent envoys . . . bearing three hundred drachmas
of silver to the sacrifice of Hercules.[24]

That this same effort at Hellenization was attempted by
the ruling class in the Roman period is clear from Josephus,
who writes:

24 II Macc. 4:11-19.

[Herod] yet more revolted from the laws of his country, and corrupted their ancient constitution, by the introduction of foreign practices, which constitution ought to have been preserved inviolable; by which means we suffered great injury afterward, while those religious observances which used to lead the multitude to piety, were now neglected; for in the first place he appointed solemn games to be celebrated every fifth year, in honor of Caesar, and built a theater at Jerusalem, as also a very great amphitheater in the plain. . . . The wrestlers also, and the rest of those that strove for the prizes in such games, were invited out of every land.[25]

From these two passages alone, the first witnessing to the Seleucid period and the second to the Roman period, we are able to detect quite clearly at least five significant resemblances. We notice first that in both periods Hellenization is regarded as contrary to the Law. We see in the second place that Hellenistic buildings are erected. Thirdly, the new Greek customs had a deleterious effect upon the cult life of Israel. We notice a fourth resemblance in the fact that in both periods the introduction of these new customs contrary to the Law is regarded as the cause of later tribulation for the nation. Finally, in both periods Jewish participation in international Hellenistic quinquennial games was fostered by the Jewish rulers. In another passage Josephus tells us concerning Herod:

As to the Olympic games, which were in a very low condition, by reason of the failure of their revenues, he recovered their

[25] *Ant.* 15.8.1 (267–69). Josephus goes on to mention "those who performed their exercises naked." It was customary, of course, for the Hellenist to participate in some athletic contests unclothed. The love of the Greek for physical beauty is well-known. Essential to the Greek idea of beauty is perfection. The sight of a man who had been circumcised would have been the occasion for ridicule if not scorn. This led to the practice of obliterating the sign of the covenant by undergoing another surgical operation, referred to as "uncircumcision." In I Macc. we read, "And they built a place of exercise in Jerusalem according to the laws of the Gentiles; and they made themselves uncircumcised, and forsook the holy covenant, and joined themselves to the Gentiles" (1:14–15). Evidently the practice of submitting to the operation of "uncircumcision" was still current in the Roman period, for Paul refers to it as if it were a well-known phenomenon in I Cor. 7:18.

reputation, and appointed revenues for their maintenance, and made that solemn meeting more venerable, as to the sacrifices and other ornaments: and by reason of this vast liberality, he was declared in the inscriptions of the people of Elis to be one of the perpetual managers of those games.[26]

Herod was, on a grand scale, a patron of Hellenism. We know that he rebuilt the temple of Apollo at Rhodes.[27] Herod carried out an extensive program of building temples in Palestine. This fact witnesses to the truth of the statement that Herod was a supporter of the emperor cult —for all the temples which Herod erected in the Holy Land were dedicated to Caesar. It will be sufficient at this point if we cite the summary statement of Josephus:

In short, one can mention no suitable spot within his realm, which he left destitute of some mark of homage to Caesar. And then, after filling his own territory with temples, he let the memorials of his esteem overflow into the province and erected in numerous cities monuments to Caesar.[28]

Returning now to the Hellenistic buildings erected in Jerusalem we notice that what was most distasteful to the pious Torah-loving Jews were the trophies—which they regarded as images—that adorned the theater. Josephus writes: "They were sorely displeased with them, because it was not the custom of their country to pay honors to such images."[29] When it was discovered to the Jews that these trophies were not actually graven images,

the greatest part of the people were disposed to change their conduct, and not to be displeased at him [Herod] any longer; but still some of them continued in their displeasure against him for his introduction of new customs, and esteemed the vio-

---

[26] *Ant.* 16.5.3 (149). Cf. parallel account in *B.J.* 1.21.2 (426–27).

[27] *Ant.* 16.5.3 (147); *B.J.* 1.21.11 (424). He also built gymnasiums at Tripoli, Damascus, and Ptolemais, temples at Berytus and Tyre, theaters at Sidon and Damascus. *B.J.* 1.21.11 (422).

[28] *B.J.* 1.21.4 (407).

[29] *Ant.* 15.8.1 (276).

lation of the laws of their country as likely to be the origin of
very great mischiefs to them, so that they deemed it an instance
of piety rather to hazard themselves [i.e., to endanger their
lives], than to seem as if they took no notice of Herod.

Some of those who opposed Herod on this account entered
into a holy covenant, pledging themselves to lay down their
lives if necessary in order to hinder Herod from carrying
on his policy of Hellenization. These men were captured
and tortured until they died. The response of the Jews who
were sympathetic with the opposition which these men
were putting up to Herod was such that when they appre-
hended Herod's spy who had discovered the proposed sedition, they pulled him to pieces limb from limb and gave
him to the dogs. All of Herod's attempts to learn who had
killed his spy failed until at last certain women succumbed
under torture and confessed what they had seen. Those who
had killed Herod's spy were executed along with their
entire families. Josephus concludes the account with these
words:

Yet did not the obstinacy of the people, and that undaunted
constancy they showed in the defence of their laws, make Herod
any easier to them until he should reign with complete security, and he resolved to encompass the multitude every way,
lest such innovations should end in an open rebellion.[30]

Opposition to the practice of erecting buildings contrary to the Law became one of the official policies of the
Jews during the great war against Rome in the time of
Vespasian and Titus, as we learn from an incident related
by Josephus in which he himself participated.

I told them [the principal men of Tiberias] that I and my asso-
ciates had been commissioned by the Jerusalem assembly to
press for the demolition of the palace erected by Herod the
tetrarch, which contained representations of animals—such a

[30] *Ant.* 15.8.3–4 (282–91). Herod at the very beginning of his career came
into conflict with the Law. *B.J.* 1.10.6 (209); *Ant.* 14.9.3 (167), 14.9.4 (174).

style of architecture being forbidden by the laws—and I requested their permission to proceed at once with the work.

Josephus goes on to say: "We were, however, anticipated in our task by Jesus, son of Sapphias," who "joined by some Galilaeans . . . set the whole palace on fire."[31] This same Jesus was not fooled by the aristocratic lukewarm Josephus, whom he suspected of having pro-Roman sympathies. On a later occasion a large crowd was collected at the instigation of Jesus, and Josephus reports the incident in the following words:

With a copy of the laws of Moses in his hands, he now stepped forward and said: "If you cannot, for your own sakes, citizens, detest Josephus, fix your eyes on your country's laws, which your commander-in-chief intended to betray, and for their sakes hate the crime and punish the audacious criminal."[32]

These passages drawn from the writings of Josephus suggest that in the Roman period, as was true in the Seleucid period, the popular resistance to the Hellenizing ruling classes was grounded in that conservative instinct which we may rightly term "loyalty to the Torah."

Willingness to Fight and Kill for the Torah

The willingness of the Jews to fight and even to die for the Torah is a characteristic feature of Jewish nationalism in both the Seleucid and Roman periods. We shall treat first the phenomenon of the willingness of Jews to fight (and kill) for the sake of the Torah, then we shall consider the phenomenon of the willingness of Jews to die (and suffer terrible torture) for the sake of the Law.

The way in which the Jews in the Seleucid period were willing to fight and kill because of their zeal for the Torah is brought out very clearly in the following passages taken from I Maccabees:

[31] *Vita* 12 (65–66).
[32] *Vita* 27 (134–35).

And when he [Mattathias] had left speaking these words, there came a Jew in the sight of all to sacrifice on the altar which was at Modin, according to the king's commandment. And Mattathias saw it, and his zeal was kindled, and his reins trembled, and he showed forth his wrath according to judgment, and ran, and slew him upon the altar. And the king's officer, who compelled men to sacrifice, he killed at that time, and pulled down the altar. And he was zealous for the law, even as Phinehas did unto Zimri the son of Salu. And Mattathias cried out in the city with a loud voice, saying, Whosoever is zealous for the law, and maintaineth the covenant, let him come forth after me. And he and his sons fled into the mountains, and forsook all that they had in the city. . . . And they mustered a host, and smote sinners in their anger, and lawless men in their wrath. . . . And they rescued the law out of the hands of the Gentiles, and out of the hand of the kings, neither suffered they the sinner to triumph.[33]

Mattathias died, and leadership passed into the hands of his son Judas Maccabeus of whom we read:

And he pursued the lawless, seeking them out, and he burnt up those that troubled his people. And the lawless shrunk for fear of him, and all the workers of lawlessness were sore troubled, and salvation prospered in his hand. . . . And he went about among the cities of Judah, and destroyed the ungodly out of the land, and turned away wrath from Israel.[34]

That this willingness to fight and kill in defense of the Torah was also very much alive in the Roman period is apparent from the passage taken from Josephus, cited above, concerning the resistance to Herod on account of his Hellenizing tendencies. There we found references to the "undaunted constancy" that the Jews "showed in defence of their laws."[35]

Philo witnesses to the fact that this willingness was characteristic of the Jews in the time of Caius Caligula, for he writes concerning the inhabitants of Judaea: "They

[33] I Macc. 2:23–28, 44, 48.
[34] I Macc. 3:5–6, 8. Cf. I Macc. 3:20; II Macc. 2:22; 8:21.
[35] *Ant.* 15.8.4 (291).

are men of great courage and spirit who are willing to die in defence of their national customs and laws with unshrinking bravery."[36] Philo poses the following question to Caius: "Are you making war upon us, because you anticipate that we will not endure such indignity [the erection of Caius' statue in the Jerusalem temple], but that we will fight on behalf of our laws, and die in defence of our national customs?"[37]

Josephus refers to this attempt of Caius Caligula to erect his statue in the Jerusalem temple in his *Bellum Judaicum*. However, he makes specific reference to only the passive resistance of the Jews, i.e., their willingness to "bare their necks," so to say.[38] This, of course, is in line with his tendency to picture the pious Jew as passive in his resistance to Rome, when he is not actively supporting Roman rule. On the whole, according to the picture Josephus paints in *Bellum Judaicum,* active resistance to Rome was inspired by self-seeking revolutionaries, and those Jews who were willing passively to lay down their lives for the sake of the Torah do not have any noticeable part in the great war against Rome. That is certainly a surface impression which is created by a first reading of *Bellum Judaicum.* That there is something wrong with this picture of Jewish resistance to Rome is indicated not only by the passage cited above from Philo, which suggests that the Jews were willing to "fight on behalf of their laws," i.e., *actively* to resist Rome in defence of their Torah, but also by what Josephus himself says in his later works, e.g., in *Contra Apionem* and *Vita.* In his *Contra Apionem* Josephus makes statements which suggest that the war with Rome was really motivated by Jewish loyalty to the Torah. He writes:

And from these laws of ours nothing has had power to deflect us, neither fear of our masters, nor envy of the institutions es-

---

[36] *Legatio ad Gaium* 31 (215).
[37] *Ibid.* (208).
[38] *B.J.* 2.10.4 (196–97).

teemed by other nations. We have trained our courage, not with a view to waging war for self-aggrandizement, but in order to preserve our laws. To defeat in any other form we patiently submit, but when pressure is put upon us to alter our statutes, then we deliberately fight, even against tremendous odds, and hold out under reverses to the last extremity.[39]

In the encomium on the Jewish laws with which Josephus ends his apology we find these words: "They [the laws of the Jews] deter them from war for the sake of conquest, but render them valiant defenders of the laws themselves."[40] As one reads these passages and considers the sincere and balanced apology for Judaism which runs throughout this literary masterpiece, he can well understand why Josephus would have desired to publish a new version of his *Bellum Judaicum*. In the version of his history of the war which has come down to us Josephus has painted a very dark picture of the Jew. He is brave and courageous, but his fanaticism is incredibly insane and barbarous. He does not act on any high principles, but rather his seditiousness is motivated by desire for self-gain. No effort is made to explain what the Torah meant to the Jew. Never a word is spoken about the promise which God had made to the Jews concerning the Holy Land. It is difficult to exaggerate the damaging effect that this history must have had upon the tense relationships which already existed between the Jewish and Gentile communities throughout the eastern Mediterranean world. One cannot resist thinking that the prodigious task of preparing the *Antiquitates Judaicae* for publication was at least partly undertaken out of a sincere desire on the part of Josephus to give a truer picture of Judaism than he had painted in *Bellum Judaicum*. Certainly, as one reads the *Antiquitates Judaicae* he gets a completely different idea of the Jew from that which is given in the earlier work. In the later work no effort is spared to tell of the way in which

39 *Contra Apionem* 2.37 (271–72).
40 *Contra Apionem* 2.41 (292).

the whole history of the Jews is rooted in and inseparably bound up with their religion. Unfortunately this history brings the reader only up to the beginning of the war with Rome. However, it should come as no surprise to learn that Josephus desired to publish a new version of the history of the war with Rome, to which project he refers at the close of his *Antiquitates Judaicae*.[41] Since he says that this new version would be brief, it is generally assumed that its purpose would have been merely that of a summary sketch, designed for readers who might find his longer version of the war too detailed and tedious to read. However, we are inclined to believe that it would have reflected a more sympathetic attitude toward the fanaticism of the Jews than is given in our version of his history of the war, and that its primary purpose would have been to counter to some extent the aid and comfort which his first history afforded those Gentiles who were only too ready to yield to the anti-Semitism of the period.

It cannot be denied that loyalty to the Law must have played a much more important part in the national resistance to Rome than is indicated in *Bellum Judaicum*. This fact is made quite clear not only by the passages cited above from *Contra Apionem*, but also by those we have referred to in his *Vita*. One might ask if the statements in *Contra Apionem* are to be relied upon very heavily in view of the fact that this work is admitted by all to be an apology for the Jews and would naturally place the Jew in as good a light as possible. We leave this question undiscussed, since a proper treatment would require more space than can rightly be given here, and because our point does not rest on these passages in *Contra Apionem* alone. Josephus' autobiography (*Vita*) is in no sense an apology for the Jews. It is designed primarily to exonerate the character and improve the reputation of its author. Therefore, it is all the more significant that in this work, in which he is constantly

41 *Ant.* 20.11.3 (267).

defending himself and attacking his enemies (the Galilaean extremists), he quite incidentally reveals that the fanatic revolutionaries like Jesus of Sapphias and John of Gischala actually represented themselves as being concerned that the war should be carried out along the lines of strict obedience to the Torah.[42] The above discussion concerning a problem of *Tendenz* in the writings of Josephus, and the way in which his various works are related to one another in this respect, has been a kind of digression. It was necessary, however, in order that the reader might understand why it is that whenever we wish to cite examples to show that the Jewish resistance to Rome was inspired by a strong loyalty to the Torah, we turn almost without exception to the later writings of Josephus and not to his *Bellum Judaicum.* We return now to our consideration of the ways in which the earlier and later periods of Jewish nationalism strongly resemble each the other.

Willingness to Suffer and Die for the Torah

We have seen above how in both the Seleucid and Roman periods there was a willingness of the Jews to fight and kill in defense of the Torah. Closely related to this phenomenon is the more extraordinary willingness of the Jews to suffer and die for the sake of the Torah. This is characteristic of both periods of nationalism. We have already noted the phenomenon of Jews throughout the Hellenistic period submitting to terrible tortures, even unto death, rather than eat food forbidden by the Law of Moses.[43] The first of the seven brothers who were martyred for refusing to eat swine's flesh is recorded as saying: "What wouldest thou ask and learn from us? for we are ready to die rather than transgress the laws of our fathers."[44]

For the Roman period we have Josephus' report con-

[42] *Vita* 12 (65), 13 (74), 27 (134).
[43] See above pp. 54–55.
[44] II Macc. 7:2. Cf. 7:11.

cerning those Jews who, "although they were tortured and distorted, burnt and torn to pieces, and went through all kinds of instruments of torture, that they might be forced either to blaspheme their legislator, or to eat what was forbidden them, yet could they not be made to do either."[45]

According to I Maccabees, when it grew time for Mattathias to die he said to his sons: "And now, my children, be ye zealous for the law, and give your lives for the covenant of your fathers . . . be strong and shew yourselves men in behalf of the law, for therein shall you obtain glory."[46]

In the Roman period it would appear that a similar teaching was very much alive, for Josephus writes that just before the death of Herod two of the most celebrated interpreters of the Jewish laws, Mattathias and Judas, exhorted their followers to "pull down all the works which the king had erected contrary to the law of their fathers, and thereby obtain the rewards which the law will confer upon them for such actions of piety."[47] They were, according to Josephus, specifically encouraged to tear down the golden eagle which, contrary to the Law, Herod had erected over the great gate of the temple. Nor were they to fear to die,

since they would die for the preservation and observation of the laws of their fathers; since they would also acquire an everlasting fame and commendation; since they would be both commended by the present generation and leave an example to life that would never be forgotten to posterity.[48]

These last words call to mind the teaching of Eleazar, one of the leading scribes in the Seleucid period, who just be-

---

[45] *B.J.* 2.8.10 (152). Translation according to D. S. Margoliouth's revised edition of W. Whiston's translation (New York: E. P. Dutton, n.d.).

[46] I Macc. 2:50, 64. Judas also exhorts his followers to die for their laws according to II Maccabees 8:21.

[47] *Ant.* 17.6.2 (150). The parallel account in *B.J.* goes on to say that "even if the action proved hazardous, it was a noble deed to die for the law of one's country (1.33.2 [650])."

[48] *Ant.* 17.6.2 (152).

fore he went to the torture wheel is reported to have said, "By manfully parting with my life now, I will show myself worthy of mine old age, and leave behind a noble example to the young to die willingly and nobly a glorious death for the reverend and holy laws."[49]

Herod's golden eagle was pulled down and cut to pieces with axes. When Mattathias and Judas were taken before the king, they said defiantly:

We have given our assistance to the majesty of God, and we have obeyed the dictates of the law; and it ought not to be wondered at, if we esteem those laws which Moses had suggested to him, and were taught him by God, and which he wrote and left behind him, more worthy of observation than thy commands. Accordingly we will undergo death, and all sorts of punishment which thou canst inflict upon us, with pleasure, since we are conscious to ourselves that we shall die not for any unrighteous actions, but for our love to religion.[50]

This noble speech reflects the same spirit as animated the earlier Mattathias who defiantly said to the agent of the Seleucids:

If all the nations that are in the house of the king's dominion hearken unto him, to fall away each one from the worship of his fathers, and have made choice to follow his commandments, yet will I and my sons and my brethren walk in the covenant of our fathers. Heaven forbid that we should forsake the law and the ordinances. We will not hearken to the king's words, to go aside from our worship, on the right hand or on the left.[51]

We are also reminded of the last words of the seventh son, who, according to II Maccabees, before he was martyred in the presence of King Antiochus said: "I obey not the commandment of the king, but I hearken to the commandment of the law that was given to our father through Moses."[52]

[49] II Macc. 6:27-28.
[50] *Ant.* 17.6.3 (158-59).
[51] I Macc. 2:19-22.
[52] II Macc. 7:30. With this we may also compare, from the Roman period, the attitude of the followers of Judas the Galilaean who according to

Herod had Mattathias and Judas and their Torah-loving followers burnt alive.[53] The Jews did not forget this act of barbarity even after Herod died.[54] During the season of Passover, those who lamented the unjust death of Mattathias and Judas raised a sedition against Archeleaus which was not quelled until three thousand Jews were slaughtered in the temple precincts.[55]

Thus we see quite clearly that in the Roman, as well as in the Seleucid period, there were courageous Jews who were willing to risk their lives in defense of the Torah. We see also that this zeal for the Law was not confined to a select few, but that on the contrary great multitudes of Jews in both periods were strongly sympathetic with the resistance put up against those practices and policies of the ruling class which were contrary to the Law. This is what we mean when we say that Jewish nationalism in both the Seleucid and Roman periods was characterized by zeal for the Torah. Josephus when writing his *Contra Apionem* was able to look back over Jewish history and after speaking of the rewards for obedience to the Torah to write: "I should have hesitated to write thus, had not the facts made all men aware that many of our countrymen have on many occasions ere now preferred to brave all manner of suffering rather than to utter a single word against the Law."[56]

Josephus said "that God is to be their only ruler and lord," and who "also make light of dying any kinds of death, nor indeed do they heed the punishment of their relatives and friends, nor can any such fear make them call any man lord" (*Ant.* 18.1.6 [23]).

[53] *Ant.* 17.6.4 (167); *B.J.* 1.33.4 (655).

[54] *Ant.* 17.9.1 (206); 17.9.3 (314).

[55] *Ant.* 17.9.3 (218).

[56] *Contra Apionem* 2 (219). At another place he writes: "We have given practical proof of our reverence for our own scriptures. For, although such long ages have now passed, no one has ventured either to add, or to remove, or to alter a syllable; and it is an instinct with every Jew, from the day of his birth, to regard them as the decrees of God, to abide by them, and if need be, cheerfully to die for them" (*ibid.*, 1 [42]). Cf. *ibid.*, 2 (218), (232), (233), (234), (283), (294).

Religious Self-Destruction

Very closely related to the willingness to suffer and die for the Torah is the most unusual phenomenon of suicide to avoid falling into the hands of the heathen. In II Maccabees we read:

Now information was given to Nicanor against one Razis, an elder of Jerusalem, as being a lover of his countrymen and a man of very good report, and one called father of the Jews for his good will. For in the former times when there was no mingling he had been accused of the Jews' religion, and had jeoparded body and life with all earnestness for the religion of the Jews. And Nicanor, wishing to make evident the ill will that he bare unto the Jews, sent above five hundred soldiers to take him; for he thought by taking him to inflict a calamity upon them. But when the troops were upon the point of taking the tower, and were forcing the door of the court, and bade bring fire and burn the doors, he being surrounded on every side fell upon his sword, choosing rather to die nobly than to fall into the hands of the wicked wretches, and suffer outrage unworthy of his nobleness.[57]

Although there is no specific reference to the Law in this passage, that Razis was a pious Jew is made clear by the reference to him as one who "had jeoparded body and life with all earnestness for the religion of the Jews." This willingness to take one's own life rather than to fall into the hands of heathen enemies is carried to an incredible conclusion in the Roman period by those Jews besieged on top of the Maccabean mountain fortress Massada. When it finally appeared that it was only a matter of time before the Romans would break through the last Jewish fortifications, according to Josephus' account, the leader of the Jews, Eleazar, a descendant of Judas the Galilaean, spoke in the following manner:

Long since, my brave men, we determined neither to serve the Romans nor any other save God, for he alone is man's true and

[57] II Macc. 14:37-42.

righteous Lord; and now the time is come which bids us verify
that resolution by our actions. . . . Our fate at break of day is
certain capture, but there is still the free choice of a noble
death with those we hold most dear. For our enemies, fervently
though they pray to take us alive, can no more prevent this
than we can hope to defeat them in battle. . . . Is a man to see
his wife led off to violation, to hear the voice of his child crying "Father!" when his own hands are bound? No, while those
hands are free and grasp the sword, let them render an honour-
able service. Unenslaved by the foe let us die, as free men with
our children and wives let us quit this life together! This our
laws enjoin, this our wives and children implore of us.[58]

According to Josephus' account Eleazar's proposal prevailed, and the Jews prayerfully and systematically carried
through the mass act of self-destruction. So that when the
Romans finally broke through the last barrier, they were
met with but deathly silence and the incredible evidence
that there was indeed no noble excess to which devoted
Jews would not go out of zeal for their God and his Torah.

Circumcision

We next consider a phenomenon which is rooted unmistakably in zeal for the Law in a very literal sense, and that
is the concern on the part of the Jewish nationalists to see
that the terms of the covenant, as prescribed in Genesis
17:9–14, are carried out even if it means that persons are
circumcised by force or violence. We find that this phenomenon is characteristic of both the Seleucid and Roman periods once the nationalists have gained the upper hand and
have the power to enforce the terms of the covenant upon
the inhabitants of the promised land.

In I Maccabees we read: "And Mattathias and his
friends went round about, and pulled down the altars; and

---

58 *B.J.* 7.8.6 (323, 326); 7.8.7 (385–87). For other references to suicide in
the Roman period, see *Ant.* 14.15.5 (429–30); *B.J.* 3.7.34 (331); 3.8.4 (355ff.);
6.5.1 (280).

they circumcised by force the children that were uncircumcised, as many as they found in the coasts of Israel."[59] It appears that the policy of enforcing circumcision on conquered peoples was followed by the second and third generations of Maccabees.[60] The logic that lay behind this policy of enforced circumcision was based on the belief that God would not fulfill the promises he had made to his people concerning the Holy Land so long as any male in it was breaking his covenant, and, according to the Torah, Yahweh had proclaimed that "the uncircumcised male who is not circumcised in the flesh of his foreskin, that soul shall be cut off from his people; he hath broken my covenant."[61]

It is quite clear that the policy of circumcision by force (if necessary) was in effect among the extremists who fought against Rome. Josephus tells us in his *Vita* that while he was a general in Galilee two Trachonite nobles came to him with their horses, arms, and money—apparently with the intention of joining forces with the Jews against Rome.[62] He goes on to write: "The Jews would have compelled them to be circumcised as a condition of residence among them."[63]

[59] I Macc. 2:45–46.

[60] *Ant.* 13.9.1 (257–58); 13.11.3 (318–19).

[61] Gen. 17:14.

[62] That they must have had some such intention is clear from *Vita* 31 (154). It is worth noting that both the Seleucids and the Romans attempted at times to prohibit the Jews from practicing circumcision. Cf. I Macc. 1:60; II Macc. 6:10; *Ant.* 12.5.4 (254, 256). We have no direct evidence from the Roman period until the time of Hadrian. Aelius Spartianus writes: "At this time [while Hadrian was in Asia] the Jews began war, because they were forbidden to practice circumcision." *Historia Augusta.* Reinach notes that the motive is not mentioned elsewhere and may be doubted. He adds that the successor of Hadrian, Antoninus Pius, expressly excepted the Jews from the prohibition against circumcision. But this could have been a reversal of Hadrian's policy.

[63] *Vita* 23 (113). We may assume with a considerable degree of probability that it was Josephus' refusal to allow this course of action carried out which comprised the specific crime with which Jesus of Sapphias charged him on the occasion when he (Jesus) took the law of Moses in his hands and said, "Have regard to these laws of your country, which your commander-in-chief intended to betray, and for their sakes hate the crime and punish the audacious criminal." *Vita* 27 (134–35). Cf. *Vita* 31 (149ff.).

On another occasion during the war some Roman soldiers surrendered themselves to the Jews, after which, according to Josephus' account, all were treacherously killed by the Jews. There was, however, one exception, namely the general of the Romans, a certain Metilius, who "saved his life by entreaties and promises to turn Jew, and even to be circumcised."[64] Josephus represents this killing of the Roman soldiers as nothing less than murder and says that the moderate Jews were greatly disturbed and felt that God would punish them because of the wickedness of their extremist compatriots—"For, to add to its heinousness, the massacre took place on the sabbath, a day on which from religious scruples Jews abstain even from the most innocent acts."[65] This reference to the sabbath leads us to a consideration of the attitude of the Jews during the Hellenistic period toward this institution of the Torah.

Sabbath Observance

In one of the laments over Jerusalem preserved in I Maccabees we read: "Her sabbaths became a reproach, and her

---

[64] *B.J.* 2.17.9 (454). Another passage which witnesses to the central importance of circumcision to Jews in the Roman period is found in *Ant.* 20.2.4 (38ff.). A certain Izates, king of Adiabene, became a proselyte to Judaism. He debated whether he should be circumcised, for he was advised that were he to submit to the operation he would hazard the loss of his kingdom, since his subjects would not bear to be governed by a man who was so zealous (ζηλωτὴν) in another religion. While he was still in doubt a Galilean by the name of Eleazar came to his court "and found him reading the law of Moses." Then Eleazar said to the king: "Thou dost not consider, O king! that thou unjustly breakest the principle of those laws, and art injurious to God himself; for thou oughtest not only to read them, but chiefly to practice what they enjoin thee. How long wilt thou continue uncircumcised? But if thou hast not yet read the law about circumcision, and dost not know how great impiety thou are guilty of by neglecting it, read it now." The king, upon hearing these words retired into another room and sent for a surgeon and did what he was commanded to do. It is a significant fact that descendants of this zealous convert to Judaism were among the most valiant of the Jewish revolutionaries in Jerusalem during the war years A.D. 66–70. *B.J.* 2.19.2 (520); 6.6.4 (356).

[65] *B.J.* 2.17.10 (456).

honor became contempt."[66] II Maccabees is more explicit when it reports: "A man could neither keep the sabbath, nor observe the feasts of the fathers, nor so much as confess himself to be a Jew."[67] Obviously Hellenization involved some measure of sabbath profanation. We obtain some insight into the conflict between the Gentile and the Jewish attitudes toward the sabbath in the Seleucid period from the following passage in II Maccabees:

But Nicanor, hearing that Judas and his company were in the region of Samaria, resolved to set upon them with all security on the day of rest. And when the Jews that were compelled to follow him said, O destroy not so savagely and barbarously, but give due glory to the day which he that beholdeth all things hath honoured and hallowed above [other days]; then the thrice-accursed wretch asked if there were a Sovereign in heaven that hath commanded to keep the sabbath day. And when they declared, There is the Lord, living himself a Sovereign in heaven, who bade [us] observe the seventh day; then sayeth the other, I also am a sovereign upon the earth, who [now] command to take up arms and execute the king's business.[68]

We also learn from II Maccabees that Judas and his followers scrupulously kept the sabbath[69] and carefully abstained from profaning it even when so to do would have been greatly to the military advantage to the Jews.[70] It is quite clear from the Gospels that in the Roman period as well there was on the part of the Jews a strong concern for strict sabbath observance. Furthermore, this concern to keep the sabbath day holy was very much alive even in time of open hostility toward the Romans.[71]

We find that some Jews were so strict in their observance

[66] I Macc. 1:39.
[67] II Macc. 6:6.
[68] II Macc. 15:1-5.
[69] II Macc. 12:38.
[70] II Macc. 8:26-27.
[71] Cf. *B.J.* 1.7.3 (146) and the parallel account in *Ant.* 14.4.2 (63); *B.J.* 2.21.8 (634); 4.2.3 (99, 100); *Vita* 32 (159, 161).

of the sabbath that they would not even defend themselves if they were attacked on that day. We read in II Maccabees that "others, that had run together into the caves near by to keep the seventh day secretly, being betrayed by Philip were all burnt together, because they scrupled to defend themselves, from regard to the honour of that most solemn day."[72] A similar if not the same incident is referred to in I Maccabees where we read as follows:

Then many that sought after justice and judgement went down into the wilderness, to dwell there, they, and their sons, and their wives, and their cattle; because evils were multiplied upon them. And it was told the king's officers, and the forces that were in Jerusalem . . . that certain men, who had broken the king's commandment, were gone down into the secret places in the wilderness; and many pursued after them, and having overtaken them, they encamped against them, and set the battle in array against them on the sabbath day. And they said . . . Come forth and do according to the word of the king and ye shall live. And they said, We will not come forth, neither will we do the word of the king, to profane the sabbath day. And they hasted to give them battle. And they answered them not, neither cast they a stone at them, nor stopped up the secret places, saying, Let us die all in our innocency . . . and they died, they and their wives and their children, and their cattle, to the number of a thousand souls.[73]

Obviously, if all Jews had taken the same attitude there would never have been a Jewish nationalism. Jewish nationalism throughout the Hellenistic period was possible only so long as the Jews were willing to fight on the sabbath. We read that Mattathias and his friends heard about the massacre of the Jews and arrived at the following decision:

If we all do as our brethren have done, and fight not against the Gentiles for our lives and our ordinances, they will now quickly destroy us from off the earth. And they took counsel on that day, saying, Whosoever shall come against us to battle

[72] II Macc. 6:11.
[73] I Macc. 2:29–38.

on the sabbath day, let us fight against him, and we shall in no wise all die, as our brethren died in the secret places.[74]

What Josephus says about this in his *Antiquitates Judaicae* is very interesting. We read as follows:

And so about a thousand with their wives and children died by suffocation in the caves; but many escaped and joined Mattathias, whom they appointed their leader. And he instructed them to fight even on the Sabbath, saying that if for the sake of observing the law they failed to do so, they would be their own enemies, for their foes would attack them on that day, and unless they resisted, nothing would prevent them from all perishing without striking a blow. These words persuaded them, and to this day we continue the practice of fighting even on the Sabbath whenever it becomes necessary.[75]

We see from Josephus' statement, "To this day we continue the practice of fighting even on the Sabbath whenever it becomes necessary," that the phenomenon of Jews fighting on the sabbath, under certain conditions, was characteristic of the Roman as well as the Seleucid period. It should not be thought that this phenomenon in the Roman period was merely dependent upon *ad hoc* decisions to be made anew whenever the Jews were in danger of being attacked on the sabbath. Evidently the original decision in the early Maccabean period was in the Roman period accepted as legally binding. Josephus when writing about Pompey's siege of Jerusalem refers to the law (νόμος) which permits the Jews to defend themselves on the sabbath.[76]

It is not at all the purpose of this chapter, in which our task is to indicate nothing more than the resemblances be-

---

[74] I Macc. 2:40–41.

[75] *Ant.* 12.6.2 (275–77). In *Vita* 32 (161) Josephus says that the Jewish laws forbade the bearing of arms on the sabbath, "however urgent the apparent necessity." But this statement is not as historically reliable as that cited above from *Ant.* 12.6.2 (277), which directly contradicts it. The context of the *Vita* passage shows that the statement under question was made by Josephus in his attempt to justify a particular course of action he had taken, and for that reason is subject to some degree of doubt. No such doubt may be attached to the passage in *Ant.*

[76] *Ant.* 14.4.2 (63).

tween the Jewish nationalism of the Seleucid and that of the Roman period, to trace the influence of the Maccabees on the Jewish nationalism of the Roman period. It is, however, a simple statement of fact that so far as we are able to tell it was the Maccabees who first put this particular compromise into effect and established it as a recognized principle for the nation to follow in its death struggle with the enemies of the Torah. The importance of this fact is difficult to exaggerate once it is seen that so long as the heathen could attack the Jews on the sabbath with impunity, just so long was the possibility of national independence out of the question. Even after the Jews had decided to compromise the Torah and to fight to defend themselves on the sabbath, that day remained the weakest point in the armor of national defense. With reference to Pompey's siege of Jerusalem Josephus writes:

> The Law permits us to defend ourselves against those who begin a battle and strike us, but it does not allow us to fight against an enemy that does nothing else. Of this fact the Romans were well aware, and on those days which we call the Sabbath, they did not shoot at the Jews or meet them in hand to hand combat, but instead they raised earthworks and towers, and brought up their siege-engines in order that these might be put to work the following day.[77]

There is ample evidence that in their tactics the generals of both the Seleucid and Roman armies did exploit this military weakness of the Jews by attacking them on the sabbath.[78] They also used the strategy of timing their sieges of Jewish cities so as to exploit the weakness of low food supplies consequent to the observance of the laws relative to the sabbath year.[79]

[77] *Ant.* 14.4.2–3 (63–64); parallel account in *B.J.* 1.7.4 (146).
[78] For the Seleucid period cf. I Macc. 2:32, 38; 9:34, 43; II Macc. 5:25; 8:26. For the Roman period cf. *Ant.* 14.4.2 (63); 18.9.2 (322), 18.9.6 (354).
[79] For the Seleucid period cf. I Macc. 6:49, 53. For the Roman period cf. *Ant.* 14.16.2 (475), 14.16.3 (487–88); 15.1.2 (7). There can be no doubt that

The willingness of the Jews to transgress the Law by defending themselves on the sabbath was no doubt partly due to the natural desire for self-preservation. However, in our opinion, it would not have commended itself as it did to Jews zealous for the Torah were it not for the fact that such a compromise was humanly speaking absolutely necessary for the preservation of the Torah as it was intended by God. Yahweh had given his people the Law that they might know how to live in accordance with his will. If His people were destroyed, then the Torah would have no meaning. For this reason it is possible to speak of the principle of Torah-expediency, namely the principle of compromising one part of the Torah in order that the whole might be preserved. Exactly how, at that time, this may have been carried out at the exegetical level we have no way of knowing with certainty. But that some such high principle lay behind the effort of the Jews to interpret the Law in such a fashion as to make it self-affirming, we cannot doubt. Whether such a principle were consciously or unconsciously followed does not matter. What is of paramount importance is to recognize that to compromise the Torah is not necessarily to abandon it, and that in the case of the Maccabees it was their zeal for the Law which sustained them even in those battles when they were transgressing the Law by fighting on the sabbath.

The dilemma that the Jewish nationalists were in is put

the Seleucids used this strategy, Antiochus IV in 170 B.C., Antiochus V in 149 B.C., and Antiochus VII in 135 B.C. Nor is there any doubt that it was used in the Roman period in 65 B.C., and twenty-eight years later when after a siege Herod finally took Jerusalem in 37 B.C. Therefore, it is highly probable that the reason the Romans did not in full force seek to crush the Jewish revolt sooner than they did after it broke out in A.D. 66 was because they preferred to press the attack at the most opportune time, namely during and right after the next sabbatical year, which was in A.D. 69. It is interesting to note that though fighting on the sabbath is not forbidden in the Dead Sea Scrolls, the Sons of Light are forbidden to wage war during "the year of remitting," because that is the "Sabbath of rest for Israel." *War of the Sons of Light against the Sons of Darkness*, col. 2, line 8.

very nicely by Josephus in the speech of Agrippa to the Jews who had revolted against Rome:

> If you observe your sabbath customs and refuse to take any action on that day, you will undoubtedly be easily defeated, as were your forefathers by Pompey, who pressed the siege most vigorously on the days when the besieged remained inactive; if, on the contrary, you transgress the law of your ancestors, I fail to see what further object you will have for hostilities, since your one aim is to preserve inviolate all the institutions of your fathers. How could you invoke the aid of the Deity, after deliberately omitting to pay him the service which you owe Him?[80]

It should be noted that Agrippa's assertion, that the one aim of the revolutionaries was "to preserve inviolate all the institutions" of their forefathers, implies an indirect admission that their "one aim" involved the preservation inviolate of the *whole Torah*. Elsewhere in *Bellum Judaicum* one will search in vain to find Josephus explicitly admitting that the aim of the revolutionaries was related in *any* way to the preservation of the Torah.

If we may judge by their actions, the revoultionaries attempted to solve their dilemma by going one step further along the road of Torah-expediency, i.e., by not only defending themselves against attack, but also by opposing *every* effort made by the Romans to effectuate the siege. Josephus' account of the siege of Jerusalem by Titus preserves no record of the Jews having given the Romans any special advantage on the sabbath, such as they had given in the days of Pompey. On the contrary, he explicitly tells us in one passage that the Jews themselves aggressively took the offensive and attacked the Romans on the sabbath.[81]

[80] *B.J.* 2.16.4 (392–94).

[81] From a military point of view such action was quite necessary. For if the Romans could count on the Jews not making an attack on the sabbath, that knowledge itself could be used to the tactical advantage of the Romans. It is sometimes as important for a general to know what his opponent will not do as it is to know what he will do.

We read in *Bellum Judaicum*:

The Jews, seeing the war now approaching the capital, abandoned the feast and rushed to arms; and, with great confidence in
their numbers, sprang in disorder and with loud cries into the
fray, with no thought for the seventh day of rest, for it was the
very sabbath which they regarded with special reverence. But
the same passion which shook them out of their piety brought
them victory in the battle; for with such fury did they fall upon
the Romans that they.broke and penetrated their ranks, slaugh-
tering the enemy.[82]

This passage brings out as clearly as any the polemic of
Josephus against the Jewish nationalists in his *Bellum
Judaicum*. They "abandoned the feast," and "with no
thought of the seventh day of rest" they "rushed to arms."
In this way Josephus is able to create the impression on
some readers that such "passionate" fighting had no positive relationship to religious zeal, but on the contrary had
its roots in the evil designs of vainglorious men. He says
that they went out to fight "with great confidence in their
numbers." Fortunately, however, Josephus is a better historian than he is a propagandist, for he himself provides
many illustrations of the fact that even when they were
overwhelmingly outnumbered the Jews fought with the
same fanaticism. Therefore, their confidence must have
been grounded in some other source than mere numbers.
We shall attempt to demonstrate in the next chapter that
their confidence was in their God who had inspired the
small hosts of the Maccabees before them by the miraculous
victory He had given the Jews over Sennacherib, whose
army was destroyed by divine intervention.

Even in the above passage from *Bellum Judaicum*, it is
clear that the Jews who went out to fight in such a frenzy

[82] *B.J.* 2.19.2 (517–18). Compare Washington's historic Christmas Eve
surprise attack upon the Hessians at Trenton. This and countless other
examples from military history, equally shocking, can be adduced to prove
that in exploiting the element of surprise the religious observances of the
armies on both sides of a conflict play an important part.

had come to Jerusalem in the first place that they might participate in a religious festival. Furthermore, Josephus himself admits that the sabbath on which they went out to fight was by them "regarded with special reverence." Therefore, we get a far more credible interpretation of this willingness to fight aggressively on the sabbath in a passage found in *Antiquitates Judaicae*. There, with reference to what befell the Jews in Babylon, Josephus tells us that two Jews, Asineus and Anileus, raised up for themselves a little semi-independent kingdom. The governor of Babylon heard about it, and, according to the account,

He then encamped around the marshes, and lay still; but, on the next day (it was the sabbath, which is among the Jews a day of rest from all sorts of work), he supposed that the enemy would not dare to fight him thereon, but that he would take them and carry them away prisoners, without fighting.

However, Asineus sent out spies, and they returned and said to him:

We are caught by their intrigues like brute beasts, and there is a large body of cavalry marching upon us, while we are destitute of hands to defend ourselves withal, because we are restrained from doing it by the prohibition of our law.

Josephus continues:

But Asineus did not by any means agree with the opinion of his spy as to what was to be done, but thought it *more agreeable to the law* to pluck up their spirits in this necessity they were fallen into, and *break their law* by avenging themselves, although they should die in the action, than by doing nothing, to please their enemies in submitting to be slain by them. Accordingly he took up his weapons, and infused courage into those that were with him to act as courageously as himself. So they fell upon their enemies, and slew a great many of them because they despised them, and came as to a certain victory, and put the rest to flight.[83]

83 *Ant.* 18.9.2 (319, 322–24). Italics mine.

We see from this passage that in his later writings it was possible for Josephus to represent the phenomenon of fighting on the sabbath as a practice which was justifiable in the eyes of those Jews who did so—justifiable on the ground that it was *more agreeable to the Torah*. There is every reason why we should assume that the revolutionaries in Jerusalem were just as convinced that their fighting on the sabbath was *more agreeable to the Torah* (than the alternative of not doing so) as were the followers of Asineus of whom we have just read. And there is no reason whatsoever why we should assume that in this particular respect these Jewish nationalists were less motivated by a sincere piety than were the Maccabees before them, who first introduced this principle of Torah-expediency.

What has been here presented strongly suggests that in the Roman period as in the Seleucid period fighting on the sabbath is not to be understood as evidence of secular motivation within Jewish nationalism but rather as an example of the degree to which pious Torah-loving Jews would go in their desperate endeavors to defend and preserve the Torah—and, we might add, the temple, as we shall see in the next chapter.

Summary

This brings to a conclusion our consideration of the resemblances between the Seleucid and Roman periods of Jewish nationalism—that is, so far as the question of the relationship between that nationalism and the Torah is concerned. Our method has been to treat the phenomena one by one, setting a phenomenon from one period alongside a similar phenomenon from the other. In this way we have attempted to demonstrate the strong resemblances between the two periods of Jewish nationalism by allowing the reader to see the evidence for himself, with only a minimum amount of interpretation.

Resemblances, however striking, do not demonstrate, conclusively, identity between the inner characters of historical movements. The resemblances with which we have been dealing are related to the inner character of the period of Jewish nationalism which they represent in the same way in which metaphysicians speak of appearance being related to reality. There is no necessary reason why these resemblances could not be largely accidental. We must admit, therefore, that it is theoretically possible that these resemblances are accidental. However, this theoretical possibility seems highly improbable. However far appearances may be removed from reality, there must be some relationship between the two. In the same way we may say that however far removed from the inner character of Jewish nationalism the phenomena of resemblance which we have exhibited may be, there must be some sense in which these resemblances witness to the true character of the Jewish nationalism which runs throughout both periods.

It should be remembered that our primary sources for the Seleucid period, namely I and II Maccabees, picture the Jewish nationalists as pious Jews, zealous for the Torah, whereas our primary source for the Roman period, namely Josephus, tends to paint a very dark picture of the extreme Jewish nationalists of his day, charging them with rebellion against God and transgression of his Torah. In contrast to this general impression, we wish to assert the following proposition: There was no fundamental change in the relationship of Jewish nationalism to the Torah in the period running from Antiochus Epiphanes to Titus. This proposition seems to us to be established as highly probable for two reasons. First, our survey of the literature has failed to uncover any significant dissimilarities between the attitude of the Jewish nationalists of the earlier and later periods, relative to the Torah. Second, the evidence presented in this chapter indicates quite clearly that the Jewish nationalists in both periods were doing and saying the same kind of things relative to the Torah.

We may go further and say that in our view there is no positive evidence whatsoever that there was any significant change in the attitude toward the Torah within the main stream of Jewish nationalism during the Hellenistic period. The burden of proof certainly rests on the shoulders of any one who, in the light of the evidence presented in this chapter, would still wish to maintain that such a change did take place.

V: JEWISH NATIONALISM
AND THE TEMPLE

We speak of the Torah and of the temple in this and the
preceding chapter as if they were two distinct entities—
which of course they were. Nonetheless, it is quite necessary
to keep in mind that they were inseparably bound up together in Jewish nationalism of the Hellenistic period. The
intimate connection between the Law and the national
sanctuary in the piety of the Jews at this time is seen clearly
in a passage which is taken from Philo:

> But all who attempt to violate their laws, or to turn them into
> ridicule, they detest as their bitterest enemies, and they look
> upon each separate one of the commandments with such rev-
> erence that, whether one ought to call it the invariable good
> fortune or the happiness of the nation, they have never been
> guilty of the violation of even the most insignificant of them;
> but above all other observances their zeal for their holy temple
> is the most predominant, and vehement, and universal feeling
> throughout the whole nation.[1]

What Philo does not make explicit in the above passage,
though it is clearly implicit in what he says, is that the centrality of the temple for Judaism of this period was fixed
in and by the Torah. Sacrifice at the Jerusalem sanctuary
in accordance with provisions set down in the Torah was
thought to be a necessary prerequisite if the Israelite was to
fulfill the conditions of the covenant made with Yahweh.

1 Philo *Legatio ad Gaium* 31 (211–12). See also Acts 6:13–14; 21:28.

This includes the annual festivals prescribed in the Torah, most if not all of which revolved around the Jerusalem sanctuary and were so very constitutive of postexilic Judaism. If these festivals with their appropriate sacrifices were not kept as prescribed in the Torah, then, of course, Yahweh could not be expected to fulfill his promises—which promises were conditional upon Israel's obedience to the Law. The promises of Yahweh to his chosen people, Israel, provided the ground for the pious hope which is so characteristic of Judaism. If we would understand Jewish nationalism in the Hellenistic period we must understand the significant place of the temple and its worship in the life of Israel at this time.

We can say neither that the temple was more important than the Torah, nor that the Torah was more influential than the temple. The two were inseparably bound up together. There were of course very real differences in the part they played in the national resistance against the heathen. The Torah, as a book, could be copied and read by any pious Jew who knew the language; while the temple was unique and could be served only by the priests. The Torah was transportable and consequently went with the nationalists into their caves in the wilderness and into their mountain retreats, sustaining their hopes in the nation's darkest hours; whereas the temple was fixed in Jerusalem and offered protection only to those who would defend it as a citadel. But these are purely physical differences. Spiritually speaking, both the power of the Torah and the power of the temple over the religious life of the Jew ultimately rested on the same foundation, namely their common role as mediating agents between Yahweh and his covenant people, Israel. The parts they played were complementary; the Torah mediated God's revelation to his people, while the temple worship mediated the nation's devotion to its God.

It has been pointed out in the previous chapter how Hellenism's challenge to the supremacy of the Torah in the religious life of Israel represented a mortal threat to post-exilic Judaism. In the same way, any radical alteration in the temple worship was bound to strike a crucial blow at the heart of the nation's religious integrity. Daniel's "abomination that maketh desolate"[2] was, quite likely, from the Hellenistic point of view, some perfectly rational, good, and just modification in the equipment and/or the ritual of the Jerusalem sanctuary. But to the pious Torah-loving Jew it was the acme of blasphemy.

The main purpose of this chapter will be to demonstrate that the temple was of central significance to nationalism in both the Seleucid and Roman periods. The importance of this fact for our main thesis—if it is not already obvious to the reader—will be brought out clearly at the end of this chapter. Before we proceed to consider the evidence which indicates that the temple *was* of crucial significance to nationalists throughout the Hellenistic period, perhaps we ought to say a word about what would seem to be the obviousness of the point which the whole chapter will be devoted to making. The reader might be led to say, "Of course the temple was of central significance in both the Seleucid and Roman periods—why should we expect it to be otherwise?" This is the kind of response that might be expected from one who is well versed in Near Eastern antiquities in general and Jewish antiquities in particular. However, *such a response does not take into consideration the fact that our main primary source for the understanding of Jewish nationalism in the Roman period is Josephus, in whose writings the nationalists are pictured as self-seeking men who transgress the Law.* Josephus charges them with desecrating the temple, which is just the opposite of the reputation earned by the nationalists in the Seleucid

2 Dan. 12:11. Cf. Dan. 11:31.

period, who were remembered because, among other things, they cleansed the temple from its defilement by Antiochus Epiphanes and rededicated it for worship according to the Law. We have shown in Chapter II that Josephus is not to be trusted too far in the interpretation he places upon the actions of the anti-Roman extremists. But that was not enough. We need to go much further if we are to build a solid foundation for our thesis. We need to give convincing evidence—much of which has to be drawn from the histories of Josephus himself—that in fact the nationalists in both the Seleucid and Roman periods were motivated by the same fundamental theology. The previous chapter was devoted to a consideration of the Torah in Jewish nationalism. In that chapter we drew attention to evidence which indicates that from the beginning to the end of Jewish nationalism of the Hellenistic period no radical change took place in the nationalists' attitude toward the Torah. In this chapter we seek to demonstrate that the same is true with reference to the temple, i.e., that the attitude toward the temple held by the Jewish nationalists did not significantly change from the time of Antiochus Epiphanes to that of Titus.

The method to be followed in this chapter will not be so rigid as that employed in the previous one. We shall, as we did in the previous chapter, show some striking parallels between the Seleucid and Roman periods. But on the whole our method will be more flexible. Sometimes we shall indulge in digression in order to bring into sharp focus the particular character of the national resistance being revealed at the moment. Though some of these excursions to the side may seem lengthy and involved, if followed with the eyes open, they will help the reader to attain that more intimate and interior point of view which is so necessary for the proper understanding of the wider historical terrain.

The Temple Is Desecrated

When Antiochus Epiphanes "presumed to enter the most holy temple of all the earth,"[3] he demonstrated to those Jews zealous for the Torah that the Seleucids could not be trusted to preserve inviolate the sanctity of the Jerusalem sanctuary. So also Pompey, at the very beginning of the Roman period, made unmistakably clear, to all who had eyes to see, that so long as the nation was under Roman rule the sanctity of the temple would be subject to the threat of profanation by the heathen. The grave seriousness of Pompey's intrusion into the sacred precincts of the temple is reflected in an account preserved by Josephus in his *Bellum Judaicum*:

Of all the calamities of that time none so deeply affected the nation as the exposure to alien eyes of the Holy Place, hitherto screened from view. Pompey indeed, along with his staff, penetrated to the sanctuary, entry to which was permitted to none but the high priest.[4]

Antiochus Epiphanes plundered the Jerusalem sanctuary.[5] Pompey himself did not go this far. However, this restraint was of little comfort to those Jews who had learned to distrust the heathen. Any people who had so little reverence for "the most holy Temple in all the earth" as to profane it by their unlawful presence could be expected to plunder the temple treasuries if it served their purposes. This actually happened ten years after Pompey's unlawful intrusion, at the time when the government of Syria passed into the hands of Crassus, of whom Josephus writes:

Crassus, intending to march against the Parthians, came to Judaea and carried off the money in the temple, amounting to

3 II Macc. 5:15. Cf. I Macc. 1:21.

4 *B.J.* 1.7.6 (152). Parallel account found in *Ant.* 14.4.4 (72).

5 I Macc. 1:21-23; II Macc. 5:16, 21. Cf. *Contra Apionem* 2 (83-85), where Josephus cites Polybius, Strabo, Nicolas of Damascus, and other ancient historians as reporting that Antiochus Epiphanes plundered the temple.

two thousand talents, which Pompey had left, and was prepared to strip the sanctuary of all its gold, which amounted to eight thousand talents. He also took a bar of solid beaten gold. . . . This bar was given to him . . . as a ransom for all the rest. . . . Crassus, however, although he took this bar with the understanding that he would not touch anything else in the temple, violated his oath and carried off all the gold in the sanctuary.[6]

A similar incident happened during the series of disturbances following the death of Herod the Great. Some Roman soldiers under the command of Sabinus, while attempting to put down a Jewish insurrection in Jerusalem, set fire to the cloisters which surrounded the temple. Then, according to Josephus, they "rushed through the fire, where it gave them room so to do, and seized on that treasure where the sacred money was reposited; a great part of which was stolen by the soldiers, and Sabinus got openly four hundred talents." Josephus goes on to say that the Jews were grieved by "this plundering of the money dedicated to God in the temple."[7]

Again, at the very outbreak of the great war with Rome, we read: "But Florus, as if he had contracted to fan the flames of war, sent to the temple treasury and extracted seventeen talents, making the requirements of the imperial service his pretext."[8]

After his account of how the Jewish revolutionaries gained the upper hand in Jerusalem, Josephus writes:

Fearing, however, that Florus might return to the attack and capture the temple by way of the fortress Antonia, the Jewish revolutionaries instantly mounted the porticoes which connect the two buildings and cut the communication. This manoeuvre cooled the cupidity of Florus; for it was God's treasures that he coveted and that had made him so eager to reach Antonia, and

[6] *Ant.* 14.7.1 (105–9). Parallel account in *B.J.* 1.8.8 (179).
[7] *Ant.* 17.10.2–3 (264–65).
[8] *B.J.* 2.14.6 (293).

now that the porticoes were broken down, his ardour was checked.[9]

More important than the illegal taking of money from the sacred temple treasuries, was the removal of the sacred furniture prescribed by the Torah as necessary for the proper temple worship. The golden altar,[10] the golden candlestick,[11] the table of the shewbread,[12] and other sacred cups and bowls used in the temple ritual were taken from the sanctuary by Antiochus Epiphanes.[13] It is a well-known fact that some of these same pieces of temple furniture were taken by Titus to Rome as war trophies to be carried in his triumphal procession.[14]

The evidence adduced above demonstrates quite clearly that not only in the Seleucid but in the Roman period as well the heathen violated the sanctity of the temple. In both periods the heathen entered the temple unlawfully, and in both periods the temple was plundered of its sacred treasuries, even including its sacred furniture. So long as Israel was subject to heathen powers, just so long was the holy house of God himself subject to heathen profanation. This is a simple lesson of Jewish history in the Hellenistic period. Are we to assume that the Jews living in that period who saw with their own eyes their temple being profaned by the heathen were oblivious to this simple lesson so obvious to us?

Perhaps even more serious than illegal entry and plundering were the alterations made in the interior of the temple to make it fit for pagan worship. Most serious of all,

9 *B.J.* 2.15.6 (330–31).
10 Ex. 30:1–6.
11 Ex. 25:31–39; 37:17–24.
12 Ex. 25:23–30.
13 I Macc. 1:20–22.
14 Josephus mentions specifically a golden table which was probably the table of shewbread, and the golden candlestick. *B.J.* 7.5.5 (148–49). There are representations of these pieces of furniture on the Arch of Titus, at Rome.

certainly, was the actual destruction of the temple and the erection on its site of a pagan sanctuary. In the Seleucid period the interior of the temple was actually changed for three years,[15] although the threatened destruction of the Jerusalem sanctuary and the erection of a pagan temple on its site[16] was never carried out. By way of comparison we may say that in the Roman period in the time of Caius Caligula pagan alterations in the interior of the temple were threatened though not carried out,[17] but, as is well-known, the Jerusalem sanctuary was actually destroyed by Titus' armies,[18] and a pagan temple was erected on the same site in the time of Hadrian.[19]

It would appear, therefore, that both under Seleucid and Roman domination the very existence of temple sacrifice according to the Torah was imperiled. The "abomination that maketh desolate" which was perpetrated in the Seleucid period was threatened again in the Roman period, and the threat reported to have been made by the Seleucids to

[15] II Macc. 10:3 reads *two years*, but the commentators generally follow the chronology of I Macc. which would seem to call for a three-year interval.

[16] Cf. I Macc. 7:35, where Nicanor threatens to burn the temple, and II Macc. 14:33, where the Seleucid general threatens that if the Jews persist in their rebellious activity he will not only level the temple even with the ground, and break down the altar, but will erect on its site a temple to the pagan god Dionysus.

[17] *Ant.* 18.8.2–3 (261–72); *B.J.* 2.10.1–5 (184–203); Philo *Legatio ad Gaium* 31 (207ff.).

[18] *B.J.* 6.4.5 (249–53).

[19] *Dio Cassius* 69 (12). The new temple was dedicated to the worship of the Capitoline Jupiter. It is quite mistaken to assume that merely because the Romans never actually forced an idolatrous change in the interior of the Jewish temple that they, therefore, represented less of a threat to the inviolate holiness of the Jerusalem sanctuary than did the Seleucids. For all the excess of the Seleucid opposition to the Jewish religion, nothing so crude and barbarous was ever actually carried out against the Jews as the destruction of their temple. The Romans did destroy the holy house of the God of the Jews. They, not the Seleucids—if comparisons must be made—were the greater enemies of the Jewish religion. And if their claim to this distinction was not fixed by their destruction of the temple, then it certainly was by their erection of a temple to Jupiter on the site holy to Yahweh.

destroy Yahweh's temple and erect on its site another to a pagan god could have been carried out by the Romans at any time—as eventually it was.

Our purpose in pointing out the above facts is to show the reader that throughout the Greco-Roman period Hellenistic heathenism, when seen through the eyes of a pious Jew, looked very much the same. The policies of the Hellenistic rulers, both Seleucid and Roman, might change somewhat from time to time. But the fact remained that the heathen were idolatrous and sooner or later could be expected to violate the holiness of the Promised Land, the sanctity of the inviolate temple, or the sacredness of the Torah. The heathen were perfidious and proved themselves quite unworthy of trust again and again.[20] Unless we are able in some measure to get inside the national life of the Jews in this Hellenistic period, and, sharing their presuppositions, try to see how the outside world would have looked to them, we shall never be able to understand the actions of the Jewish nationalists or the course of their history. It does not matter that to some of us moderns the policy of the Romans toward the Jews seems quite moderate and reasonable. The important historical question to ask if we are to understand Jewish nationalism is, "How did the Jews regard the Romans?" So far as we are able to tell, they had very little if any reason to regard them in any different way from that in which they regarded the Seleucids. From the point of view of the pious Jew, both the Romans and the Seleucids threatened the supremacy of the Torah and the inviolate sanctity of the national temple.

We turn now to a consideration of the attitude of the Jews toward their national sanctuary in the Hellenistic period. We notice first of all that when the heathen threaten

20 Cf. I Macc. 6:62; 7:8ff. (especially vv. 16, 18, 27, 30); 11:53; 13:17; 19; II Macc. 3:8; 4:34ff.; 5:25; 14:22, 29; 15:10. For the Roman period cf. *B.J.* 1.11.8 (234); 1.12.7 (246); 2.9.4 (176); 3.10.10 (532–42); 4.1.10 (82); 7.8.7 (373); *Ant.* 14.7.1 (109); 14.13.2 (329); 18.3.2 (61–62); 20.8.5 (161).

to violate the sanctity of the temple, there are pious Jews who are willing to appeal to the pity of the heathen in order to hinder them in their unlawful designs. They do this by prostrating themselves and uttering supplications *en masse.*

Nonviolent Resistance

In II Maccabees we read that Antiochus Epiphanes appointed as his agent a certain Heliodorus, who was sent to effect the removal of some money deposited in the Jerusalem temple. The Jews objected to this procedure and answered "that it was altogether impossible that wrong should be done unto them that had put trust in the holiness of the place, and in the majesty and inviolable sanctity of the temple, honoured all over the world." However, Heliodorus said that he had his orders from the king and that the money must be confiscated. The account continues:

So having appointed a day, he entered in to direct the inquiry concerning these matters; and there was no small distress throughout the whole city. And the priests, prostrating themselves before the altar . . . called upon him that gave the law concerning deposits, that he should preserve these [treasures] safe for those who had deposited them. . . . And those that were in the houses rushed flocking out to make a universal supplication, because the place was like to come into contempt. And the women, girt with sackcloth under their breasts, thronged the streets. . . . And all, stretching forth their hands toward heaven, made their solemn supplication. Then it would have pitied a man to see the multitude prostrating themselves all mingled together, and the expectation of the high priest in his sore distress.[21]

With this story from II Maccabees may be compared that found in Josephus, who, writing concerning events in the Roman period, tells us that the emperor Gaius Caesar did send as his agent a certain "Petronius to Jerusalem to in-

---

[21] II Maccabees 3:7–21.

stall in the sanctuary statues of himself."[22] The response of
the Jews to this proposed violation of the sanctity of their
temple was fully proportionate to the enormity of the sacrilegious design. Josephus writes:

> But there came many ten thousand of the Jews to Petronius, to
> Ptolemais, to offer their petitions to him, that "he would not
> compel them to transgress and violate the law of their fore-
> fathers; but if," said they, "thou art entirely resolved to bring
> this statue, and erect it, do thou first kill us, and then do what
> thou has resolved on; for, while we are alive, we cannot permit
> such things as are forbidden us to be done by the authority of
> our legislature, and by our forefathers' determination, that such
> prohibitions are instances of virtue."

Like Heliodorus, Petronius said that he had his orders from
the emperor and that these must be carried out. The account continues:

> Then the Jews replied, "Since therefore, thou art so disposed,
> O Petronius! that thou wilt not disobey Caius's epistles, neither
> will we transgress the commands of our law; and trusting in the
> power of God, and by the labours of our ancestors having con-
> tinued until now without transgressing them: we dare not now
> by any means be so timorous as to transgress those laws out of
> the fear of death, which God hath determined are for our ad-
> vantage; and if we come to a trial of fortune, we will bear it in
> order to preserve our laws, as knowing that if we expose our-
> selves to dangers in such a case, we have good hope of escaping
> them, because God will stand on our side, when out of regard
> to him we undergo afflictions, and knowing also the uncertainty
> of fortune. But, if we should submit to thee, we should be
> greatly reproached for our cowardice, as thereby showing our-
> selves ready to transgress our law; and we should incur the
> great anger of God also, who, even thyself being judge, is su-
> perior to Caius."

Apparently Petronius perceived that he would not be able
to carry out the emperor's orders without provoking a war
with the Jews which would involve "a great deal of blood-

---

[22] *B.J.* 2.10.1 (184).

shed," for he did not proceed directly to Jerusalem but hastened to Tiberias to take counsel and determine what his next step should be. Josephus writes:

And many ten thousands of the Jews met Petronius again, when he was come to Tiberias. Those thought they must run a mighty hazard if they should have a war with the Romans, but judged that the transgression of the law was of much greater consequence, and made supplication to him, that he would by no means reduce them to such distress, nor defile their city with the dedication of the statue. . . . Thus they continued firm in their resoluton, and proposed to themselves to die willingly, rather than to see the dedication of the statue.[23]

In the parallel account in his *Bellum Judaicum,* Josephus concludes this part of the story with the following observation: "These words filled Petronius with astonishment and pity at the spectacle of the incomparable devotion of this people to their religion and their unflinching resignation to death."[24]

Both of these stories, the first from the Seleucid and the second from the Roman period, show marks of legendary accretion. None the less, it is an important fact that the two different proposed violations—the one temple plundering and the other the erection of a graven image in the temple—when seen through the eyes of a pious Jew have the appearance of being much the same kind of thing,[25] to be responded to in much the same manner. The close kinship between the two events in the view of the pious Jew comes out very clearly at the end of both stories, where the inviolability of the temple is maintained through divine intervention.[26]

After Heliodorus had been prevented by the miraculous intervention of God from plundering the temple, he re-

[23] *Ant.* 18.8.2 (263–72).
[24] *B.J.* 2.10.4 (198).
[25] Only, of course, the proposed violation of the Romans was much the more serious of the two.
[26] II Macc. 3:24–30; *Ant.* 18.8.6 (285–88); 18.8.9 (305–6); *B.J.* 2.10.1 (186).

turned to his king and said, "Of a truth there is about the place a power of God. For he that hath his dwelling in heaven himself hath his eyes upon that place, and helpeth it; and them that come to hurt it he smiteth and destroyeth."[27] This literary device of making a pagan witness to the truth of a particular religious belief of the author is well-known to the student of the New Testament.[28] This particular passage gives expression to a deep-felt religious certainty characteristic of the Jews in the Hellenistic period; namely, that so long as the temple stood and the sacrifices were carried out in accordance with the Torah, God would protect his holy house and sustain his people in their fight against the heathen attacks—no matter how great the odds were against the Jews. Perhaps this faith that God would intervene to protect his temple had its origin in that miraculous deliverance of Jerusalem from the mighty hosts of Sennacherib in the days of the pious Hezekiah. According to the account in II Kings, the king of Assyria sent his agent, a certain Rabshakeh, with an army to Jerusalem. This Assyrian general, like Petronius in the Roman period,[29] impressed on the Jews the invincible power of his imperial master. The pious Jews responded by covering themselves with sackcloth,[30] while their king went into the temple to supplicate the God of Israel to deliver his people out of the hands of the enemy. The story ends with the following divine intervention:

And it came to pass that night, that the angel of Yahweh went forth, and smote in the camp of the Assyrians a hundred fourscore and five thousand; and when men arose early in the morning, behold these were all dead bodies. So Sennacherib king of

27 II Macc. 3:28–39.
28 Cf. Mark 15:39, where the Roman soldier in response to the miraculous signs accompanying the Crucifixion of Jesus cries out at the end, "Truly this man was a son of God." See also Matt. 27:54, and Luke 23:47.
29 *B.J.* 2.10.3 (193).
30 Cf. II Macc. 3:19, where some Jews wore sackcloth in response to Heliodorus' threatened violation of the sanctuary.

Assyria departed, and went and returned, and dwelt at Nine-veh.[31]

The Importance of Sennacherib

It is quite clear that the story concerning the fate of Sennacherib served as a literary and theological framework for the authors of I and II Maccabees. In I Maccabees we read that the Seleucid king sent his agent, Nicanor, to destroy the Jews. Nicanor threatened to burn the house of God. In response the priests went wailing into the temple and prayed, saying:

Thou didst choose this house to be called by thy name, to be a house of prayer and supplication for thy people: take vengeance on this man and his army, and let them fall by the sword: remember their blasphemies, and suffer them not to live any longer.[32]

At this point the author of I Maccabees introduces a member of that family, "into whose keeping was entrusted the power of saving Israel."[33] Judas, who elsewhere is described as the "saviour of Israel,"[34] before leading his small hosts against the imperial army is made to pray:

When they that came from the king blasphemed, thine angel went out, and smote among them a hundred and fourscore and five thousand. Even so discomfit thou this army before us to-day, and let all the rest know that he hath spoken wickedly against the sanctuary, and judge thou him according to his wickedness.

Then follows an account in which Nicanor is the first to fall in battle, after which there is a complete annihilation of his army with apparently no casualties to the Jews.[35]

---

[31] II Kings 18:17–19:36.
[32] I Macc. 7:37–38.
[33] I Macc. 5:62, following the translation of Sidney Tedesche, *The First Book of the Maccabees* (New York, 1950). The Greek text reads: οἷς ἐδόθη σωτηρία Ισραηλ διὰ χειρὸς αὐτῶν.
[34] I Macc. 9:21 (σῴζων τὸν Ισραηλ).
[35] I Macc. 7:41–46.

The same story is told in II Maccabees with the kind of variations we have learned to expect from its author. Nicanor with a flourish of his right hand is made to declare upon his oath: "I will lay this temple of God even with the ground, and will break down the altar, and I will erect here a temple unto Dionysus for all to see."[36] Having properly dramatized the sacrilegious character of the heathen threat, the author of II Maccabees heightens the note of divine intervention on the side of the Jews by introducing into the story a vision occurring in a dream which Judas had, in which Jeremiah delivers to the leader of the Jews a gold sword with the following words: "Take the holy sword, a gift from God, wherewith thou shalt smite down the adversaries."[37] Then, to make it quite clear that the forthcoming deliverance is of divine origin, it is pointed out that Judas knew that salvation is not won by arms but that God gives victory to those who deserve it. Therefore Judas called upon the Lord, who works wonders, in these words:

Thou, O Sovereign Lord, didst send thine angel in the time of Hezekiah king of Judaea, and he slew the host of Sennacherib as many as a hundred fourscore and five thousand; so now also, O Sovereign of the heavens, send a good angel before us to bring terror and trembling; through the greatness of thine arm let them be stricken with dismay that with blasphemy are come hither against thy holy people. And as he ended with these words, Nicanor and his company advanced with trumpets and paeans; but Judas and his company joined battle with the enemy with invocation and prayers. And contending with their hearts, they slew no less than thirty and five thousand men, being made exceeding glad by the manifestation of God.[38]

The above story in II Maccabees also contains a passage which points unmistakably to the centrality of the temple for those Jews who looked to the Maccabees as great na-

[36] II Macc. 14:33.
[37] II Macc. 15:16.
[38] II Macc. 15:22-27.

tional heroes. After Judas tells the Jews about his vision in which he was given the gold sword as a holy gift from God we read:

And being encouraged by the words of Judas, which were of a lofty strain, and able to incite unto virtue and to stir the souls of the young unto manly courage, they determined not to carry on a campaign, but nobly to bear down upon [the enemy], and fighting hand to hand with all courage bring the matter to an issue, because the city and the sanctuary and the temple were in danger. For their fear for wives and children, and furthermore for brethren and kinsfolk, was in less account with them; but greatest and first was their fear for the consecrated sanctuary.[39]

The great importance of this story concerning the miraculous defeat of Sennacherib's army for writers seeking to archaize their histories of the Maccabees is perfectly apparent once it is recognized that there is really no other scriptural parallel which remotely resembles the marvelous victories of the Maccabees. The deliverance at the Red Sea is marvelous enough, but it has no connection with a threat to the holy city, Jerusalem, by an imperial army of overwhelming numbers. Nor do any of the many stories of the victories of Israel's great warriors have such a connection with Jerusalem except—as we have just said—the miraculous deliverance of the holy city from the hands of Sennacherib. For this reason we ought not to be surprised to find that the author of II Maccabees has recourse to the story again in chapter eight of his epitome of Jason of Cyrene's history.[40]

In all likelihood, if we had histories of the war of the Jews against Rome written by men sympathetic with that national resistance to heathen dominion, we should find that those Jews also—outnumbered as they were by the imperial armies of Rome with their nation and sanctuary

39 II Macc. 15:17-18.
40 II Macc. 8:19.

imperiled—would have been portrayed in such histories as
having been inspired by the story of the miraculous defeat
of Sennacherib's overwhelming hosts, before the very gates
of Jerusalem. In fact we have good evidence—indirect
though it is—that the Jewish nationalists in the Roman
period *were* inspired by this story. We do not have any direct expression of their views from their own hands. Nevertheless, we do have their thoughts more or less clearly reflected in those speeches which Josephus places in the
mouths of the Jewish moderates who carry on a debate with
their more extremist countrymen and try to convince them
to come to terms with the Romans. These speeches, in accordance with the conventions of Hellenistic historiography, reflect, as accurately as is consonant with the clear
expression of the true intent of the speaker, exactly what
was said—or, if not what was actually said, then what ap-
propriately could have been spoken under the circumstances. The literary purpose of the speeches is to bring out
the true import of the events being described, and as such
they can be expected to reflect not only the thoughts of the
speaker but, if he is attempting to confute the views of
others, to some degree the thoughts of his opponents as
well. This is exactly the kind of speeches we have at certain
crucial points in the histories of Josephus. Like the great
Thucydides, who had given classical expression to this form
of historiography, Josephus was an eyewitness of many of
the events he describes. Therefore, in dealing with those
speeches which he places in the mouths of personages active
in the great war with Rome we are handling sources of the
greatest historical significance. Their importance—if not
their reliability and literary merit—is quite comparable to
the famous speeches of Thucydides preserved in his celebrated history of the Peloponnesian War.

Let us turn, therefore, to the speech placed by Josephus
upon his own lips, in which he seeks to persuade the fanatic

defenders of Jerusalem to surrender to Rome. We shall look not only for indications that the story about Sennacherib's defeat provided inspiration to the besieged defenders of Jerusalem but shall move carefully through the whole speech seeking to learn whatever we can about the attitude of those extreme Jewish nationalists toward their temple.

Josephus begins with an appeal to the Jews to spare themselves, their country and their temple. Obviously this appeal presupposes that among other realities, the Jerusalem sanctuary is of some concern to the besieged. Josephus proceeds to speak of the desperate plight of the besieged Jews and of the invincible power of the Romans. This suggests to us that in their continued resistance under such obviously adverse circumstances the besieged Jews may have been feeding on some unusual hope of deliverance. What could this hope have been? Even if we assume that some of them might have hoped that a terrible plague would come over the Roman army and decimate the ranks of the legions—an eventuality which moderns might regard as not at all unnatural—we would still have to admit that such a turn of events would have been interpreted by them as witnessing to divine intervention. Thus the relevance to their situation of the story about Sennacherib's miraculous defeat is apparent at once.

This direct appeal to the Jews proved ineffective. Therefore, Josephus turned to reminiscences of the nation's history. He asks the challenging question: When, if ever, did the Jews conquer their enemies by force of arms?[41] Then he proceeds to cite some cases in which it is clear that the Jews were delivered from their enemies not by resort to

[41] And lest any be tempted to think of the victories of the Maccabees, Josephus points out that it was precisely mighty Rome which formerly had been an ally of the Jews. The suggestion was, we presume, that the military victories of the Maccabees would have been fruitless without the support of Rome—which is an astute historical judgment.

arms but by the intervention of God. When he comes to Sennacherib, king of Assyria, he asks:

Was it by human hands he fell? Were not those hands at rest from arms and raised in prayer, while God's angel, in one night, destroyed that countless host? And when the Assyrian arose next morning, did he not find 185,000 corpses, and with the remainder flee from the Hebrews who were neither armed nor pursuing?[42]

One need only compare the use to which this story is put by the authors of I and II Maccabees to see the kind of haggadic exegesis Josephus is attempting to refute. Josephus' clever treatment of this story in II Kings—a treatment which sharply contrasts with that given in the Maccabean literature—strongly suggests that the besieged Jews *were* deriving comfort, if not hope, from the knowledge that in times past God had miraculously delivered his people when they were under quite similar circumstances. If this story had no significance for the besieged Jews, how are we to explain the fact that Josephus chose to speak of it? The most natural explanation would seem to be that it was a story which was of tremendous significance to them, and Josephus has for that very reason taken great pains to show that the scriptural account, stripped of the kind of haggadic interpretation we see developing as early as I and II Maccabees, does not provide grounds for the use of arms by the Jews. It is a tour de force which we need not suppose was accorded validity by those who stood over against Josephus and scoffed at him and scorned his apostasy. Perhaps, adroit as it is, Josephus may never have used this exegesis in a speech actually addressed to the besieged fanatics— knowing how unreasonable men are in such circumstances. But we may well imagine that it reflects the kind of answer he would have afforded any zealous Jew who sought to find in this story divine sanction for the religious hope that God would assist the nation in its rebellion against the Romans.

42 *B.J.* 5.9.4 (387–88).

And if he did not refer to this story in an actual speech, we must still regard its presence—plus its peculiar interpretation—in the literary unit of which it is a part as reflecting an actual historical situation in which the story was being used by the besieged to sustain their hopes for some kind of divine intervention in their behalf. That the besieged did hope for divine intervention and did believe that it would come in time to save the temple we shall see later in this chapter.

Josephus continues his survey of the nation's history and refers to the Jews in exile. He points out that the exiled Jews had never revolted, yet they were sent back to re-establish the temple worship by the heathen Cyrus. Then he concludes:

> In short, there is no instance of our forefathers having triumphed by arms or failed of success without them when they committed their cause to God: if they sat still they conquered, as it pleased their Judge, if they fought they were invariably defeated.[43]

The speech rolls on: "Take the case of Zedekiah"—if we may paraphrase Josephus—"He resisted the Babylonians against the advice of Jeremiah, the prophet of God, and consequently was taken captive and saw the city and the temple demolished."

It should be fairly clear to the reader that all these references to Israel's past history would have been meaningless if the besieged Jews did not know and take that history seriously. Yet that history was a religious history. Therefore, the implication would seem to be that the besieged Jews had at least some concern for God and his purposes for Israel.[44]

We come now to a most interesting part of the speech.

[43] *B.J.* 5.9.4 (390).

[44] Of couse, if we take the extreme view that the speech is entirely un-related to any actual historical situation, and is in every respect a free literary composition by Josephus intended as pure propaganda to convince his Greco-Roman public that the Jews' resistance to Rome was in no way

Josephus says that when the Jews took up arms against Antiochus Epiphanes while he was besieging Jerusalem, they were badly beaten in battle.[45] As a consequence of this defeat, according to Josephus, the city was plundered, and the temple lay desolate for three and one half years. This single reference to the Seleucid period is highly significant.[46] In the first place, it suggests that the figure of Antiochus Epiphanes was well-known to the Jewish rebels; for he is mentioned along with the other prominent heathen kings, like Sennacherib and Cyrus, without any hint that he was less well-known than they were. But if Antiochus Epiphanes was well-known in the Roman period, how can we doubt that the Jews who led Israel to ultimate victory over his armies were equally well-known? This is, of course, a point we shall seek to demonstrate conclusively in the following chapter, namely, that the Maccabees were remembered in the Roman period. In the second place, this single reference to the Seleucid period in Josephus' speech assumes that the history of Israel during this period was of some importance to the besieged Jews. It is not difficult to guess what this importance was; for the wonderful victories of the Maccabees over the armies of the Seleucid empire

---

sanctioned by the true Jewish religion as expressed in the sacred scriptures of the Jews, then we could not make the kind of analysis in which we are now engaging. Our own view is that while this propaganda motive was probably present in the mind of Josephus as he wrote the speech as we now have it, nonetheless the speech does reflect the historical realities as they are known to us from many other sources and, therefore, can be used in attempting to get some understanding of the actual attitude of the Jews to whom the speech is ostensibly addressed.

45 We know of no other reference to such a battle.

46 No less significant is the fact that Josephus fails to make any reference to the Maccabean *victories* over the Seleucids—especially the victories over Heliodorus and Nicanor. One might argue that the Seleucids were known to the Jews only because of the veiled references to them in Daniel, in which references only Antiochus Epiphanes figures with any prominence. But this line of reasoning breaks down once it is realized that Josephus himself tells us in his *Ant.* that the Jews were still celebrating the thirteenth of Adar every year in commemoration of the great victory over the imperial forces led by the Seleucid general, Nicanor.

provided an unambiguous historical affirmation and validation of the theological tenet that if those Jews who were zealous for the Torah and the temple would take up the sword and strike a blow for Yahweh, he would give them the victory—no matter what the odds against them.[47] It is, precisely, confidence in this theological doctrine which Josephus seems to us to be trying to undermine in the speech which we are at present considering.

Josephus continues his address by pointing to the bloody hands of the besieged and asking: "Did your king lift up such hands in prayer to God against the king of Assyria, when he destroyed that great army in one night?"[48] This return to the story of Sennacherib supports our previous conclusion that the besieged quite likely derived comfort if not hope from the knowledge that God had miraculously delivered his holy city from the hands of the Assyrian army. Josephus, we suggest, has returned to this apparently crucial story in order to reiterate his point that the Jews in the days of Hezekiah did not resist the Assyrians by force of arms; for it seems his exegesis once again attempts to point out that the story provides no ground for hope of divine deliverance so long as the besieged Jews continue to resist the Romans with weapons of war.

Josephus proceeds to ask: "And do the Romans commit such wickedness, as did the king of Assyria, that you may

---

[47] This is the positive way in which to put the teaching of Judas of Galilee whom Josephus charges with having started the revolutionary movement which eventuated in the great open war with Rome in the time of Vespasian and Titus. The teaching is negatively stated as it is preserved to us in *Ant.* 18.1.1 (5): "They also said, that God would not otherwise be assisting to them, than upon their joining with one another in such counsels as might be successful, and for their own advantage; and this especially, if they would set about great exploits, and not grow weary in executing the same."

[48] *B.J.* 5.9.4 (404), following D. S. Margoliouth's revised ed. of Whiston's translation (London, n.d. [1905?] This excellent edition, by a first-rate scholar, is a revision based upon the critical edition of the Greek by B. Niese and J. von Destion (Berlin, 1887-94)—though its editor does not claim it to be as thoroughgoing a revision as that of A. R. Shilleto.

hope to have like vengeance upon them?"[49] This question suggests to the reader that the besieged Jews did hope that the miraculous defeat administered to Sennacherib would be served by God upon the Romans.[50] Now comes a question which is designed to point out an important difference between what the Assyrians under Sennacherib did and what the Romans are doing and intend to do. (Here again, the purpose is to demonstrate that there are no grounds for the hope that God will treat the Romans in the same way he dealt with the armies of Sennacherib.) Josephus asks whether it is not true that the Assyrian king accepted money from Hezekiah, promising that he would leave the city undamaged, and yet, in violation of his oath, later threatened to "burn the Temple?"[51] In contrast, says Josephus, the only thing that the Romans want is tribute.

Next, Josephus argues the justice of the Roman cause and proceeds as follows:

It is surely madness to expect God to show the same treatment to the just as to the unjust. Moreover, he knows how, at need,

[49] *Ibid.*

[50] It does not seem at all probable that Josephus would have written this statement in his *B.J.* if the speech were merely composed for propaganda purposes; for it suggests that the Jewish revolutionaries *were* sustained in their fanatic resistance by hopes which fed upon the sacred scriptures of Judaism—a fact that Josephus, for the most part, omits in his history. This continual reference to the Sennacherib story is not necessary if the only purpose of Josephus is to persuade his Greco-Roman readers that the Jewish revolution was not a true expression of Judaism. We conclude that the repeated reference to the story of the miraculous defeat of the Assyrian army before Jerusalem, and especially the above rhetorical question, indicate quite clearly that this speech does reflect the realities of an historical debate.

[51] *B.J.* 5.9.4 (405). There is no reference in II Kings to Sennacherib's intention to *burn the temple*. This statement by Josephus indicates that in the Roman as well as in the Seleucid period this story had come to be closely associated with the concern of the Jews to keep the temple inviolate —and was kept alive by the Jews because it inspired belief that God would miraculously intervene when and if the heathen threatened to burn his holy house. We will see later in this chapter that when the Romans did finally break through the desperate defense of the Jews and set fire to the temple and God did *not* intervene, then the behaviour of the Jews changed in a very curious way.

to inflict instant vengeance, as when He broke the Assyrians on the very first night when they encamped hard by; so that had he judged our generation worthy of freedom or the Romans of punishment, He would, as he did the Assyrians, have instantly visited them—when Pompey intermeddled with the nation, when after him Sossius came up, when Vespasian ravaged Galilee, and lastly now, when Titus was approaching the city. And yet Magnus and Sossius, far from sustaining any injury, took the city by storm; Vespasian from his war against us mounted to a throne.[52]

The logic which Josephus is pressing home here is that God has not punished the Romans as we would expect him to do if he were classing them with the perfidious Assyrians. After continuing in this vein for a few more lines Josephus concludes with this remark: "My belief, therefore, is that the Deity has fled from the holy places and taken His stand on the side of those with whom you are now at war."[53] There follows only his final appeal. It is addressed to the concern of the besieged Jews for their temple. The appeal is made on the ground that continued resistance to the Romans means the eventual destruction of that which they hold so dear.

In the light of the above evidence derived from an analysis of certain passages in this speech of Josephus, we suggest first, that the temple was of crucial concern to those Jews who had rebelled against Rome and were besieged in Jerusalem; second, that their apparently hopeless resistance to their heathen besiegers in the face of incredible difficulties must have been inspired to some extent by the faithful hope that God would intervene in some miraculous manner and deliver them from the hands of the Romans— as he had from the Assyrians in the days of pious Hezekiah, and from the Seleucids in the days of the pious and zealous Maccabees.

[52] *B.J.* 5.9.4 (407-9).
[53] *Ibid.* (412).

With reference to the Hellenistic period as a whole we conclude that the scriptural account of the miraculous defeat of Sennacherib's imperial army provided a story which was of special significance to Jewish nationalists in both the Seleucid and Roman periods. We also observe that there is evidence that in both periods this story was associated with the idea that God would preserve his temple from destruction by sending assistance of some kind to strike down the heathen armies which threatened it.

Throughout this discussion which has brought in so much about Sennacherib, the reader's mind may have been asking: "Did no one in those days remember Nebuchadnezzar? He had burned the temple and broken down the walls. He carted off the temple furniture and even its brass pillars, and when Nehemiah came back he found that Eliashib had set up a chamber for Tobiah in the courts of the temple. Did no one ever remember these things?" The answer is, of course these things were remembered. And no doubt such memories made it easier for Jews like Josephus to capitulate to the Romans. (After all the prophet Jeremiah had advised the Jews not to resist the Babylonians.) But at this point we are not seeking to explain the behavior of Josephus. Rather we are seeking to understand the actions of those Jews who stood *over against* Josephus and repudiated him as an apostate. (Perhaps they saw Nebuchadnezzar and Titus through the eyes of Daniel more than through the eyes of Jeremiah!) In the case of the defeat of Sennacherib we have a story which we *know* was remembered by Jews who glorified the Maccabees. We have shown how this story makes sense out of the otherwise inexplicable behavior of these zealous Jews. It enables us to see that their motivations were in part rooted in religious hope.

It is true, as Josephus pointed out, that in the story about Sennacherib in II Kings there is no reference to the use of arms on the part of the Jews. However, that did not keep

the authors of I and II Maccabees from seeing a close parallel between the deliverance which had been granted from
the Assyrians and that from the Seleucids. There can be
no doubt, therefore, that there were Jews who looked upon
the Maccabean victories as having been made possible
through divine assistance. In the course of time—as II
Maccabees makes perfectly clear—these victories were surrounded by an aura of legendary accretion in which the
miraculous intervention of God on behalf of the Jews was
increased to the point that it practically matched that found
in the story of Sennacherib's defeat. We may assume that
the Maccabean victories—so much closer in point of time
than the defeat of Sennacherib—if they *were* remembered,
were still remembered as victories in which faith in divine
assistance was combined with the most zealous use of the
sword in defence of the Torah and the temple. If the Maccabean victories *were* remembered, then it becomes quite
clear that the Jewish nationalists in the Roman period
would have derived comfort and hope from the stories of
those wonderful deliverances just as they did from the story
of the miraculous defeat of Sennacherib. However, in contrast to the story of Sennacherib's defeat, the stories from
the Seleucid period probably carried a very activistic moral;
for in the Maccabean victories God had assisted Jews who
were *zealously active in defense* of his interests. We can
see how the victories of the Maccabees would have been of
tremendous importance to the nationalists in the Roman
period, *if* they were remembered. But *were* they remembered? That is the crucial question. In the following chapter we shall establish that they were.

Our suggestions, made on the basis of the indirect evidence derived from the speech of Josephus analyzed above,
that the Jews were sustained in their fanatical resistance to
the Romans by belief that God would intervene to save
his temple, is strikingly supported by a direct statement

which Josephus places in the mouths of the besieged Jews. At a later point in the siege Titus is described as having appealed to the Jews to surrender and not to compel him to destroy Jerusalem and its temple. Josephus continues:

To this message the Jews retorted by heaping abuse from the ramparts upon Caesar himself and his father, crying out that they scorned death, which they honourably preferred to slavery; that they would do Romans every injury in their power while they had breath in their bodies . . . [as for the Temple] it would yet be saved by Him who dwelt therein, and while they had Him for their ally they would deride all menaces unsupported by action; for the issue rested with God.[54]

Did the besieged Jews really believe that God dwelt in the Jerusalem sanctuary? Did they really believe that he would save his temple? Was their fanatical resistance to the Romans grounded in the belief that "the issue rested with God? We must be careful not to say "yes" too quickly to these important questions; *for so to answer would involve us in a radically different evaluation of the Jewish resistance to the Romans from that made in our chief primary historical source.* Josephus again and again pictures these very same Jews as callous toward God, his Torah, and his Temple. He describes them as self-seeking, hypocritical, deceitful. He never once compares them to the Maccabees who figure in his histories as great leaders of the Jewish nation. *If we answer "yes" to the above questions, then the whole picture needs to be seriously revised in the direction of portraying these revolutionists as religiously motivated —in a fundamental sense—in their fanatical last-ditch stand against the legions of Rome.*

Fortunately the issue is not one that need remain unsettled in our minds. There is historical evidence of the most reliable nature which strongly supports an affirmative answer to all three of these questions. In order to bring

54 *B.J.* 5.11.2 (458-59).

out this evidence we are once again to be involved in a careful analysis of certain passages of Josephus' *Bellum Judaicum.*

A Last-Ditch Stand

Until the temple was destroyed the zealous Jews were absolutely uncompromising. They would surrender under no conditions, nor would they allow their compatriots to surrender. Those Jews who tried to go over to the side of the Romans, if caught while trying to escape from the city, were killed by their more zealous brethren. Neither famine, pestilence, nor incredible battle casualties could deter the Jews from their apparently insane refusal to surrender. But the moment the temple was set aflame—in spite of their every desperate effort to prevent the calamity—the defense of the city collapsed. Thereafter, the Jews showed no interest in defending Jerusalem, though there were almost impregnable defenses within the upper city in which they could have held out indefinitely. How can we explain this sudden change in the attitude of the zealous Jews toward the defense of Jerusalem? Since the firing of the temple coincided in time with the apparent change in attitude, we may assume that there was some kind of causal relationship between the two. The most natural explanation would seem to be that the fanatic defense of Jerusalem was rooted in the belief that God was in his temple and would eventually destroy the Romans, if only a righteous remnant would fulfill Israel's part of the covenant and be zealous in keeping up the sacrifices and in observing the Torah strictly. Such a belief would explain why the Jews chose to make a last-ditch stand before the temple instead of retiring to the tactically more defensible fortifications in the upper city, once it became clear, from a military standpoint, that the fall of the temple defenses was only a matter of time.

The fall of the temple not only made it impossible to offer
the sacrifices prescribed by the Torah, it also would have
undermined any belief the Jews might have had that God
wanted them to defend the city any longer. The logic is
obvious. If God has not saved his temple, he will not save
his city. Or, put another way: if God has left the temple,
he has left the city. This being so, we may wonder, once
the temple fell, why the Jews did not capitulate to the
Romans? We shall seek to answer this question later on,
but first let us go over briefly those events of the last dramatic days of the defense of Jerusalem.

After the armies of Titus had broken through the outer
walls of the city, the Jews took a suicidal stand between
the temple and the Romans. Josephus writes that they
sought to stem the advance of the Romans

with a prodigious exhibition of strength and spirit; for they
held that the entry of the Romans into the sanctuary meant
final capture, while the latter regarded it as the prelude to victory. So the armies clashed in desperate struggle round the en-
trances, the Romans pressing on to take possession also of the
temple, the Jews thrusting them back upon Antonia.[55]

Josephus continues his account of the desperate struggle
of which he probably was an eyewitness—perhaps standing
alongside Titus on Antonia, from where he could look
down upon the battle below and follow its course. He
writes:

Missiles and spears were useless to both belligerents. Drawing
their swords, they closed with each other, and in the mêlée it
was impossible to tell on which side either party was fighting,
the men being all jumbled together and intermingled in the
confined area, and their shouts, owing to the terrific din, falling confusedly on the ear. There was great slaughter on either
side, and the bodies and armour of the fallen were trampled
down and crushed by the combatants. And always, in which-
ever direction rolled the veering tide of war, were heard the
cheers of the victors, the wailings of the routed. Room for

[55] *B.J.* 6.1.7 (72–74).

flight or pursuit there was none; dubious turns of the scale and shifting of position were the sole incidents in the confused contest. Those in front had either to kill or be killed, there being no retreat; for those in rear in either army pressed their comrades forward, leaving no intervening space between the combatants. At length, Jewish fury prevailing over Roman skill, the whole line began to waver. For they had been fighting from the ninth hour of the night until the seventh of the day; the Jews in full strength, with the peril of capture as an incentive to gallantry, the Romans with but a portion of their forces, the legions upon whom the present combatants were dependent having not yet come up. It was therefore considered sufficient for the present to hold Antonia.[56]

Titus sent Josephus to make a last desperate appeal to the Jews in their own tongue. He was to offer them terms for sparing the temple and to threaten that if the Jews insisted on defending the temple the Romans would burn it. According to the account, the answer came back that there was no fear of capture "since the city was God's."[57]

The bloody battle raged on day after day. Josephus tells us that at last Titus, perceiving that his endeavor to spare the temple "led only to the injury and slaughter of his troops, issued orders to set the gates on fire."[58] The response of the Jews to this action of the Romans is very interesting. Josephus writes:

The Jews, seeing the fire encircling them, were deprived of all energy of body and mind; in utter consternation none attempted to ward off or extinguish the flames; paralyzed they stood and looked on. Yet though dismayed by the ravage being wrought, they learnt no lesson with regard to what was left, but, as if the very sanctuary were now ablaze, only whetted their fury against the Romans.[59]

Titus ordered his troops to extinguish the fire and then called a council of war that he might decided what should

56 *B.J.* 6.1.7 (75-80).
57 *B.J.* 6.2.1 (98).
58 *B.J.* 6.4.1 (228).
59 *B.J.* 6.4.2 (233-34).

be done about the temple. His staff was divided over the question. Some argued that the temple should be destroyed since the Jews would never cease from rebellion so long as it stood. Other were of a more moderate view. Josephus says that Titus concurred in opinion with the latter.[60] Nevertheless, in the ensuing course of the fighting the temple was set afire by the Roman soldiers. "As the flame shot up," Josephus writes, "a cry, as poignant as the tragedy, arose from the Jews, who flocked to the rescue, lost to all thought of self-preservation, all husbanding of strength, now that the object of all their past vigilance was vanishing."[61] We have no reason to doubt that this is, so far as it goes, a true picture of how the Jewish rebels felt about their national sanctuary.

While the Temple Burns

The flames which the Jews were trying so desperately to extinguish were burning the temple buildings adjacent to the main structure of the sanctuary. Before the fire destroyed the actual temple itself, Titus and his soldiers entered it and removed its sacred treasures. Thus the climax of the dramatic conflict was marked by a supreme affront to the holiness of God. If ever God intended to save his temple, the time was at hand. The ἔσχατον had come! But

[60] However, we may doubt the trustworthiness of Josephus at this point. We know that he was disposed to paint a favorable picture of his patrons Vespasian and Titus. It is not unlikely, therefore, that Josephus would have wished to free the Flavian house from any charge of barbarity which might arise from the impious temple-burning. Nor are we dependent on mere suspicion in our distrust of Josephus at this point; for there is another account of the matter which has been preserved for us in the writings of the fourth-century Christian, Sulpicius Severus, who is thought by some scholars to be dependent at this point—as it is known he was at others—on the writings of Tacitus. (We cannot be certain, for the corresponding section in the history of Tacitus is lost.) Sulpicius Severus says that Titus, at the council of war, sanctioned the destruction of the temple. Sulpicius, *Chron.* 2. 30. Cf. Thackeray's Introduction to *Bellum Judaicum* in the Loeb Classical Library ed. of the works of Josephus, II, xxiv-xxv.
[61] *B.J.* 6.4.5 (253).

God did *not* intervene. The Jews watched their sanctuary burn amid "lamentations and wailing."[62]

That the Jews had hoped for divine intervention cannot be doubted. Josephus himself tells us that the besieged were encouraged by the hope of divine deliverance promised by numerous prophets (οἱ προφῆται) who bid the faithful to "await help from God."[63] Perhaps the final blow to any last hope the Jews might have had for some miraculous turn of events occurred when the Romans perpetrated an "abomination that maketh desolate"[64] before the flaming temple—with perfect impunity. Without the slightest interpretation Josephus objectively records the following occurrence:

The Romans, now that the rebels had fled to the city, and the sanctuary itself and all around it were in flames, carried their standards into the temple court and, setting them up opposite the eastern gate, there sacrificed to them, and with rousing acclamations hailed Titus as imperator.[65]

Once this final act of blasphemy had been consummated, on holy ground, with no divine intervention, there could no longer be any doubt that God had indeed abandoned Zion. Whether or not the besieged Jews could have observed this desecration from the towers of the upper city, we may assume that they soon learned of it. What now was to be their course of action? The description which Josephus gives of their ensuing behavior provides us with convincing evidence that these Jews were strongly motivated by religious beliefs. From the practically impregnable fortifications in the upper city they could have held out against the Romans indefinitely.[66] But instead of continuing their

---

[62] *B.J.* 6.5.1 (274).

[63] *B.J.* 6.5.2 (286).

[64] The wording from Daniel thus applied is my own. However, Eusebius *Ecclesiastical History* III.v.4 regards this act as the fulfillment of the prophecy in Dan. 9:27. Cf. Matt. 24:15 and Mk 13:14.

[65] *B.J.* 6.6.1 (316). Cf. Ps. 74:4. Was this verse written before A.D. 70?

[66] Josephus in looking back on the strange action of the besieged Jews reflects as follows: "Here may we signally discern at once the power of

mad resistance to the Romans from these towers, they—for the first time—desired to treat with Titus by word of mouth. Titus offered them reasonable terms which they rejected on the grounds that they had sworn never to accept a pledge from him and that they wanted nothing more than "permission to pass through his line of circumvallation with their wives and children, undertaking to retire to the desert and to leave the city to him." [67] What is the meaning of this strange desire of the Jews to go out into the wilderness (ἡ ἔρημος) with their wives and their children? In the Semitic idiom the "wilderness" need not mean more than uncultivated land beyond the town or city limits. But it is exceedingly unlikely that all that these zealous Jews wanted was to get to the outskirts of metropolitan Jerusalem. The "wilderness" was remembered by the scriptural authors as that place where Yahweh first found Israel and "made him to suck honey out of the rock." We cannot take lightly the request of these zealous Jews that they be allowed to go out with their wives and children into the wilderness—for when it was refused them by Titus they neither surrendered nor retreated to the strong fortifications in the upper city but rather made suicidal attempts to break through the Roman lines. [68]

Into the Wilderness

Once before in the history of Israel, when the sanctuary had fallen into the hands of the heathen and had been

---

God over unholy men and the fortune of the Romans. For the tyrants stripped themselves of their security and descended of their own accord from those towers, whereon they could never have been overcome by force, and famine alone could have subdued them; while the Romans, after all the toil expended over weaker walls, mastered by the gift of fortune those that were impregnable to their artillery. For the three towers, which we have described above, would have defied every engine of war" (*B.J.* 6.8.4 [399–400]). *Cf. B.J.* 6.9.1 (409–13).

[67] *B.J.* 6.6.3 (351).
[68] *B.J.* 6.8.5 (401–2).

polluted by unlawful sacrifice, pious Jews had gone out into the wilderness with their wives and children. We read in I Maccabees: "Then many that sought after justice and judgment went down into the wilderness (τὴν ἔϱημον), to dwell there, they, and their sons, and their wives, and their cattle; because evils were multiplied upon them."[69] Nor was this phenomenon confined to the Maccabean period. There was in the Roman period during the procuratorship of Fadus the case of Theudas of whom Josephus writes:

Theudas persuaded a great part of the people to take their effects with them, and follow him to the river Jordan; for he told them he was a prophet, and that he would, by his own command, divide the river, and afford them as easy passage over it: and many were deluded by his words.[70]

During the procuratorship of Felix there was great unrest among the Jews. Josephus in reference to certain leaders of the Jews writes, "And now these impostors and deceivers persuaded the multitude to follow them into the wilderness (τὴν ἐϱημίαν), and pretended that they would exhibit manifest wonders and signs, that should be performed by the providence of God."[71] In reference to the same leaders Josephus wrote in *Bellum Judaicum:*

Deceivers and impostors, under pretense of divine inspiration fostering revolutionary changes, they persuaded the multitude to act like madmen, and led them out into the desert (τὴν ἐϱημίαν) under the belief that God would there give them tokens (σημεῖα) of deliverance.[72]

---

[69] I Macc. 2:29-30. Cf. Psalms of Solomon 17:19, which possibly refers to a similar situation at a later time.

[70] *Ant.* 20.5.1 (97).

[71] *Ant.* 20.8.6 (167–68).

[72] *B.J.* 2.13.4 (259). In connection with these episodes in which great multitudes of faithful Jews are in the desert in response to the message of some prophet of God we ought to mention certain events recorded in the Gospels. On one occasion when a great multitude had gathered around Jesus he is remembered to have told his disciples to prepare a meal for the crowd which had been with him for three days. His disciples ask: "How can one feed these men with bread here in the desert (ἐπ' ἐϱημίας)?" Mark 8:4.

During the procuratorship of Festus the same phenomenon recurred. Josephus writes:

So Festus sent forces, both horsemen and footmen, to fall upon those that had been seduced by a certain impostor, who promised them deliverance and freedom from the miseries they were under, if they would but follow him as far as the wilderness (μέχρι τῆς ἐρημίας). Accordingly those forces that were sent destroyed both him that deluded them and those that were his followers also.[73]

The opposition of the heathen officials, responsible for maintaining law and order in Palestine, to gatherings of this kind was always the same. In every instance referred to above, whether in the Seleucid or the Roman period, the crowds which went out into the wilderness were followed by royal troops and put to the sword. Obviously the Seleucids and Romans regarded these religious gatherings as politically dangerous. Therefore we need not wonder that Titus refused the request of the besieged Jews who wanted to pass through his lines and go out into the desert. But the important point for the student of Jewish nationalism to see is that all the relevant parallels indicate that this desire on the part of the besieged Jews to go out into the wilderness with their wives and children arose out of religious considerations. We see no reason to think that this indication is aught but true. Otherwise we would be unable to explain why these Jews did not accept the reasonable surrender terms offered by Titus but rather preferred to spend their lives in a suicidal effort to break through the Roman lines. The most natural way in which to understand

---

But the miracle was performed, and John writes: "When the people saw the sign (σημεῖον) which he had done, they said, 'This is indeed the prophet who is to come into the world!' Perceiving then that they were about to come and take him by force to make him king, Jesus withdrew again to the hills by himself." (John 6:14–15).

[73] *Ant.* 20.8.10 (188). Cf. Ant. 18.5.2 (116–119), where the crowds which went down to hear John the Baptist were regarded as politically dangerous.

the otherwise inexplicable behavior of these zealous Jews is to assume that their conviction that Yahweh had abandoned his temple did not convince them that their God had abandoned his people. Before there was a temple on Zion—long before—Yahweh had manifested his power over nature and kings. If in his wrath he had now abandoned his city, then the only thing a zealous Jew could do was to go into the wilderness where Yahweh had first tabernacled with Israel. The Torah read:

> Remember the days of old,
> Consider the years of many generations:
> Ask thy father, and he will show thee;
> Thine elders and they will tell thee.
> When the Most High gave to the nations their inheritance,
> When he separated the children of men,
> He set the bounds of the peoples
> According to the number of the children of Israel.
> For Yahweh's portion is his people;
> Jacob is the lot of his inheritance.
> *He found him in a desert land,*
> *And in the waste howling wilderness;*
> He compassed him about, he cared for him,
> He kept him as the apple of his eye
>
> .   .   .   .
>
> *Yahweh alone did lead him,*
> *And there was no foreign god with him.*
> He made him ride on the high places of the earth,
> And he did eat the increase of the field;
> And he made him to suck honey out of the rock,
> And oil out of the flinty rock;
> Butter of the herd, and milk of the flock,
> With fat of lambs,
> And rams of the breed of Bashan, and goats,
> With the finest of the wheat;
> And of the blood of the grape thou drankest wine.[74]

---

[74] Deut. 32:7–14. The LXX reads ἔρημος for desert.

Israel could still exist as a covenant community by interpreting the fall of the temple as the judgment of God upon the sins of his people.[75] This judgment was not to be understood as a repudiation of his people by Yahweh. The covenant God had not chosen Israel for the sake of the temple, but the temple for the sake of Israel.[76] God allows calamity to fall upon the nation not that it may be destroyed but that it may be chastened.[77] The mercy of God is never completely withdrawn from his people. God may punish, but he never abandons Israel.[78] That which has been destroyed will be rebuilt in God's due time. The temple which has been forsaken by God in his wrath will be restored in all its glory when he becomes reconciled.[79] "Meanwhile, the Torah remains—in our hands, and written in our hearts. Let us go out into the wilderness where we can keep his Law free from interference by the heathen!" Or if one thinks that something more soul-stirring in the way of a vital religious hope must have motivated those zealous Jews to make their request that they be allowed to pass through the Roman lines and go out into the desert with their wives and children, then perhaps we ought to consider the possibility that they were inspired by some kind of Messianic hope in which Messianic deliverance was associated with the wilderness.[80]

[75] Cf. II Macc. 7:18, where the pious Jew interprets his and his brothers' suffering as divine punishment because of sin, in spite of the fact that he and his brothers are giving up their lives rather than transgress the Torah.

[76] II Macc. 5:19.

[77] II Macc. 6:12.

[78] II Macc. 6:16.

[79] II Macc. 5:20.

[80] There can be no doubt that there were Messianic expectations associated with the wilderness during this general period. Cf. Matt. 24:15-25. "So when you see the desolating sacrilege spoken of by the prophet Daniel, standing in the holy place, then let those who are in Judea flee to the mountains. . . . Then if any one says to you, 'Lo, here is the Christ!' or 'There he is!' do not believe it. For false Christs and false prophets will arise and shew great signs and wonders so as to lead astray, if possible, even the elect. . . . So, if they say to you, *'Lo, he is in the wilderness,'* do not go out." The possibility that the setting up of their standards in the holy

In whatever way the reader may choose to explain the final actions of those Jewish nationalists, there is one explanation which is quite incredible in face of all the facts to which attention has been brought in this chapter, viz., that they were primarily motivated by self-interest, and that they had no sincere concern for their God, nor his Torah, nor his temple. On the contrary, there is every indication that these Jews were strongly motivated by religious beliefs.

If the reader wonders why so much space has been devoted to the attempt to demonstrate that these fanatical Jews were religiously motivated, we say as we have before, *he has not taken seriously the problem involved in the use of our main primary source.* We have no right as historians to ignore the picture of these people which Josephus has given us. That is a very dark picture indeed, and we have indicated in Chapter II why it is to be distrusted. But if we were to proceed with our research carefully, basing our work on sound historical evidence, then it was absolutely

---

place, and sacrificing to them by the Roman soldiers, could have been regarded as the "desolating sacrilege" ought not to be ignored. It may have been interpreted as a sign for the Jews to flee, not, as this particular apocalypse exhorts, to the mountains, but "into the desert," where they would find the Messiah. It is interesting to note in this connection that the "Manual of Discipline" of the Dead Sea Scrolls has the "community" going into the wilderness in obedience to the command in Isaiah 40:3; "In the wilderness prepare the way of the Lord, make straight in the desert a highway for our God." According to the Manual, there in the wilderness the way for the Lord's coming is to be prepared through the study of the Torah of Moses and through obedience to all that has been revealed by his Holy Spirit to the prophets. There in the wilderness (at Qumran?), united by a special discipline, the "community" shall constitute a "holy of holies," in which atonement is made for the guilt of transgression through sacrifices of praise and perfect obedience. Set apart in this way, the "community" shall serve as a house of holiness for Aaron and a house of community for obedient Israelites until the coming of a prophet and the Messiahs of Aaron and Israel. Col. 8, line 13 to col. 9, line 11. The activity of John the Baptist in the wilderness, Jesus' baptism by John, and Jesus' temptations in the wilderness all point to the fact that there were well-recognized messianic expectations associated with the wilderness of Judea.

necessary that we labor very hard and long to establish with as high a degree of probability as possible that Jewish nationalism in the Roman period was rooted, not in secularized self-interest, as Josephus suggests, but rather in pious devotion to the God of the Torah who was also the God of the national sanctuary.

So far as we can tell, these zealous Jews were no different in their motivation from their earlier compatriots, the Maccabees, of whom the author of II Maccabees was able to say that in their fanatic fight against the Seleucids they were, of course, motivated to some extent by fear for their families, "but greatest and first was their fear for the consecrated sanctuary." [81]

"Zeal for Thy House Will Consume Me"

The Maccabees were not only willing to fight to defend the temple. They were ready, if need be, to die in behalf of the national sanctuary. The author of I Maccabees places the following words in the mouth of Judas as words of exhortation to his army:

Gird yourselves, and be valiant men, and be in readiness against the morning, that ye may fight with these Gentiles, that are assembled together against us to destroy us, and our holy place: for it is better for us to die in battle, than to look upon the evils of our nation and the holy place. Nevertheless, as may be the will in heaven, so shall he do. [82]

We have given abundant evidence that the Jewish nationalists during the last weeks and days of their defense of the temple against the Romans appear to have been just as willing to lay down their lives for the sanctuary as were the Maccabees. [83] Nor is this willingness to fight and die in

[81] II Macc. 15:18.
[82] I Macc. 3:58–60. Cf. I Macc. 3:43; 13:3; 14:29, 32, 36, 42.
[83] See especially *B.J.* 6.1.7 (71–80); 6.2.6 (143); 6.4.2 (234); 6.4.3 (239); 6.4.5 (253).

behalf of the Temple characteristic of Jewish nationalism only at the *end* of the Roman period. We find evidence *throughout* the Roman period which indicates a willingness on the part of the Jews who resisted Rome to defend the temple with their lives if necessary. Working backwards in time we notice first that when Petronius attempted to erect Caius Caligula's statue in the Jerusalem temple, great multitudes of Jews were ready to die rather than see the national sanctuary defiled.[84] Earlier, in the time of Herod, Judas and Mattathias along with their followers died willingly out of their concern to keep the temple from being profaned by Herod's idolatrous golden eagle. After Herod's death, Josephus writes that those Jews bent on revolution assembled in large numbers and asserted that Judas and Mattathias "had in defence of their country's laws and the temple perished on the pyre."[85]

This concern for the temple among those Jews zealous for the Torah did not originate in the time of Herod. As we have indicated, it characterized the Maccabees as well.

Summary

We conclude this chapter by observing that there is no evidence whatever that the Jewish nationalists of the Roman period had a different attitude toward the temple from that of the Maccabees. On the other hand, as we have indicated in this chapter, there is considerable evidence which indicates that in *both* periods the temple was of central concern to the nationalists. We see no reason why this central concern for the temple should have had different roots in one period from that which it had in the other. The Torah prescriptions with reference to sacrifice made

[84] *B.J.* 2.10.1–5 (184–203); *Ant.* 18.8.1–6 (257–88); Philo, *Legatio ad Gaium* 31 (207ff.). Philo in effect says that the Jews would have gone to war to prevent the erection of the statue in the temple.

[85] *B.J.* 2.1.1 (6). Note the close association of Torah and temple.

the temple central in the cult life of the nation. Since the Jewish nationalists in both the Seleucid and Roman periods seem to have had the same attitude toward the Torah, as we have demonstrated in the previous chapter, we believe that we are on firm ground in asserting that the centrality of the temple for the nationalists in both periods must have been rooted in their common concern for the Law. What alternative is there?

It would follow, therefore, that fundamentally the same attitude toward the temple prevailed among the Jewish nationalists of the Roman period as prevailed among their counterparts in the Seleucid period. This conclusion further strengthens our thesis that the Jewish nationalists of the Roman period were motivated by the same kind of theology which inspired the Maccabees, and that these earlier national heroes were the nearest counterparts to the later Zealots,[86] if not their actual prototypes. They were their nearest counterparts, for they did and said the same kind of thing—as we have demonstrated in this and the previous chapter. But whether the Maccabees were actually "prototypes" for the Zealots depends on whether they were actually remembered in the Roman period. We are now ready to consider that question in the next chapter. Were the Maccabees forgotten heroes in the New Testament period, or were they still remembered and was their memory still associated with the soul-stirring victories over the imperial armies of the Seleucids? If they were so remembered, then that is a fact of tremendous importance to students interested in the Jewish background of the New Testament—as we have indicated in the Introduction and shall bring out more clearly in our concluding chapter.

[86] "Zealot" is used here and throughout the book not in the strict sense with which Josephus uses it, but in its more general meaning—i.e., extreme nationalist.

VI: WERE THE MACCABEES
REMEMBERED?

We have demonstrated in the two previous chapters that
the Maccabees were historical counterparts to the Jewish
nationalists of the first century A.D. However, we want to
know whether they were consciously held as prototypes by
the later Jewish nationalists. This is important to know
because if they were, it would indicate that the example
and teaching of the Maccabees was very influential in the
New Testament period. For the Maccabees to have been
held as prototypes by the Zealots it would have been necessary for them to have been remembered by Jews in the
first century A.D. Were they so remembered?

There are certain apparent difficulties which seem at
first to stand in the way of an affirmative answer to this
question. We shall first state what those difficulties are and
then attempt to show that they are not really difficulties
at all but that, when properly understood, they harmonize
very well with the hypothesis that the Maccabees were remembered. After we have done this we shall consider the
positive evidence which indicates very strongly that the
Maccabees *were* remembered during the first century A.D.

The difficulties which seem to go against the possibility
that the Maccabees were remembered resolve themselves
into the simple fact that no reference either to the Maccabean heroes or to their achievements is found in the great

body of Jewish and Christian literature which comes to us from the first century A.D.

The Argument from Silence

It is well-known that the Maccabees are not explicitly mentioned in the Mishnah. However, it is not only the Mishnah which is silent regarding the Maccabees. Josephus never speaks of the example or teaching of the Maccabees as having any influence on the Jews in the Roman period. Furthermore, with the possible exception of Hebrews 11:35–38, the New Testament does not refer to the Maccabees in any way. If the Maccabees were remembered and were great national heroes in this period, why is it that they do not figure more prominently in this literature? All of the objections to the main thesis of this dissertation, which are known to its author, can be reduced, in the final analysis, to one or another form of this grand "argument from silence." It is imperative, therefore, that we deal with this question.

We have already devoted one whole chapter to the writings of Josephus in which we sought to explain why, in our view, the author has obscured the connection between the Maccabees and the Jewish nationalists who fought against Rome. Briefly stated, the reasons why we think that Josephus would have obscured such a connection are as follows: *politically*, as a pro-Roman Jewish apologist, while he could praise the Maccabees who had been allies of Rome, he had to blame those Jews who in his day were the enemies of Rome; *theologically*, he could glorify the Maccabees as the saviours of Israel; but the victory of Rome over the Jews proved in his view that the Jewish leaders were rebels against the will of God; *personally*, Josephus was linked by descent to the royal house of the Hasmoneans; naturally proud of the great achievements of his famous ancestors, he could hardly admit that his most bitter enemies were their true spiritual heirs. For these three reasons, and perhaps for others unknown to us, we dare not argue from the "silence" of Josephus that the example and teaching of the Maccabees had no influence on the action and thought of those Jews whom he describes in the most contemptuous and bitter language as "brigands."

With regard to the New Testament it should be pointed out that not only is it silent about the Maccabees, it is also silent about Shammai and Hillel and all the other pre-Tannaitic Rabbinical teachers. We know, however, from the literature of Jews for whom the teaching and example of these men were important that their memory and influence was very much alive during the first century A.D. Nor should we look to the Mishnah to get a picture of the influence of Jesus of Nazareth or John the Baptist among Jews during the latter half of the first century A.D. We have no aerial photographs of the history of the Jews in Palestine during this period. We have only some highly stylized paintings, all of which have been made from particular points of view. The Jewish nationalists lost the war, and, therefore, paintings from their particular point of view were either never produced or if produced, not preserved.[1]

The New Testament, generally speaking, is concerned with but one central subject, Jesus of Nazareth as the Messiah. All matters which are not, from the point of view of the New Testament authors, directly related in some way to that central subject, should be regarded by the historian as background material—sometimes detailed, generally reliable, but inevitably selective and highly fragmentary.

---

[1] *Megillath Taanith* may be an exception. It will be discussed at the end of this chapter. It is too early to determine the exact bearing of the sectarian scrolls from the Judean wilderness upon this particular argument. They do not mention the Maccabees, though in important respects they give expression to the same kind of theology which apparently motivated the Maccabees. See Chapter VII.

The proper response to the fact that the Maccabees do not figure prominently in the New Testament is to assume, not that they were unimportant to Jews in this period, but that they were unimportant to the early Christian church —and even that might be to some extent an unwarranted assumption since there is not a single New Testament author whom we can regard as a qualified spokesman for the *prewar* Jerusalem or Palestinian church.[2]

With regard to the point that the Mishnah is silent about the Maccabees, it should be remembered that this particular body of Rabbinic literature was codified by Jews who submitted to Roman authority. Johanan ben Zakkai, the founder of the school at Jabneh, is said to have been smuggled out of Jerusalem during the siege. In Jabneh men gathered around him who were willing to work with the Romans. The head of this school of scholars was recognized as the accredited representative of the defeated nation, and it sometimes was necessary for him to journey to Rome on matters of state. It was Rabbi Judah the Holy who edited the Mishnah and in large part gave it its final form. He is remembered as an apt student of Greek and a trusted friend of the Romans.[3] Therefore, the fact that the warlike Maccabees do not figure prominently in the Mish-

[2] The evidence for the very late tradition that the Christians left Jerusalem before the war and migrated to Pella provides us with too thin a thread on which to hang any sound historical judgment regarding the extent to which the Jewish Christians may have shared the national hopes and aspirations of their fellow countrymen and/or been involved in the struggle for national independence. The much earlier tradition that the disciples continued to worship in the Jerusalem temple is, historically speaking, decidedly more reliable. The Jerusalem church, led by those who were of the highest repute within the early apostolic church, was a very vital and influential force when Paul wrote Galatians. The mystery of what ever happened to this once aggressive Christian community may never be solved. But one cannot avoid noticing that its disappearance from the scene of history coincides with the crushing defeat of national hopes at the hands of the Romans. Cf. Brandon, *The Fall of Jerusalem and the Christian Church.*

[3] Cf. Herbert Danby, *The Mishnah, translated from the Hebrew with Introduction and Brief Explanatory Notes* (London, 1933), pp. xix–xxi.

nah should suggest to us, not that they were unimportant to Jews during the first century A.D., but that their example and teaching was not normative for those Rabbis whose views have been preserved to us in the Mishnaic discussions—and even that might be in some ways a misleading suggestion since in many cases that which has been preserved of the teachings of certain Rabbis cited in the Mishnah is too fragmentary to enable one to decide what their attitude toward the Maccabees was.[4]

We conclude that the fact that the Maccabees do not figure as some would expect in the writings of Josephus, the Mishnah, and the New Testament provides no grounds for the assumption that these great national heroes were forgotten during the first century A.D. None of this literature is written from the point of view of those extreme nationalists who would most naturally have looked to the example and teachings of the Maccabees for inspiration. Literature from their hands quite possibly would reveal that the Maccabees played a very influential role in their thinking and acting. It is possible that we do have one document which comes from the hands of these nationalistic Jews, *Megillath Taanith*. We shall discuss this document rather fully later in this chapter.

The Maccabees Were Remembered

We turn now to consider the evidence which indicates that the Maccabees were remembered by the Jews in Pales-

---

[4] One also needs to contend with the fact that the Mishnah in at least some cases seems to acknowledge the authority of Halakic principles first established by the Maccabees. See, for example, *Yoma* 8.6. Louis Finkelstein regards this teaching of the Mishnah as an extension of the rule first established in Maccabean times, of setting aside the sabbath law when life is in danger (I Macc. 2:41). "Some examples of the Maccabean Halaka," *Journal of Biblical Literature*, XLIX (1930), 29. One must say, however, that on the whole the tendency of the Mishnah is to soften the rigorous demands of the Torah as understood by the Maccabees.

tine during the first century A.D. In the first place it should be pointed out that since there is no real evidence against the possibility that the Maccabees were remembered, there is no sound historical reason why one should think that the Maccabees were forgotten heroes. On the contrary, since they were such great examples of religious piety and military excellence, we have every reason to suppose that the stories about their marvelous victories were one of the most popular features of Palestine folk tradition during the Roman period.

But what positive evidence do we have that at certain definite points in time and place the Maccabean heroes were remembered? There are, of course, certain obvious instances to which we can point. Thus, for example, the Maccabees were remembered when the author of I Maccabees composed his history. So were they remembered when Jason of Cyrene wrote his five-volume work on the achievements of the Maccabees. At a somewhat later date the Epitomizer, known as the author of II Maccabees, abridged Jason's five volumes into one. The Maccabees were remembered then—and, we might add, they were highly glorified.

In spite of the fact that Josephus is silent with reference to any influence the Maccabees may have had on the Jews during the first century A.D., it is still true to say that these great national heroes were remembered by him when, in composing his histories, he wrote about their exploits against the Seleucids. In fact, in his *Antiquitates Judaicae,* which was written long after his *Bellum Judaicum,* Josephus makes a statement which seems to suggest that the Maccabees were remembered in his day not only by the historian but also by Jews in general, and especially by those Jews who were interested in achieving national independence from the Romans. After describing the victories of the Jews under the leadership of Judas, in which he seems to be following closely the accounts given in I Maccabees, Josephus writes as follows:

Such was the end of Judas, who had been a valiant man and a great warrior, and mindful of the injunctions of his father Mattathias, had had the fortitude to do and suffer all things for the liberty of his fellow-citizens. And such was the prowess of this man that he left behind him the greatest and most glorious of memorials—to have freed his nation and rescued them from slavery to the Macedonians.[5]

These remarks are not found in our I Maccabees and presumably reflect the view of Josephus himself as he looks back to the time of the Maccabees. The final statement certainly suggests that Judas was remembered for precisely those qualities which would have made him a national hero in the eyes of those who sought to rescue Israel from slavery to the Romans.

In spite of the fact that the Mishnah is silent concerning the Maccabees, it is well known that the Rabbis did remember the Maccabean family as well as their great victories over the Seleucids.[6] None of these considerations, however, amount to positive evidence of a very strong character. With reference to I and II Maccabees, it should be pointed out that we have no way of knowing whether this literature circulated in Palestine during the first century A.D. or not. We may assume that it did, but we cannot prove it.

As for Josephus' statement that Judas Maccabeus left behind him a glorious memorial, we dare not place too much weight on that since Josephus, as a descendent of the royal Hasmonean house, might have been expressing his

---

[5] *Ant.* 12.11.2 (433–34).
[6] Cf. *Shab.* 21b; *Yom.* 16a; *R.Sh.* 18b; *Taan.* 18b; *Meg.* 6a, 11a. The Rabbis referred to the Maccabees as the Hasmoneans. The name Maccabee was borne by only one member of the family, Judas. Later this name came to be used for the whole family. This extension in the use of the name Maccabee seems to have occurred first in Christian circles, though it may have had its origin in Alexandrian Jewish circles.

own private judgment at this point and not giving voice to a popular attitude.

As far as the memories of the Rabbis are concerned, we have no right to question this important tradition. However, one must admit that evidence from Talmudic literature is not decisive in this case. Fortunately we do have much more significant and decisive evidence to present; and to that evidence we now turn our attention.

We rest the case for our thesis that the Maccabees were remembered by the Jews in Palestine during the first century A.D. on the fact that there were national holidays celebrated annually by the Jews in this period which commemorated certain great events from the time of the Maccabees. There is nothing new or startling about this fact. It is known to all students of Jewish history. But it is a fact which, in our view, has never been properly evaluated by those who have written about Jewish history. In one sense the primary purpose of the preceding chapters of this dissertation has been to prepare the reader to see this well-accepted fact in its true light.

Hanukkah

Until this very day, the Jews still celebrate Hanukkah every year for eight days. All other great feasts celebrated by the Jews are prescribed by the Torah. Hanukkah alone has survived through the centuries without justification in the Bible. What is it that can account for the way in which this popular festival has gripped the hearts of the Jewish people and lived on as an annual observance? Every year during Hanukkah the Jews pray:

We thank thee also for the miracles, for the redemption, for the mighty deeds and saving acts, wrought by thee, as well as for the wars which thou didst wage for our fathers in days of old, at this season. In the days of the Hasmonean, Mattathias

son of Johanan, the High Priest, and his sons, when, the iniqui-
tous power of Greece rose up against thy people Israel to make
them forgetful of thy Law, and to force them to transgress the
statutes of thy will, then didst thou in thy abundant mercy
rise up for them in the time of their trouble; thou didst plead
their cause, thou didst judge their suit, thou didst avenge
their wrong; thou deliveredst the strong into the hands of the
weak, the many into the hands of the few, the impure into the
hands of the pure, the wicked into the hands of the righteous,
and the arrogant into the hands of them that occupied themselves with thy Law: for thyself thou didst make a great and
holy name in thy world, and for thy people Israel thou didst
work a great deliverance and redemption as at this day. And
thereupon thy children came into the oracle of thy house,
cleansed thy temple, purified thy sanctuary, kindled lights in
thy holy courts, and appointed these eight days of Hanukkah
in order to give thanks and praises unto thy great name.[7]

No one questions the fact that the festival of Hanukkah
was instituted in the time of the Maccabees to commemorate the rededication of the temple after it had been recovered and cleansed from the defiling hands of the Seleucids by the victorious Judas and his brothers.[8] Hanukkah
means "dedication." We read in I Maccabees:

But Judas and his brethren said, Behold, our enemies are
discomforted: let us go up to cleanse the holy place, and to dedi-
cate it afresh. And all the army was gathered together, and they

[7] *The Standard Prayer Book,* authorized English Translation by S. Singer
(New York: Bloch Publishing Co., 1949), pp. 63-64.

[8] There have been various theories propounded as to the relationship
of Hanukkah to earlier religious celebrations. Cf. O. S. Rankin, *The Origins
of the Festival of Hannukkah, the Jewish New Age Festival* (Edinburgh,
1930); S. Zeitlin, "Hanukkah," *Jewish Quarterly Review,* new ser., XXIX
(1938), 1-36; J. Morgenstern, "The Chanukkah Festival and the Calendar
of Ancient Israel," *Hebrew Union Annual,* XX (1947), 1-136 (the continuation of this article in Vol. XXI adds little and is mostly devoted to a study of the calendar). The above-mentioned literature provides
abundant references to the work of other scholars who have written on
Hanukkah. The latest statement on the subject is that given in Zeitlin's
Introduction to *The First Book of the Maccabees,* English Translation by
Sidney Tedesche, Introduction and Commentary by Solomon Zeitlin (New
York: Harper, 1950), pp. 50-54. Zeitlin discusses the factors which suggest

went up to mount Zion. And they saw the sanctuary laid desolate, and the altar profaned, and the gates burned up, and
shrubs growing in the courts as in a forest or as on one of the
mountains, and the priest's chambers pulled down; and they
rent their clothes, and made great lamentation, and put ashes
on their heads, and fell on their faces to the ground, and blew
with the solemn trumpets, and cried toward heaven. Then
Judas appointed certain men to fight against those who were
in the citadel, until he should have cleansed the holy place.

And he chose blameless priests, such as had pleasure in the
law: and they cleansed the holy place, and bear out the stones
of defilement unto an unclean place. And they took counsel
concerning the altar of burnt offerings, which had been profaned, what they should do with it: and there came into their
mind a good counsel, that they should pull it down, lest it
should be a reproach to them, because the Gentiles had defiled
it: and they pulled down the altar, and laid up the stones in

---

an origin differing from that traditionally ascribed to Hanukkah, and then
argues for the priority of Biblical precedents. It matters not to our thesis
what the origins of Hanukkah were in the pre-Maccabean period, so long
as it is held that the form in which it was observed in post-Maccabean
times was determined by and associated with the great Maccabean victories.
This fact is evidently not under dispute. Morgenstern writes: "Very ap-
propriately the Temple at Jerusalem was rededicated by the Maccabees on
IX/25, the very same day on which, three years earlier, it had been dedicated by the Syrians to their supreme deity. But instead of making their
Jewish festival the climactic and closing day of an eight day religious
celebration, coinciding exactly in time with the Syrian festival, and perhaps even to distinguish their festival clearly from the Syrian festival,
and so, to avoid the suggestion that they had borrowed the Syrian festival
directly, or had even actually adopted a heathen, non-Yahwistic festival to
their cult practice, they made this day of Dedication . . . the opening day of
an eight day festival. . . . Thus they made their Dedication Festival, their
Chanukkah, contrast markedly with its immediate antecedent" ("The
Chanukkah," p. 115). Zeitlin seeks to undermine *any* attempt to theorize on
the pagan origins of Hanukkah by observing that "the choice of a date for
Hanukkah to coincide with the date of the defilement of the Temple need
cause no surprise. Actually Judah might have purified the Temple any
time after 23 Heshvan, when Antiochus' stone *Sorega* was pulled down;
he purposely waited until the anniversary of the defeat to lend greater
brilliance to the celebration of the victory: 'At the same time on the same
day on which the heathen profaned it, on that very day it was consecrated
with songs and harps and lutes and with cymbals (I Macc. 4:54).' This also
explains the coincidence of the date with the Feast of Dionysus, for Antiochus had doubtless chosen that date for dedicating the Temple to Zeus
Olympius" (*The First Book of the Maccabees,* Introduction, p. 52).

the mountain of the house in a convenient place, until there should come a prophet to give an answer concerning them. And they took whole stones according to the law, and built a new altar after the fashion of the former; and they built the holy place, and the inner parts of the house; and they hallowed the courts. And they made the holy vessels new, and they brought the candlestick, and the altar of burnt offerings and of incense, and the table into the temple. And they burned incense upon the altar, and they lighted the lamps that were upon the candlestick, and they gave light in the temple. And they set loaves upon the table, and spread out the veils, and finished all the works which they made.

And they rose up early in the morning, on the five and twentieth day of the ninth month, which is the month Chislev, in the hundred and forty and eighth year, and offered sacrifice according to the law upon the new altar of burnt offerings which they had made. At what time and on what day the Gentiles had profaned it, even on that [day] it was dedicated afresh, with songs and harps and lutes, and with cymbals. And all the people fell upon their faces, and worshipped, and gave praise unto heaven, which had given them good success. And they kept the dedication of the altar eight days, and offered burnt offerings with gladness, and sacrificed a sacrifice of deliverance and praise. And they decked the forefront of the temple with crowns of gold and small shields, and dedicated afresh the gates and the priests' chambers, and made doors for them. And there was exceeding great gladness among the people, and the reproach of the Gentiles was turned away. And Judas and his brethren and the whole congregation of Israel ordained, that the days of the dedication of the altar should be kept in their seasons from year to year by the space of eight days, from the five and twentieth day of the month Chislev, with gladness and joy.[9]

We have cited this passage in full because we want the reader to see the kind of evidence which exists in a first-rate historical source for the institution of an eight-day festival beginning on the twenty-fifth of Chislev to be observed annually in commemoration of the rededication of the temple after its defilement by pagan worship. It is gen-

[9] I Macc. 4:36–59.

erally thought that the author of I Maccabees had access to eyewitness accounts in composing his history. This may be true in the present passage. But it is also true that there is a certain literary unity to I Maccabees which makes it quite clear that our author has not simply pieced together a collection of eyewitness accounts without exercising his discriminating editorial prerogatives. The moment this is admitted, however, it follows that the account above not only reflects the original intention of the Maccabees in instituting the festival, but also, to some extent, the true meaning of the festival in the eyes of the author of I Maccabees. This means that at some date after the original institution of the festival it was possible for a first-rate historian, whose reliability has been attested by corroborating evidence from many other sources, to refer to the ordinance that the festival be observed annually beginning on the twenty-fifth of Chislev without the slightest suggestion that the Jews in his day were not observing this festival.

In II Maccabees we read:

And Maccabaeus and they that were with him, the Lord leading them on, recovered the temple and the city; and they pulled down the altars that had been built in the market place by the aliens, and also [the walls of] sacred inclosures. And having cleansed the sanctuary they made another altar of sacrifice; and striking stones and taking fire out of them, they offered sacrifices, after [they had ceased for] two years, and [burned] incense, and [lighted] lamps, and set forth the shewbread. And when they had done these things, they fell prostrate and besought the Lord that they might fall no more into such evils; but that, if ever they should sin, they might be chastened by him with forebearance, and not be delivered unto blaspheming and barbarous heathen. Now on the same day that the sanctuary was profaned by aliens, upon that very day did it come to pass that the cleansing of the sanctuary was made, even on the five and twentieth day of the same month, which is Chislev. And they kept eight days with gladness in the manner (of the feast) of tabernacles, remembering how that not long afore, during the feast of tabernacles, they were wandering in the mountains and in the caves after the manner of wild beasts. Wherefore bearing wands wreathed with leaves, and fair boughs, and palms also, they offered up hymns of thanksgiving to him that had prosperously brought to pass the cleansing of his own place. They ordained also with a common statute and decree, for all the nation of the Jews, that they should keep these days every year.[10]

The relationship between these two accounts of the institution of Hanukkah is not one of literary dependence. No one has ever suggested that. Yet there is no mistaking the fact that the same historical event lies behind both accounts. The theological references are much more explicit, and come much more to the fore in the account of II Maccabees. But the essential form of the festival is the same as in the account preserved in I Maccabees. (1) The event is made possible by the victories of the Maccabees. (2) The event was to be commemorated annually by a festival. (3) This festival was to last eight days. (4) These eight days were to begin on the twenty-fifth of Chislev.

In the letters, ostensibly addressed to the Jews in Egypt from the Jews in Jerusalem, which are found at the beginning of II Maccabees, reference is made to a festival in the month Chislev. These references are generally understood to refer to Hanukkah, and the interpretation usually placed upon the letters is that their purpose was to get the Jews in Egypt to celebrate a festival which, though it was not prescribed in the Torah, was celebrated by the Jews in Palestine.[11] There is one point at which we can be quite dogmatic, and that is in saying that there is not the slightest suggestion in the whole of either I or II Maccabees that the annual eight-day dedication festival instituted by the Maccabees was later dropped by the Jews. Therefore, however early one may wish to date this literature, we do have reliable documents which indicate, when interpreted in the

10 II Macc. 10:1-8.
11 II Macc. 1:1–2:18.

most natural way, that Hanukkah was accepted by the Jews
as one of their recognized annual observances. That this
was the case not only when I and II Maccabees were written but also at the end of the first century A.D., when Josephus wrote his *Antiquitates Judaicae,* is proved (and we
use the word advisedly) by the following considerations.

After describing the defeats of the Seleucids by the Jews
under the leadership of Judas Maccabeus and the consequent rededication of the temple—in all of which he seems
to regard the account in I Maccabees as a reliable source—
Josephus adds these significant words:

> So much pleasure did they find in the renewal of their customs
> and in unexpectedly obtaining the right to have their own
> service after so long a time, that they made a law that their
> descendents should celebrate the restoration of the temple serv-
> ice for eight days. And from that time to the present we observe
> this festival, which we call the festival of Lights, giving this
> name to it, I think, from the fact that the right to worship ap-
> peared to us at a time when we hardly dared hope for it.[12]

Though Josephus calls this festival the Festival of Lights,
it is clear that he has in mind the same celebration which
is referred to in I and II Maccabees.[13] From the point of
view of our thesis it is difficult to exaggerate the historical
significance of this statement by Josephus that from the
time the festival was first instituted by the Maccabees until
his own day there had been no interruption in its annual
observance. The Greek is quite clear: "καὶ ἐξ ἐκείνου μέχρι

[12] *Ant.* 12.7.7 (324–25).

[13] We will find that in all other sources from the first and second centuries A.D. in which the festival is mentioned it is known by the name
"Feast of Dedication," Hanukkah. Zeitlin thinks that these two different
names for the same festival "need cause no surprise, for all Jewish festivals
had two names, to correspond to their two-fold character as public and
private celebrations. So 'Passover,' 'Pentecost,' and 'Tabernacles' refer to
the public, religious character of those festivals; while the corresponding
designations—'Festival of Unleavened Bread,' 'Festival of First Fruits' and
'Festival of Ingathering'—refer to their popular character" (Tedesche,
The First Book of the Maccabees, Introduction, p. 51).

τοῦ δεῦρο τὴν ἑορτὴν ἄγομεν." Literally translated it reads: "And from that [time] until now we keep [or: we are keeping] the festival." The continuous action carried by the present tense of the verb in Greek, combined with the meaning of the preposition μέχρι ("until," denoting continuity in time) make it quite clear that the meaning of the Greek requires that, as of the time when Josephus was writing, there had been no interruption of the annual observance of the festival since its institution in the days of the Maccabees. It is also to be noted that, according to Josephus, the Jews made it a *law* (νόμον) that the festival be observed annually. Neither of the authors of I and II Maccabees went so far as to refer to the Maccabean decree as a "law." But Josephus uses language which suggests that by *his time* the decree of the Maccabees had attained the status of a law among the Jews. Perhaps that was one reason why, in spite of the fact that there was no justification for Hanukkah in the Torah, the festival was never abandoned by the Jews.

It is also worth noting that the form of the festival described by Josephus is exactly the same as that described by the authors of I and II Maccabees. (1) There is the same recognition that the rededication was made possible by the Maccabean victories. (2) It was the Maccabees who led the nation throughout the whole event, and it was through their instigation that the occasion was ordained to be an annual observance. (3) This rededication took place on the twenty-fifth of Chislev. (4) The festival was eight days in length.

We have stated above that it could be "proved" that Hanukkah was one of the recognized annual observances of the Jews during the first century A.D. We used the much abused word "proof" in the only proper sense it can be used in the discussion of historical questions. To prove that something happened in the past is to establish *with a very high degree of probability* that it happened.[14] One never attains the goal of absolute certainty in the solution of historical problems. For that reason we readily admit that the passage quoted above from Josephus does not establish with absolute certainty that Hanukkah was observed annually by the Jews during the first century A.D. On the other hand, we do claim that it makes it *very highly probable*. We make this claim for the following reasons: (1) This is clearly what the statement implies. (2) There are no reasons why we should doubt whether the statement authentically represents Josephus' thought. (3) He was in an excellent position to know what festivals the Jews observed annually during the first century A.D.

It is extremely significant that we find that the New Testament provides corroborating evidence that Hanukkah was observed by the Jews during the first century A.D. With reference to the ministry in Judea the three synoptic gospels confine their attention to the one momentous journey of Jesus up to Jerusalem. That journey, by the unanimous agreement of all four gospels, took place during the festival of Passover.[15] Therefore, we cannot expect to learn from

[14] It should not be necessary to make the above kind of statement. However, it *is* necessary for the very simple reason that even in the highest circles of scholarship, this word "proof" is used in more than one sense with the most disastrous results. On the one hand the claim is made that one has proved his case when all that has been done is to establish its probability—without reference to the fact that there are degrees of probability. On the other hand the charge is not infrequently made, "He has shown that the truth of his thesis is very highly probable, but he has not proved it." The error in this latter case lies hidden in the assumption that there is a distinction between a *very high degree of probability* and a *proof*. In historical discussions, there is no such distinction. Actually, the word "proof," in the minds of many people carries the meaning of "logical proof," or "mathematical proof." What these people mean by "proof" is "absolute certainty." This may be possible to attain in the realm of logic or mathematics and possibly other realms as well, but it is not attainable in the realm of historical research.

[15] Luke refers to a childhood visit to Jerusalem which also, significantly enough from a literary point of view, takes place on Passover—perhaps included in the gospel as a foreshadowing of the end of his ministry in Jerusalem during the same festival.

the synoptics whether or not Jesus ever went up to Jerusalem during a festival called Hanukkah. And in view of
the fact that all the gospels have the movements of Jesus as
their central temporal and geographical theme, it follows
that we cannot expect to learn anything from the synoptics
about any of the other Jerusalem festivals. But the fourth
gospel—unlike the other three—refers to journeys of Jesus
to Jerusalem other than the final one. On one occasion
Jesus is represented as being in Jerusalem during the Feast
of Dedication, i.e., Hanukkah.[16] It is a matter of no consequence to our thesis how one evaluates the historical probability that Jesus did make the journey to which John refers. The significant point is that the New Testament, in
the only gospel where we have any right to expect a reference to feasts other than Passover, does actually witness to
the fact that the Jews observed a festival called Hanukkah.
Even if one takes the extreme view of regarding the journey as a pure literary invention, one would still have to
admit that the author's reference to the Feast of Dedication
witnesses to the fact that he knew something about a Jewish
festival called the Feast of Dedication. In fact, he must
have known a good deal more than the bare minimum that
there was a Jewish feast so named, for he places the feast in
the correct season of the year.

What is the testimony of the Rabbis concerning the question of whether Hanukkah was recognized as one of the set
annual observances of the Jews? We can say without any
reservations that they did regard it as one of the *received*
festivals.[17] The Rabbis taught that Hanukkah: (1) began
on the twenty-fifth of Chislev; (2) continued for eight days;
(3) and was instituted in the time of the Maccabees. The
Rabbis also knew that Hanukkah was connected with the
victory of the Maccabees over the Seleucids who had defiled

16 John 12:22.
17 Cf. *Shab.* 21b; *R.Sh.* 18b; *Taan.* 28b; *Meg.* 29b, 31a; *M. Kat.* 27b.

the temple—which of course is a very crucial point. They tried to explain the reason why the festival was eight days in length by what has the appearance of being a legendary story. But this does not alter the fact that their understanding of the origin of Hanukkah corresponds essentially with that given in I and II Maccabees and in *Antiquitates Judaicae*.[18]

Hanukkah is referred to in the Mishnah several times.[19] It is always mentioned with respect and as if its status were like that of festivals prescribed in the Torah. That Hanukkah is not prescribed in the Torah is something the Mishnah never explicitly refers to.[20] Nor is there in the Mishnah the slightest suggestion that Hanukkah had been recently instituted or reinstituted. The most natural interpretation of the passages which mention Hanukkah leads one to suppose that, at the time the Rabbinic discussions which are preserved in the Mishnah took place, this Feast of Dedication was a well-recognized and generally accepted religious festival of the Jews.

We have been considering certain evidence from the writings of Josephus, the New Testament and Rabbinical literature. We have found that these three distinct bodies of literature all agree in witnessing to the fact that Hanukkah *was* observed by the Jews in Palestine during the first cen-

[18] *Shab.* 21b. If this Rabbinical account corresponded more closely than it does to the earlier accounts, we might have grounds for suspecting some kind of literary dependence. As it is, the variations are sufficient to suggest that the Rabbinical accounts witness to the existence of a tradition—written or oral—which was in some ways independent from these particular written sources. The existence of such a tradition does, of course, strengthen our thesis that the Maccabees were never forgotten by the Jews—at least not until after the Rabbinic period, and then they could never be completely forgotten since they are mentioned by the Rabbis.

[19] *Bikk.* 1.6; *R. Sh.* 1.3; *Taan.* 2.10; *Meg.* 3.4.6; *M. Kat.* 3.9; *B.K.* 6.6.

[20] However, the fact is recognized indirectly in that there exists no Mishnah tractate on Hanukkah. If Hanukkah had been prescribed in the Torah, there would have been such a tractate on the laws relating to its institution and observation.

tury A.D. While it may be theoretically conceivable to some that such a convergence of evidence from admittedly independent sources could be due to pure chance, such an opinion cannot be accepted as a sound historical judgment. The *only* defensible historical hypothesis that can account for such unanimous testimony from such varied and unbiased[21] sources is to assume that their agreement arises from the correspondence of their reports to the actualities of history. We do not rest our case on any one passage alone but rather on the total complex of evidence which converges to establish for us an unshakable historical foundation on which to build our argument. That historical foundation is that Hanukkah, an eight-day festival commemorating an event which took place in the days of the Maccabees, was observed by the Jews during the New Testament period.

But, one might ask, does it follow that because Hanukkah was observed, the *origin* of Hanukkah was remembered? We think that it does so follow. Let us consider, for a moment, an example from our own time. No one thinks that simply because Americans observe Halloween every year on October thirty-first that the general populace understands the origin of this day. On the other hand, the fourth of July is generally recognized as a day for celebration of American Independence. In time of war or threat of war the meaning of the historical event which the Fourth of July commemorates is brought home to the people through press and radio, from public platforms erected in cemeteries and before national monuments in every little and big town all over the land. Whenever there is a real national crisis, then in school rooms, cathedrals, and to some extent in churches and synagogues, some recognition is generally given to the historic meaning of this day. The

[21] Unbiased with respect to the question under discussion.

radical difference between Halloween and the Fourth of July for the American people is that the former has no vital connection with any crucial period in the history of our nation, whereas the latter does have such a connection. Now in the case of Americans we are dealing with a people who are notorious the world over for their lack of historical consciousness. Americans are, as a nation, still largely dominated by the frontier mentality which seeks meaning almost wholly in the future. But with older nations it is different, and with the Jews it is very different. Israel, from the time of the prophets, if not before, has always been an historically minded people. That which an historically minded people remembers is that which they commemorate annually in public and private acts of worship and festivity. When that which is commemorated is an event which is crucially related to the history of that people, it will be especially remembered and influential in those periods when that people is going through similar historical times. As we have demonstrated in the previous two chapters, there were many striking similarities between the time of the Roman occupation and the time of the Seleucids. Speaking from a nationalistic religious point of view, there were no essential differences between the two periods. It is absolutely inconceivable that any historically minded people—and especially the Jews—could commemorate for eight days every year the redemption of their national sanctuary without remembering those through whose hands God had made the redemption possible. To suppose that is to go against all we know about the Jews today, and to violate all that historical criticism has been able to tell us about the character of Jewish mentality in antiquity. The Jews were and are a people who remember. They remember especially the redemption, mighty deeds and saving acts wrought by God, as well as those wars which Yahweh waged for their forefathers.[22] The memory of their past is never more alive to them as a people than it is during one of their great festivals. This is true today; therefore, why should we assume that it was not also true during the first century A.D.?

Having said all this, it is still true to say that Hanukkah, for all its associations with military victory is and probably always has been primarily a religious festival. The very word "hanukkah," referring to the dedication of the sanctuary for holy worship of the one true God, suggests the religious character of the eight-day observance.[23] We have shown in the previous two chapters that the Jewish nationalists of the first century A.D. were religiously motivated. Therefore, there cannot be any doubt that the Maccabees would have served as prototypes for them in their pious zeal for the Torah and the temple.

Nicanor's Day

But is this all we can say? Is there no evidence to indicate that the Maccabees were also remembered for their great

[22] This is a paraphrase of Jewish Hanukkah liturgy, in which liturgy, as we have seen, the Maccabees *are* remembered.

[23] There are indications that Hanukkah, for many modern Jewish Zionists, has taken on more and more political connotations. It is reported, for example, that Hanukkah is *the* great patriotic festival of the Israeli calendar, and that as part of the eight-day observance, Israeli youth, starting from the most remote parts of the new national state, carry lighted torches by relay to Modin, the ancestral home of the Maccabees. The climax of the celebration comes at the moment when the torch bearers converge on Modin and light a fire atop a nearby mountain. This fire can be seen from afar in all directions, and is designed to rekindle in the hearts of all Israelites the burning desire for national independence through the inspiration of the example of the great Jewish national heroes, the Maccabees. It would be a tragic mistake for a historian to read back into the first century A.D. the practice and ideology of modern Zionism. I make reference to these practices of the modern Zionists only by way of qualifying my statement that Hanukkah is primarily a religious festival—apparently for a large number of Jews it has become something else besides that.

military victories over the Seleucids? Our answer, once again, is affirmative. There *is* such evidence. We read in I Maccabees that

Nicanor went forth from Jerusalem, and encamped in Beth-horon, and there met him the host of Syria. And Judas encamped in Adasa with three thousand men: and Judas prayed and said, When they that came from the king blasphemed, thine angel went out, and smote among them a hundred and four-score and five thousand. Even so discomfit thou this army before us to-day, and let all the rest know that he hath spoken wickedly against thy sanctuary, and judge thou him according to his wickedness. And the thirteenth day of the month Adar the armies joined battle: and Nicanor's army was discomfited, and he himself was the first to fall in the battle. Now when his army saw that Nicanor was fallen, they cast away their arms, and fled. And they pursued after them a day's journey from Adasa until thou comest to Gazara, and they sounded an alarm after them with the solemn trumpets. And they came forth out of all the villages of Judea round about, and closed them in; and these turned them back on those, and they all fell by the sword, and there was not one of them left. And they took the spoils, and the booty, and they smote off Nicanor's head, and his right hand, which he stretched out so haughtily, and brought them, and hanged them up beside Jerusalem. And the people was exceeding glad, and they kept that day as a day of great gladness. And they ordained to keep this year by year, [to wit], the thirteenth day of Adar.[24]

From this passage it appears that not only the rededication of the temple was decreed to be remembered by an annual festival, but also the marvelous victory over the Seleucid general, Nicanor. We note also that the date on which the observance was to be kept was the thirteenth of Adar. Turning to II Maccabees we read:

[But then Nicanor] when he became aware that he had been bravely defeated by the stratagem of Judas, came to the great and holy temple, while the priests were offering the usual sacrifices, and commanded them to deliver up the man. And when

[24] I Macc. 7:39–50.

they declared with oaths that they had no knowledge where the man was whom they sought, he stretched forth his right hand toward the sanctuary, and sware this oath: If ye will not deliver up to me Judas as a prisoner, I will lay this temple of God even with the ground, and will break down the altar, and I will erect here a temple unto Dionysus for all to see. . . . And Nicanor, bearing himself haughtily in all vaingloriousness, had determined to set up a monument of complete victory over Judas and all them that were with him: but Maccabaeus still trusted unceasingly, with all hope that he should obtain help from the Lord. And he exhorted his company not to be fearful at the inroad of the heathen, but, keeping in mind the help which of old they had ofttimes received from heaven, so now also to look for the victory which would come to them from the Almighty; and comforting them out of the law and the prophets, and withal putting them in mind of the conflicts that they had maintained, he made them more eager [for the battle]. And when he had aroused their spirit, he gave them [his] commands, at the same time pointing out the perfidiousness of the heathen and their breach of their oaths. . . . And calling upon [God] he said after this manner: Thou, O Sovereign Lord, didst send thine angel in the time of Hezekiah king of Judea, and slew of the host of Sennacherib as many as a hundred fourscore and five thousand; so now also, O Sovereign of the heavens, send a good angel before us to bring terror and trembling: through the greatness of thine arm let them be stricken with dismay that with blasphemy are come here hither against thy holy people. And as he ended with these words, Nicanor and his company advanced with trumpets and paeans; but Judas and his company joined battle with the enemy with invocation and prayers. And contending with their hands and praying to God with their hearts, they slew no less than thirty and five thousand men, being made exceeding glad by the manifestation of God.

And when the engagement was over, and they were returning again with joy, they recognized Nicanor lying dead in full armor. . . . And he that in all things was in body and soul the foremost champion of his fellow citizens . . . commanded to cut off Nicanor's head, and his hand with the shoulder, and bring them to Jerusalem. And when he had arrived there, and had called his country men together and set the priests before the altar, he sent for them that were in the citadel; and showing the head of the vile Nicanor, and the hand of that profane man, which with proud brags he had stretched out against the holy house of the Almighty, and cutting out the tongue of the impious Nicanor, he said that he would give it by pieces to the birds, and hang up the rewards of his madness over against the sanctuary. And they all [looking up] unto heaven blessed the Lord who had manifested himself, saying, Blessed be he that hath preserved his own place undefiled. And he hanged Nicanor's head and shoulder from the citadel, a sign, evident unto all and manifest, of the help of the Lord. And they all ordained with a common decree in no wise to let this day pass undistinguished, but to mark with honour the thirteenth day of the twelfth month (it is called Adar in the Syrian tongue), the day before the day of Mordecai.[25]

This very long quotation—which is really an abridgment of an account which itself is said to be an epitome of a longer work—has been included in order that the reader may get some idea of the way in which military victories of the Maccabees were remembered by some of the later Jews. In this case all credit for the victory is ascribed to divine assistance—*but the human agent is not forgotten.* On the contrary it is remembered and highly glorified. Judas is remembered as one who "in all things was in body and soul the foremost champion of his fellow citizens." The followers of Judas are remembered as preserving that perfect blend of piety and rigorous action in the interests of Yahweh—"And contending with their hands and praying to God with their hearts, they slew no less than thirty and five thousand men. . . ."

In spite of the fact that the thirteenth of Adar marked a victory so memorable that, as is shown by the above evidence from I and II Maccabees, it was decreed to be observed annually, it eventually was abandoned by the Jews. No modern Jew gives any special recognition to the thirteenth of Adar. But *when* was this festival abandoned by

25 II Macc. 14:31–33; 15.6–11; 15: 22–36.

the Jews? Was it abandoned before the first century A.D.?
No, it was not. Josephus explicitly tells that it was still observed by the Jews when he wrote his *Antiquitates Judaicae:* "Now the victory took place on the thirteenth of the
month which is called Adar by the Jews, and Dystros by
the Macedonians. And the Jews celebrate their victory
every year in this month, and observe this day as a festival."[26] It is clear from this passage and from the account
which precedes it in *Antiquitates Judaicae* that the Jews in
the first century A.D. did observe the thirteenth of Adar as
a festival commemorating a great Maccabean victory.

The discussions that the Rabbis had concerning Nicanor's Day reveal the following facts about their understanding of the festival: first, at the time the Rabbinic discussions were taking place it was known that the thirteenth
of Adar was Nicanor's Day; second, it was known that
Nicanor was one of the Greek generals, that he had waved
his hand against Jerusalem and threatened to destroy it;
third, it was known that the Maccabees defeated him in battle, and it was believed that they cut off his thumbs and
toes and suspended them from the gates of Jerusalem.[27]
This Rabbinic passage, in all essential respects, corresponds
with the accounts given in I and II Maccabees and Josephus concerning Nicanor's Day. Therefore, except for the
silence of the New Testament, we have a similar convergence of evidence from all the relevant bodies of literature,
as we had in the case of the festival of Hanukkah. We know
of no reason why we should not regard the fact that the

[26] *Ant.* 12.10.5 (412).
[27] *Taan.* 18b. This final legendary touch is an interesting variation which
suggests that rather than literary dependence upon I Macc. (where head
and right hand were amputated), or upon II Macc. (where head, hand
with the shoulder, and tongue were cut off), or upon Josephus (who omits
all reference to this offensive mark of barbarousness), this Rabbinic passage
is derived from an independent written or/and oral tradition. The existence
of such a tradition, as we have said before, adds support to our thesis that
the Maccabees were *not* forgotten.

Jews *did* observe Nicanor's Day during the first century A.D. as historically well founded.

Although this military victory certainly had religious meaning for the Jews—as comes out clearly in the versions of the event cited above—nevertheless, compared to Hanukkah it was quite unambiguously a *military* victory. Or at least we can say that whereas the emphasis in Hanukkah would seem to us most naturally to have fallen on the religious character of the event, the emphasis in Nicanor's Day would have tended to bring out the fact that this day commemorated a great military victory. The central religious meaning of the event as remembered was that God avenges his holy city.[28] No doubt it was the combination of military victory and theological meaning which gave this particular event its special character. In whatever way we understand Nicanor's Day, we must acknowledge the importance that the skillful and devoted use of the sword played in the particular act of deliverance which was commemorated thereon. This means, quite simply, that the Maccabees were remembered not only as *religious* leaders who had recaptured the temple, cleansed it and rededicated it, but they were also remembered as *military* leaders who led the Jews to glorious victories over the imperial armies of the Seleucids. There was no discrepancy between the two roles they played. They were zealous for God, his Torah, and his temple to the point that they were willing to fight and die in his interests. In this respect they served as the perfect prototypes for the Jewish nationalists of the Roman period. They were "all things to all zealous nationalists." Their religious devotion was well enough attested to satisfy the most pious Jew. Their skill and zeal in battle must have been an inspiration to every Jew who was ready to take up the sword and strike a blow for God and freedom.

---

[28] Josephus discreetly omits explicit reference to this "politically dangerous" theological interpretation—though it is brought out clearly in all the other versions.

We have demonstrated in the two previous chapters that
the Maccabees were the nearest historical counterparts to
the Jewish nationalists of the Roman period. We have
demonstrated in this chapter that the Maccabees were remembered by the Jews during the first century A.D. The
fact that the Maccabees did and said the same kind of
things, combined with the fact that the memory of their
achievements was still alive in the first century A.D. establishes the very high historical probability of the further
fact that the Maccabees were consciously regarded as prototypes of religious zeal and valor by the Jewish nationalists
in the Roman period. Consequently it follows, as does the
night the day, that the example and teaching of the Maccabees must have exerted a tremendous influence upon the
thought and action of the extreme nationalists in the New
Testament period.

Thus, for example, if we would better understand the
motivation and inner conflict of a disciple of Jesus who
may have been of Zealot tendencies, we should do well to
consider not only the hypercritical picture of these men
painted by Josephus but also the more sympathetic portrait of their prototypes given us in the Maccabean literature, in which we are able to see genuine religious devotion
set in a theological framework that makes some sense out of
so-called "fanatical" Jewish nationalism.

Megillath Taanith

On various occasions in the preceding chapters we have
referred to the possibility that in *Megillath Taanith* we do
have a document which has come to us from the hands of
the Jewish nationalists of the Roman period. We have made
no detailed reference to this document thus far, not because literature from the hands of the war party is irrelevant to the question whether the Maccabees were remembered, but because we chose to follow a certain order of

priority in dealing with the evidence being analyzed. It is our view that the combined evidence and arguments presented in Chapters IV and V and in the preceding part of this chapter establishes beyond any reasonable doubt that the Maccabees *were* remembered—and that the Jewish nationalists in the Roman period regarded them as their prototypes. The evidence for this demonstration has been drawn from documents whose historical value is well-known to all students of Jewish history.

We turn now to consider *Megillath Taanith,* an historical document of great importance, with which many students of the New Testament have little or no acquaintance. *Megillath Taanith* is the English transliteration of the Aramaic מגלת תענית which means "Scroll of Fasts." But this title is probably not that originally borne by the document, and it is certainly misleading. What we actually have is a list of days on which fasting (and sometimes mourning also) was *forbidden.* Thirty-five such days are mentioned, and for most of these there is given a very brief description of what happened on that date. Sometimes nothing is said except, "It is a good day (*yom tob*) whereon we are not to fast." When the event is described and can be identified, it is seen to be an occasion for joy and rejoicing. What we really have, therefore, is a kind of calendar on which are recorded thirty-five dates which recall to the mind of the reader certain events of the past when something good happened. The reason why fasting and mourning are prohibited is that these particular days are occasions, not for fasting and mourning, but for rejoicing.

This calendar is written in Aramaic.[29] However, in all the manuscripts which have come down to us the Aramaic entries are commented on by a scholiast who wrote in

[29] George Foot Moore has suggested that it was written in Aramaic, "presumably because it was meant for the guidance of the unlearned as well as the educated" (*Judaism in the First Centuries of the Christian Era: The Age of the Tannaim* [Cambridge, Mass., 1927], I, 160).

Hebrew. The scholarly consensus is that the scholia are for the most part post-Talmudic in date and of distinctly less historical value than the Aramaic portion itself. In the discussion to follow, whenever we refer to *Megillath Taanith,* we shall have reference to the Aramaic portion only.

As to the question of the date of this document there seems to be general agreement among those who have written on the subject during the past seventy-five years or so that the Aramaic calendar was edited in the latter half of the first or the beginning of the second century A.D.[30]

We cannot review all the literature which embodies the findings of research which has been carried through by those who have tried to identify the individual entries in this calendar with particular historical events from other sources.[31] There seems to be general agreement that the list of thirty-five days mentioned in *Megillath Taanith* in-

---

[30] So J. Derenbourg, *Essai sur l'histoire et la géographie de la Palestine d'après les Talmuds et les autres sources rabbiniques* (Paris, 1867), I, 439f.; Emil Schürer, *Geschichte des jüdischen Volkes im Zeitalter Jesu Christi,* 3d and 4th ed. (Leipzig, 1901), I, 156–57; J. Z. Lauterbach, "Megillat Taanit," in *The Jewish Encyclopedia* (New York, 1904), VIII, 427f.; Gustaf Dalman, *Grammatik des jüdisch-palästinischen Aramäisch,* 2d ed., (Leipzig, 1905), pp. 8ff.; Solomon Zeitlin, *Megillat Taanit as a Source for Jewish Chronology and History in the Hellenistic and Roman Periods* (Philadelphia, 1922), pp. 1–4; George Foot Moore, *Judaism in the First Centuries of the Christian Era: The Age of the Tannaim* (Cambridge, Mass., 1927), I, 160; Hermann L. Strack, *Introduction to the Talmud and Midrash* (Philadelphia, 1931), p. 15; Hans Lichtenstein, "Die Fastenrolle: Eine Untersuchung zur jüdisch-hellenistischen Geschichte," *Hebrew Union College Annual,* VIII–IX (1931–1932), 257f.; M. Abel, *Les Livres des Maccabées,* 2d ed. (Paris, 1949), p. xvii. See Appendix for a review of evidence bearing on the question of dating *Megillath Taanith.*

[31] The reader can find the various problems more or less fully discussed in the above-cited works of the following authors—Derenbourg, I, 439–42; Zeitlin, pp. 72–118; Lichtenstein, pp. 267–307—and in Gustaf Dalman, *Aramäische Dialektproben* (Leipzig, 1896), pp. 31–34. Both Zeitlin and Lichtenstein have given detailed discussions to each entry. The latter has presented us with the definitive work to date, but the former's monograph is also quite indispensable. More or less detailed bibliographies of earlier French and German works on *Megillath Taanith* are given by Schürer, Lauterbach, Strack, and Lichtenstein in their works cited in Note 30 above. The bibliography supplied by Lichtenstein is the most complete and up-to-date.

cludes some entries which are to be identified with events dated in the Maccabean period. The thirty-five days are arranged under twelve headings corresponding to the twelve months of the Jewish year. Thus for the month Chislev, the calendar reads:[32]

בעשרין וחמשה ביה הנכתא תמניא יומין דילא למספד בהון:

"On the twenty-fifth thereon, Hanukkah; [for] eight days it is forbidden to mourn thereon." Whether the meaning be, "On the twenty-fifth of Chislev begins the eight-day festival Hanakkuh, on which it is forbidden to mourn," or "On the twenty-fifth of Chislev is the festival Hanukkah; for eight days it is forbidden to mourn," the statement still clearly refers to the dedication of the temple by the Maccabees after it had been cleansed from its profanation by the Seleucids, which dedication began on the twenty-fifth of Chislev and lasted for eight days. As we have shown, this festival was decreed to be observed annually, on those dates, and evidence from Rabbinic literature, the writings of Josephus, and the New Testament indicate that is was observed annually by the Jews during the period from which *Megillath Taanith* is presumed to have come. Therefore, it should not be surprising to learn that all commentators agree on the historical identification of this particular entry.

Let us take another entry. Under the month Adar our calendar reads:

בתלת עשר ביה יום ניקנור:

"On the thirteenth thereon [is] Nicanor's Day." Once again there seems to be no difficulty in identifying this entry. It seems most naturally to refer to that day instituted as an annual holiday in the time of the Maccabees in commemoration of the great victory over Nicanor. As we have shown, that day was decreed to be observed annually on the thirteenth of Adar and in time came to be known to the Jews

---

[32] All citations of the Aramaic text are from Lichtenstein's critical edition. The English translations are based upon this text, though the text and translation of Zeitlin has been carefully compared.

as Nicanor's Day. All commentators agree on this identification for this entry.

Under the month of Iyyar we find the following:

בעשרין ותלתא ביה נפקן בני חקרא מן ירושלם:

"On the twenty-third thereon, departed the sons of the
Acra from Jerusalem." In I Maccabees we read that Simon
besieged the men of the Acra in Jerusalem (οἱ ἐκ τῆς ἄκρας
ἐν Ιερουσαλημ) and starved them into submission. Apparently these men were either Seleucids or Hellenized Jews
of the opposition party. They were banished from the city,
and Simon cleansed the Acra from its pollution. The account continues:

And he entered into it on the three and twentieth day of the
second month [Iyyar], in the hundred and seventy and first year,
with praise and palm branches, and with harps, and with cymbals, and with viols, and with hymns, and with songs: because
a great enemy was destroyed out of Israel. And he ordained
that they should keep that day every year with gladness.[33]

There seems to be no reason to doubt that this entry in
Megillath Taanith refers to the annual holiday instituted
by Simon Maccabeus. Incidentally, if we deny the historical
authenticity of *Megillath Taanith* at this point, it would
appear that we would have to assume that somehow a marvelous coincidence has occurred in the accounts of two
documents which have two widely separated histories of
literary transmission. By far the simplest and most natural
way in which to account for this coincidence in date and
data is to assume that there actually was such an annual
holiday (observed by at least some of the Jews, if not by the
entire nation) and that the account in I Maccabees and the
entry in *Megillath Taanith* reflect historical fact and not
literary fiction.[34]

[33] I Macc. 13:51-52.

[34] It is theoretically conceivable, though not historically probable, that
some individual or group might have accidentally discovered a copy of I
Maccabees or some other document containing the same information and

Not all of the thirty-five entries in our calendar are as easy to identify as those we have considered. Nonetheless, there is a considerable area of agreement among scholars who have studied this document. We are primarily concerned with the entries which are usually identified with events occurring in the Maccabean period.

Those entries which have been identified with historical events mentioned in I and/or II Maccabees number as follows: Derenbourg eight, Dalman seven and possibly eight, Zeitlin eleven, Lichtenstein eleven, and Abel six. Besides the unanimity of these authors on the proper identification of the three entries mentioned above, there is an agreement of four to one on three other entries. Once there is disagreement over the precise identification of an entry, though there is agreement that it is to be identified with one of two events, both of which occurred in the Maccabean period. The above figures do not include entries which are sometimes identified with events which occurred during the reign of John Hyrcanus. These entries might in some respects be considered as belonging to the Maccabean period; they number three or four, varying with the authors. Lichtenstein, who claims to have made an effort to identify each entry solely on the basis of historical evidence, without allowing preconceptions to influence him, identifies fifteen of the entries with events occurring during the reigns of Judas, Jonathan, Simon, and John Hyrcanus.

---

for some reason decided to enter these dates on a calendar. But it is difficult to see why this kind of action would be taken unless it was thought that there was some special value in observing these days as holidays. Such a calendar would have no meaning unless those who were to read it had at least some latent memory of the days being commemorated. They would have to know, for example, who Nicanor was, and something about what happened to him, before they could understand why it was that on the thirteenth of Adar they were forbidden to fast. But if the Jews could remember Nicanor, and what happened to him, why not also Judas Maccabeus and his part in the same event? It turns out that this theoretical possibility is no escape at all but leads us around by another way to the same conclusion, namely that the Maccabees must have been remembered in the first century A.D.

What, we may ask, is the general view as to the purpose of this calendar? Lauterbach thinks that "This calendar of victories was intended to fan the spark of liberty among the people and to fill them with confidence and courage by reminding them of the victories of the Maccabees and the divine aid vouchsafed to the Jewish nation against the heathen."[35] Zeitlin believes that the purpose of the scroll "was to show the people that if they were fully resolved to throw off the yoke of the Romans they had as great prospect of success as the Hasmoneans and their followers had of throwing off the yoke of the Syrians."[36] At another point, Zeitlin observes:

Of all the feast-days recorded in the scroll, few are still observed. The other festivals have sunk into oblivion. This was quite natural. Their origin, as we shall see, was connected with the victories of the Jews over the Syrians in the Hasmonean period and over the Roman armies in the beginning of the war with Vespasian. When, therefore, the sanctuary was destroyed and Jewish independence lost, their *raison d'être* was gone.[37]

Abel writes: "Ce calendrier destiné à relever le moral des Juifs après leurs épreuves a été mis à jour jusqu'au temps d'Hadrien."[38] The other authors we have cited make no explicit reference to the purpose of *Megillath Taanith*. However, in so far as they accept the tradition that the scroll was compiled by Eleazar ben Hananiah, and identify him with the Eleazar who was one of the leaders of the Jewish nationalists in the war with Rome, both Derenbourg and Lichtenstein would seem to subscribe to the view that the purpose of the document was to inspire the Jews in their war with the Romans by reminding them of the great Jewish victories of the past.

What are our own conclusions about *Megillath Taanith?*

[35] *Jewish Encyclopedia*, VIII 427.
[36] *Megillat Taanit*, p. 4.
[37] *Ibid.*, pp. 2–3.
[38] *Les Livres des Maccabées*, p. xvii

First, the judgment of scholarship that *Megillath Taanith* is an authentic historical document originating in Palestine in the last half of the first or at the beginning of the second century A.D. seems to us to be an acceptable working hypothesis. Second, the suggestion that the purpose of *Megillath Taanith* was to inspire the Jews in their resistance to Rome by reminding them of the Maccabean victories may not give an adequate account for the *origin* of such a document, but, for whatever reason it was compiled, one of the practical effects it would have had among the Jews in the Roman period would have been to remind them of the Maccabean victories. Third, if this document had not included any days from the Maccabean period, it would have raised serious doubts as to the validity of our thesis that the Maccabees were remembered in Palestine during the first century A.D. Fourth, since it does include some and is thought to include several days from the Maccabean period, it serves as striking corroboration of our thesis.

If what we have asserted is true, namely that the Maccabees were influential prototypes for the Jewish nationalists in the Roman period, then we would expect any calendar listing days on which Jews were forbidden to mourn to include days commemorating the great Maccabean victories. This is precisely what we find in *Megillath Taanith*.

VII: WAR OF THE SONS OF LIGHT AGAINST THE SONS OF DARKNESS

No discussion of Jewish nationalism in the Greco-Roman period would be complete without some reference to certain documents which have come to light in recent years. These documents are part of the material generally referred to as the Dead Sea Scrolls. The great controversy over the authenticity of these now famous scrolls is gradually subsiding with the verdict of the scholarly world going in favor of regarding the documents as authentic Jewish writings from the Greco-Roman period. The important contribution which has been made by insistent dissent on the part of leading scholars, both in England and America, concerning the authenticity and early dating of these scrolls cannot be overestimated. But merely to see firsthand the thousands of fragments of scrolls from one particular cave (No. 4) which are being worked over in the Palestine Archaeological Museum, enables one to understand why there is no sound ground for thinking that these discoveries are forgeries.

The question of date is being carefully determined by the combined disciplines of paleography, archaelogy, and textual, literary, and historical criticism. There is an international team of scholars charged with the responsibility of carrying out the original research involved in editing this material from Cave No. 4. One can only express gratitude for what has been done and encouragement for what is yet to be done. In general it may be said that the work of this team of scholars is corroborating in principle the pioneer work done by those Israeli and American scholars responsible for editing the scrolls found in the first cave (No. 1).

The present state of the various discussions in progress indicates quite clearly that these documents belonged originally to a tightly organized community of highly religious Jewish patriots which at least during part of their history lived together near the mouth of the Wadi Qumran, overlooking the north end of the Dead Sea and the hills of Moab to the east. The community center has been excavated by competent archaeologists and without any question belongs to the Greco-Roman period of Jewish history. The cave in which the initial discoveries were made is at some distance from this site, but subsequent discoveries have been made in caves which are literally only a stone's throw from the community buildings. In spite of the fact that no manuscripts have been found within the Qumran buildings there is no sound reason to doubt that the community which occupied the buildings is also responsible for the presence of the scrolls in the surrounding caves.

In general it may be said with some confidence that the scholarly research and debates now being carried on will establish in principle the following broad outlines of the community's history.

The spiritual and historical origins of the Qumran community are to be found in the national resistance to the Hellenizing policies of the ruling classes in the Seleucid period, while the end of the community is closely associated with the Jewish nation's fatal struggle against the Roman occupation forces.

It is too soon to say with finality what the exact relationship was between this community and other known Jewish groups. But there is nothing now known about the community which would go against the following summary statement. In the beginning of its history the sect probably had spiritual affinities with the early Maccabees, especially the Hasidim and whatever circle produced the book of Daniel. Later, under the leadership of a Teacher of Righteousness, in the days of Alexander Jannaeus, the sect made a definite break with the Hasmoneans, and established a community center at Qumran. The Covenanters of Qumran stood over against the Sadducees on many counts. They were close to the Pharisees in some respects, though quite different from them in others. Their relationship to the Essenes was one of close kinship, if indeed they are not to be considered an Essene community. It is altogether probable that this is the community refered to by Pliny when he writes of the Essenes living on the west shore of the Dead Sea. The relationships between this sect and the John the Baptist movement and the early Christian community are quite significant, though as yet undefined. The members of the Qumran community probably joined other patriotic groups like the Zealots in the national struggle against Rome, if not as a community then possibly as individuals. At any rate we know from archaeological evidence that the community headquarters at Qumran was destroyed during the war of A.D. 66–70. The fate of their postwar membership is problematical. Some may have participated in the sporadic but continued resistance to Rome which did not end until Hadrian's crushing of the Bar Cochba revolt of A.D. 132–135. Ultimately their membership was probably assimilated by the Jewish Christian community and other Jewish groups which survived the prolonged struggle with Rome.

While we cannot yet spell out exactly what part this community played in the two great national resistance movements in the Seleucid and Roman periods, one thing is perfectly clear: this community did cherish a certain literature which in the careful and balanced judgment of Millar Burrows "breathes a militant spirit that would have satisfied the Maccabees and Zealots."[1] Burrows, in these words, has reference to the community's Battle Manual, the *War of the Sons of Light against the Sons of Darkness.* Fragments of enough manuscripts of this composition have been found in one of the caves (No. 4) close by the community headquarters to remove all doubt concerning the question whether this document really belonged to what otherwise might have passed as a passive and pacifist religious order. We cannot say with certainty that this War Scroll was first produced by the community at Qumran, nor that other patriotic groups might not also have valued it highly, but we can say that this particular Jewish religious order had a high regard for this scroll and, we presume, for the theology it expresses. Since the theology of this scroll is highly nationalistic, it is important for us to get some impression of its contents.[2]

While important fragments of other copies of this Battle Manual are now in the hands of the scholars working in the

[1] *The Dead Sea Scrolls* (New York, 1955), p. 292.

[2] In all that follows in this chapter I gratefully acknowledge the close cooperation of my esteemed colleague Lawrence Toombs, who has prepared for my use with introduction and critical notes a translation of selected passages of the War Scroll, or as he has taught me to refer to it, the Battle Manual. It is Toombs's translation which appears in this chapter and in the following. This translation has been made with the work of previous translations in view. Credit for producing the first complete translation in English goes to Simon J. De Vries of Union Theological Seminary, New York, to whose yet unpublished pioneer work I am indebted for having my eyes first opened in a definite way to the importance of this document for this book. Burrows has given a translation of most of the scroll in *The Dead Sea Scrolls,* pp. 390–99. See also, M. Avi-Yonah, "The 'War of the Sons of Light and the Sons of Darkness' and Maccabean Warfare," *Israel Exploration Journal,* Vol. II, No. 1 (1952); J. Van der Ploeg. "La Règle de la guerre," *Vetus Testamentum,* V (October, 1955), 395ff.; Yigael Yadin, *The Scroll of the War of the Sons of Light against the Sons of Darkness* (Jerusalem, 1955).

Palestine Archaeological Museum in Jerusalem, Jordan, the only manuscript available to scholars at large is that which came with the initial discoveries from the first cave (No. 1). This manuscript, edited by the late E. L. Sukenik, has been published in splendid style in *The Dead Sea Scrolls of the Hebrew University.*

The bottom of each of the scroll's nineteen columns is broken off, and there are numerous lacunae in the surviving portions of the text, so that in all not more than two thirds of the document survives. In addition there are many repetitions and closely similar passages in the text, and the exact relationship of its parts to one another is difficult to determine. Since, then, the principles of organization of the document itself are doubtful, it seems best to try to capture the flavor and peculiar emphasis of this writing by a careful selection from its best-preserved sections of those portions in which the spirit of the Holy War is most vigorously and typically expressed.[3]

These selected portions of the document have been arranged in such a way as to give the reader an unfolding picture of the war—the announcement, the period of preparation, the battle itself, and the celebration of victory.

War of Sons of Light against the Sons of Darkness

A WAR OF ANGELS AND MEN
(Col. 1, Lines 9–12)

On the day when the Kittim fall there shall be a battle and a tremendous slaughter before the God of Israel, for He has appointed a day for Himself from of old for a war of annihilation against the Sons of Darkness. In it there shall gather to-

---

[3] So Toombs, who further notes that in the translation which follows a line of dots indicates a lacuna which could not be restored; also that in his translation he has aimed at clarity rather than literalness and thus has sometimes changed the word order and at times rendered the same Hebrew word by several English equivalents.

gether for the great slaughter a congregation of angels and an assembly of men—the Sons of Light and the Portion of Darkness, doing battle together to reveal the might of God, with the sound of a great tumult and the battle cry of angels and men at the day of destruction. It shall be a time of sore distress for those whom God ransoms, and in all their distresses a similar anguish shall not be until the final eternal deliverance comes.

THE TRUMPETS OF THE HOST
(Col. 3, Lines 1–11)

Rules for the war; and for the trumpets which summon them when the war gates are opened so that the soldiers may go out, the trumpets for the alarm of war over the slain, the trumpets of ambush, the trumpets of pursuit when the enemy has been defeated, and the trumpets of assembly on the return from battle.

On the trumpets for summoning the congregation they shall inscribe, "The Called of God:" On the trumpets for summoning the nobles they shall inscribe, "The Princes of God." On the trumpets of the supervisors they shall inscribe, "The Rule of God." On the trumpets of the men of renown they shall inscribe, "The Chief Fathers of the Congregation." When they gather at the house of meeting, they shall inscribe on the trumpets, "The Instructions of God for the Holy Council." On the trumpets for the camps they shall inscribe, "The Peace of God in the Camps of His Saints." On the trumpets for their marches they shall inscribe, "The Mighty Acts of God in Scattering the Enemy and Putting to Flight All Those Who Hate Righteousness." (He brings shame on those who hate God). On the trumpets for the battle arrays they shall inscribe, "Arrays of the Standards of God for His Wrathful Vengeance on All the Sons of Darkness." On the trumpets for summoning the soldiers when the war gates are opened that they may go out against the battle line of the enemy they shall inscribe, "Memorial of Vengence at God's Appointed Time." On the trumpets of the slain they shall inscribe, "The Hand of God's Might in Battle to Strike All Treacherous Men Dead." On the trumpets of ambush they shall inscribe, "The Mysteries of God to Destroy Wickedness." On the trumpets of pursuit they shall inscribe, "God's Smiting of All the Sons of Darkness." (His anger will not return until they are completely destroyed). When they return from the battle to enter the battle line they shall inscribe on the trumpets of return, "God's Gathering." On the trumpets of the march back from battle against the enemy in order to enter the congregation at Jerusalem they shall inscribe, "The Joys of God at the Peaceful Return."

THE PURITY OF THE TROOPS
(Col. 7, Lines 1–7)

The men who enforce discipline shall be forty to fifty years old. The supervisors of the camp shall be fifty to sixty years old. The officers also shall be forty to fifty years old. Those who strip the slain, who take the plunder, who clean the land, who guard the equipment, and who serve the rations—all of these shall be twenty five to thirty years old. No mere lad or woman shall come into their camps from the time when they leave Jerusalem until their return. No one who is lame, blind, or paralytic, no one who has a permanent defect in his flesh, no one who is afflicted with an uncleanness in his flesh—none of these shall go with them to battle. They shall all be volunteers for the war, perfect in spirit and body, and ready for the day of vengeance. No one who is not cleansed from his semen shall go down with them on the day of battle, for holy angels are with their hosts. There shall be a distance of two thousand cubits between each of their camps and the latrines, and no nakedness, an evil thing, shall be seen in the neighborhood of any of their camps.

EXHORTATION BEFORE THE BATTLE
(Col. 15, Lines 1–12)

For it is a time of anguish for Israel, and a time of . . . . of battle against all the nations. Those of God's portion will receive eternal deliverance, and there will be an end of every wicked nation.

All the battle formations shall come and encamp before the King of the Kittim and the whole army of Beliel which is mustered with him on the day of their destruction by the sword of

God. Then the Chief Priest shall take his place, and with him his brother priests, and the Levites, and all the men of authority, and he shall read aloud the prayer for the destined time of battle, as it is written in the Manual for this particular time, as well as all the words of their psalms. And he shall set all the battle lines in order there as it is written in the Battle Manual. Then the priest who is chosen by the decision of all his brothers for the destined time of vengeance shall walk to and fro and he shall encourage the men . . . . and he shall speak as follows:

"Be strong! Be bold! Be valorous men! Fear not, neither . . . . in the battle. Do not be alarmed nor tremble before them. Do not retreat, and do not . . . . , for they are the congregation of wickedness, and all their deeds are done in darkness and all their desire is directed to it . . . . Their defenses and their power are dissipated like smoke, and all the assembly of their multitude . . . . will not be found, and every last vesture of their being will quickly fade away . . . . Strengthen yourselves for the battle of God, for this day is the destined time of battle!"

THE CONDUCT OF THE BATTLE: THE INFANTRY ATTACK
(Col. 6, Lines 1b–6)

They shall return to their positions, and after them three battalions of soldiers shall go out and take their places between the battle lines. The first battalion shall launch seven war javelins against the enemy battle line. On the blade of the javelins they shall inscribe, "The Lightning Flash of a Spear for the Power of God." Upon the weapons of the second group they shall inscribe, "Bloody Missiles to Bring down Those Slain by God's Anger." Upon the javelins of the third group they shall inscribe, "A Sword Flash Devouring the Wicked Who Are Slain by God's Judgment." Each of these battalions shall make seven casts and then return to its position. After them two battalions of soldiers shall go out and take their places between the two battle lines, the first battalion carrying spear and shield and the second battalion carrying shield and dart, to bring down those slain by the judgment of God and to subdue the enemy battle line by the power of God, in order to bring to every worthless nation a recompense for its evil.

But to the God of Israel shall the kingdom be; and by the saints of His people He shall do valiantly.

THE ATTACK CONTINUES
(Col. 16, Lines 5b-9)

The priests shall give a second blast for them . . . . and, when they are in position near the Kittim battle line as thick as the night mist, each man shall raise his hand with his weapons of war, and six priests shall sound the trumpets of the slain; a sharp, continuous blast, in order to control the battle. Then the Levites and all the people shall sound the ram's horns . . . . with a loud noise, and when the sound is heard, they shall defile their hands with the corpses of the Kittim in striking them down, and all the people shall make haste at the sound . . . . shall be blasts on the trumpets of the slain, and the battle against the Kittim will continue.

THE ROUT OF THE ENEMY
(Col. 9, Lines 2-7)

The priests shall sound the trumpets of the slain to control the battle until the enemy is defeated and turns his back. The priests shall sound the trumpets to control the battle. When the enemy is defeated before them, the priests shall sound the trumpets of assembly, and all the soldiers shall go out to them from the front of the lines of battle. Six battalions shall take up their positions, along with the battalion of shock troops, seven battle lines in all, twenty-eight thousand men of war and six thousand charioteers. All of these will take up the pursuit in order to exterminate the enemy in the battle of God in an eternal annihilation. The priests shall sound the trumpets of pursuit for them, and they shall divide themselves against all the enemy for a final pursuit, and the charioteers shall beat back the enemy along the flanks of the battle until he is wiped out. When the slain are falling, the priests shall keep sounding the trumpets from a distance, but they shall not come among the corpses so as to pollute themselves with their unclean blood, for they are holy men, and shall not defile the oil of their anointing as priests with the blood of a worthless nation.

THE CELEBRATION OF VICTORY
(Col. 14, Lines 2–7a)

After they leave the corpses to go back to the camp, they shall all shout together the Psalm of the Return. In the morning they shall cleanse their garments and wash away the blood of the guilty dead. Then they shall return to the position where they had drawn up their battle line before the enemy was cut down. There they shall all bless the God of Israel and joyfully exalt his name together; speaking as follows:

Blessed be the God of Israel,
> who keeps steadfast love for his covenant
> and testimonies of salvation for the people of his redemption.

He called men who were staggering to come forth from the prison house;
But he gathered the assembly of the nations to bring them to an end without a remnant;
> to establish by justice the heart of the faint,
> to open the mouth of the dumb that he might declare aloud his mighty acts,
> to teach feeble hands to make war.

He gives the trembling knees a firm standing place,
> and muscular power to the shoulder of those who strike.

EXPRESSION OF CONTINUED CONFIDENCE
(Col. 11, Lines 1–13)

For the battle is thine, and by the strength of thine hand their carcasses have been dashed to pieces without a burial. Goliath of Gath, a mighty man of valor, thou didst deliver into the hand of thy servant David, because he trusted in thy great name, and not in sword or spear—for thine is the battle. The Philistines thou hast subdued time without number by thy holy name. Moreover by the hand of our kings thou has saved us time without number, because of thy mercies and not in accordance with our deeds, which we have done wickedly, and our acts of rebellion. The battle is thine and from thee comes the power. It is not our own, and neither our strength nor the vigor of our hands did valiantly, for we acted in thy strength and in the power of thy great valor, as thou hast declared to us from of old, saying, "A star shall come forth from Jacob, a sceptre shall rise from Israel, and shall crush the forehead of Moab and break down all the sons of Seth, and he will come down from Jacob and destroy the survivor of the city. The enemy will be conquered, and Israel will do valiantly." Through thine anointed ones, who had a vision of the testimonies, thou didst declare to us the times of the battles of thine hand—to fight against our enemies, to strike down the troops of Beliel (seven worthless nations) by the hand of the poor whom thou hast redeemed with strength and peace, as a marvelous act of power; and the melted heart shall be as a door of hope. Thou hast dealt with them as with Pharaoh and the officers of his chariotry at the Red Sea. The smitten of spirit thou hast burned up like a blazing torch in a swath of grain, devouring evil. Thou wilt not turn back until wickedness is annihilated. From of old thou hast proclaimed the appointed time for thy deed of power, saying "Assure shall fall by a sword, not of man, and a sword not of man shall devour him."

A careful reading of these selected portions of the scroll of the *War of the Sons of Light against the Sons of Darkness* makes it perfectly clear that in the Qumran community we are dealing with a group of Jewish patriots for whom there is absolutely no conflict between religion and patriotism, piety and nationalism, prayer and the sword. Their patriotism grows out of their religion, their nationalism out of their piety, and the sword with which they fight is a consecrated weapon. The very strength with which they strike is strength from God.

It is of the greatest significance that the history of this community spans the Greco-Roman period of Jewish history. Here is evidence that there was living continuity between the period of the Maccabees and the period of the Zealots. Ideals cherished in the earlier period were cherished in the later period. In fact, the very difficulty experienced by the scholars in identifying the Kittim referred to in this and other documents of the sect, witnesses indirectly to the point we have been making throughout this book, namely that to the pious Jew the Seleucids and the Romans looked very much alike. Both represented heathen culture of a unified type, that is, Hellenism.

All of this is of importance for our main thesis, namely that the Maccabees were remembered and their example and teaching was of considerable influence in the New Testament period. Because if there could be continuity of life for the patriots of Qumran, why not for others? If this sect's Teacher of Righteousness could be remembered and honored, why not others? Were the country people around the village of Modin likely to forget the name and deeds of Mattathias and Judas Maccabaeus? It is a mistake to reason, as some do, that because the Hasmoneans became worldly and were corrupted by power and by contact with the Hellenized ruling classes in Jerusalem, the love of the nation for their illustrious ancestors would have been destroyed. On the contrary, the example and teachings of the early Maccabees could have been appealed to by the conservative opponents of the high-living Hasmoneans to shame them and recall to their minds their true heritage. David's glory was not tarnished by the sins of his later descendents, nor was that of the early Maccabees tarnished by the wickedness of the Hasmoneans.

James C. G. Greig has argued that the two most likely known historical persons with whom the Teacher of Righteousness of the Qumran Community might be identified are Mattathias and his son Judas Maccabeus.[4] Other scholars have argued that the Teacher of Righteousness lived earlier than this, and still others that he lived later. There is even some indication that there may have been more than one Teacher of Righteousness in the history of the sect. The point is simply this: that scholars are now having

[4] "The Teacher of Righteousness and the Qumran Community," *New Testament Studies*, Vol. II, No. 2 (November, 1955).

their minds opened to the possibility that some of the great men of the Seleucid period could have exercised an influence upon the Roman period through groups of Jews who cherished and preserved their teachings and kept alive the memories of certain creative events in which these great men participated. Certainly the early Maccabees were among the heroic Jewish figures participating in important events in Jewish history of the Seleucid period. It is the most natural thing in the world to think that in one or more of a number of different ways their influence could have extended on into the Roman period. The Dead Sea Scrolls have drawn our attention to merely one possible way in which men from the earlier period had an influence upon the later period.

But perhaps more important than the men themselves is the theology which motivated them. At its deepest level our thesis is that there is a basic continuity between the two periods in that it was the same dynamic militant zeal for the covenant God of Israel which motivated both the uprising against the Seleucids and the uprising against the Romans. We call this phenomenon Jewish nationalism, and assert that in essence there was no change between the time of the Maccabees and the time of the Zealots. This War Scroll of the Qumran community has some interesting testimony to bear at this point. Scholars have all agreed that there are some remarkable parallels between certain passages in this scroll and certain passages in I and II Maccabees. We shall have occasion to draw attention to some of these in the concluding chapter. However, at this point we would simply note that in the judgment of some scholars who have studied this scroll it is quite possible that the earliest portions (and these scholars have in mind certain of the battle hymns) date from the time of the Maccabean war. If so, then it may well be that we are closer to authentic Maccabean theology in this scroll than we are in the more formal and tendentious histories of I and II Maccabees. The fact that material of this kind, expressing this militant spirit, was being copied and read in the wilderness of Judah while the Roman legions were in the land is of the greatest importance.[5] How great we shall see in the next and final chapter.

[5] Paul Winter has shown that there are good reasons for weighing carefully the possibility that the Benedictus (Luke 1:68–75) was originally a "Dedication Prayer Before Battle" from the Maccabean period, and that the Magnificat (Luke 1:46b–55) was a "Hymn of Thanksgiving After Battle" from the same time. These Maccabean war songs found their place in the Third Gospel by way of "a Jewish-Christian (Nazarene) adaptation of the 'Baptist Document,' i.e., a first century literary record emanating from the circle of followers of John the Baptist and dealing with John's birth," according to Winter. After all the dust which has been stirred up by the Dead Sea Scrolls has finally settled, we may well find that John the Baptist, spiritual activity in the Judean Wilderness, and the Maccabean heritage are all far more important for an understanding of Christian origins than we have ever expected.

PART THREE

CONCLUSIONS

VIII: JEWISH NATIONALISM AND JESUS

Jewish Nationalism

This inquiry into Jewish nationalism has indicated that the Zealots were not, as Josephus pictured them, purely selfish and secularly motivated. But rather, like their prototypes the early Maccabees, they were deeply patriotic and motivated by a dynamic theology of zeal for the Torah. As we have already seen, this zeal for the Law included zeal for the Jerusalem temple. But equally important—and until now we have not dealt with this point—this zeal for the Torah presupposed an undying confidence in God's promise of the Land.

THE PROMISED LAND

The land of Canaan had been promised to Abraham. It was this promise which sustained the Israelites during their forty-year sojourn in the wilderness. It emboldened them in their conquest of Canaan under Joshua, and later it strengthened them in their resistance to the incursions of the Philistines. One cannot begin to appreciate the full depth of the ground swell of Jewish patriotism in the days of the Maccabees and the Zealots if he does not recognize the importance of their belief that God had promised to them the land on which they lived and on which their fathers had lived for generations before them.

As von Rad has shown in his important study of the
Holy War concept in Deuteronomy, Jewish nationalism in
the days of Josiah was firmly rooted in the farming population of the rural areas.[1] This was no less true of Jewish
nationalism in the Greco-Roman period. To some extent
Jewish nationalism was an expression of the conservative
rural reaction to the more extreme cultural changes taking
place in urban centers, especially in Jerusalem. But it was
much more than this! Leadership for the Holy War in the
time of Josiah as well as in the Maccabean period came
from priestly circles in the rural areas bent on reforming
the national life and assuring the correct observance of
cultic rites in the Jerusalem temple. These cultic rites,
especially the great agricultural festivals, were of great importance to the Jewish farmer, whose relationship to his
land was a covenant relationship. It was "promised" land.
But this promise was conditional upon complete obedience
to the commandments to the covenant God, including
strict compliance with the divine prescriptions for sacrifice
and worship in the Jerusalem temple.

The divine promise of the Land must also be viewed
from the perspective of the further extension of this promise found in Deuteronomy 15:6. After reminding the
Israelites of God's promise of the Land, and calling their
attention to the necessity for strict obedience to his commandments, Moses went on to add this fateful promise of
God: "You shall rule over many nations, but they shall not
rule over you." Jewish resistance to foreign rule in the days
of the Maccabees and the Zealots cannot be separated from
their confidence that God would fulfill his promises concerning the inheritance of the Land, and political sov-
ereignty for his covenant people.

It is a fatal mistake for the modern interpreter of Jewish

[1] Gerhard von Rad, *Deuteronomium-Studien* (Göttingen, 1947), pp. 42-48.

history to expect the Jews in the days of the Maccabees and Zealots lightly to set aside as of no worth these promises of God. To trust in God, was to trust in his promises. He had promised his people the Land free of foreign domination. The Maccabees and Zealots were Jews who so believed these promises that they were willing to risk their lives and the lives of their wives and children in life-and-death struggles for religious freedom and political independence against overwhelming odds.

THE MACCABEES AND THE ZEALOTS

The importance of the Maccabees for the Zealots was simply this: the Maccabees had been obedient to the commandments of God—they had been zealous for his Law and his temple—and he had given them victory over the great hosts of the heathen. Was not God faithful to accomplish in the present what he had accomplished in the past? Would he do less now that his people were oppressed by the Romans, than he had done while they were oppressed by the Seleucids? What more was needed than zealous obedience to the Law and eager readiness to take up the sword and strike a blow for God—as Phineas, the prototype *par excellence* for all Zealots, had done to Zimri and the Midianite whore, and as Mattathias, the father of the Maccabees, had done to the apostate Israelite who went up to offer sacrifice on the idolatrous altar in Modin?[2] God had accounted Phineas righteous on account of his zealous act.[3] The same God had saved his people through the zealousness of his servants the Maccabees.[4] Would he not strengthen the arm of every Zealot who, in the footstep of

[2] Numbers 25:6–15; I Macc. 2:23–27.
[3] Ps. 106:30–31.
[4] I Macc. 2:27.

Phineas and the Maccabees, was ready to advance now against the Romans?[5]

A study of the Hebrew קנא, which lies behind the Greek ζηλόω, from which our word Zealot is derived, indicates that a man who is zealous for God is one who is active for God— but active in a particular way. He is a man who gives himself over to God to be an agent of his righteous wrath and judgment against idolatry, or apostasy, or any transgression of the Law which excites God's jealousy (jealousy and zeal both having the same Hebrew root). Furthermore there is something essentially redemptive in this zealous activity. Numbers 25:10–13 makes this quite clear: "And Yahweh spake unto Moses, saying, Phineas . . . hath turned my wrath away from the children of Israel, in that he was jealous with my jealousy among them . . . and made atonement for the children of Israel."

We cannot understand the full power and theological depth of zealous Jewish nationalism until we see that in the Phineas-Maccabean tradition of zeal for the Law, the sword of those who love God is a redemptive instrument, and its zealous use is capable of turning away the wrath of God from his disobedient people, by making atonement for the sins of the nation.[6]

However, to strike down an apostate Jew is one thing,

[5] Phineas is mentioned as the forefather of the Maccabees in I Macc. 2:54. That the author of I Maccabees saw a special connection between the early Maccabean heroes and the figure of Phineas is clear from 2:26: "Thus he [Mattathias] showed his zeal for the Law, as Phineas had done toward Zimri, son of Salom."

[6] Dare we suggest that the Zealot (or *Sicarii*) saw in the spilled blood of the apostate Israelite an atoning sacrifice to expiate the sins of national apostasy? Is this a legitimate theological context within which to ponder the acts of one who was willing to persecute the Christians "even unto death" (Acts 22:4)? It is incredible to assume that the figure of Phineas was unknown to Paul, who tells us in the first chapter of Galatians that he advanced beyond many of his own age in Judaism because of his extreme zeal (*zelotes*) for the traditions of his fathers, and in the same connection tells us that in his former life in Judaism he persecuted the church violently and tried to destroy it. In the third chapter of Phillipians Paul makes this connection between zeal and active persecution of transgressors of the

but to take on the armies of a great world empire is quite another matter. In the days of Antiochus Epiphanes this note of realism was not entirely lost in the clamor of war. We read that faced by overwhelmingly superior forces some of the early Maccabean followers exclaimed, "What? Shall we be able, being a small company, to fight against so great and strong a multitude?" Whereupon Judas is remembered to have replied: "It is an easy thing for many to be shut up in the hands of a few; and it makes no difference with heaven, to save by many or by few: for victory in battle standeth not in the multitude of a host; but strength is from heaven." There were ample scriptural "testimonia" to support this kind of implicit faith in the power of the covenant God.

Had not God delivered the hosts of the Midianites into the hands of the three hundred stouthearted Israelites under the leadership of Gideon?[7] Had not Jonathan spoken the truth when he said, "There is no restraint to the Lord to save by many or by few"?[8] Indeed, had not God stopped the giant Goliath by the hand of the boy David?[9] There is no reason to doubt the reliability in substance of the following account of Judas' prayer before leading his forces into a battle in which they were greatly outnumbered:

Blessed art Thou, O Saviour of Israel, who staved off the charge of the mighty man by the hand of Thy servant David, and didst deliver the camp of the Philistines into the hands of Jonathan son of Saul, and his armor bearer. In the same way

---

Law quite explicit when, in describing his former high achievements within Judaism, he writes, "As to zeal, a persecutor of the church" (kata zelos diokon ten ekklesian). We do not know what transgression of the Law was being committed by the churches which evoked Saul of Tarsus' zealous response of persecution even unto death. But ironically and significantly enough, it might well have been the table fellowship between Gentile and Jewish Christians, which he later came to see as an essential mark of the true Israel. Cf. W. R. Farmer, "The Patriarch Phineas," Anglican Theological Review, XXXIV (1952), pp. 26–30.

[7] Judges 7.
[8] I Samuel 14:6.
[9] I Samuel 17:40–54.

hem in this camp by the hand of Thy people Israel, and let them be put to shame in spite of their army and their horsemen. Make them cowardly. Melt the boldness of their strength. Let them quake at their destruction. Cast them down with the sword of those that love (ἀγαπώντων) Thee, and let all who know Thy name praise Thee with hymns.[10]

As we know from the preceding chapter, liturgical material like this was being copied and read in the wilderness of Judah in the days of the Romans. We read in the scroll of the *War of the Sons of Light against the Sons of Darkness:*

For the battle is thine, and by the strength of thine hand their carcasses have been dashed to pieces without a burial. Goliath of Gath, a mighty man of valor, thou didst deliver into the hand of thy servant David, because he trusted in thy great name, and not in sword or spear—for thine is the battle. The Philistines thou hast subdued time without number by thy holy name. Moreover by the hand of our kings Thou hast saved us time without number, because of thy mercies and not in accordance with our deeds, which we have done wickedly, and our acts of rebellion. The battle is thine and from Thee comes the power. It is not our own, and neither our strength nor the vigor of our hands did valiantly, for we acted in thy strength and in the power of thy great valor.[11]

The recognition that victory in battle for the Israelites was due to the strength of their covenant God, mighty in war, whether that recognition be made in prayer before battle or in hymn after battle, is an authentic note of Jewish nationalism in the Greco-Roman period reaching back into the pre-exilic history of Israel. So long as their war was a Holy War, the Israelites were encouraged to believe that ultimate victory was assured in spite of the odds against them. We have every reason to think that the Zealots also, along with the Covenanters of Qumran, shared this ancient belief which had meant so much to the Jews in the days of the Maccabees.

10 I Macc. 4:30–33, as translated by Sidney Tedesche.
11 1QM 11:2–5, as translated by Lawrence Toombs.

INTERVENTION OF ANGELS

This confidence in divine assistance in time of battle receives dramatic expression in the belief in intervention of angels on the side of the Israelites. The cooperative activity of the heavenly and earthly armies of the Lord appears to have been an ancient element in Israel's conception of the Holy War. In II Samuel 5:17-25 we read that when the Philistines came up to the valley of Rephaim and took up positions against the Israelites, David enquired of the Lord what he should do. Having received his orders and having executed them with success, David said, "The Lord hath broken forth upon mine enemies before me." Later when the Philistines returned, David once again enquired of the Lord and was told not to make a frontal attack but rather to go around behind the enemy and lie in ambush among the mulberry trees. "Then when thou hearest the sound of marching in the tops of the mulberry trees, bestir thyself, for then shall the Lord go out before thee, to smite the host of the Philistines." The "sound of marching" in the tops of the mulberry trees indicates the presence of the "hosts" of the Lord. So that from very early times the Israelites seem to have been prepared to think of the Lord's assistance in battle in so to say "pluralistic" terms.

By the Maccabean period, it had become more or less conventional for pious Jews to think of their transcendent Lord as dealing with his people through the mediating agency of angels. Both I and II Maccabees picture Judas praying for angelic intervention on the eve of battle.[12]

In the Roman period the members of the Qumran community believed that God's angels would go with them into battle against their enemies the Kittim:

We will come with the holy ones of thy greatness, an army of angels in our visitations; and great will be the battle against our company. But a host of. His spirits are with our footmen

[12] I Macc. 7:41-42; II Macc. 15:22-24.

and horsemen, like clouds and like mists of dew to cover the land, even like an outpouring of showers of rain to water fittingly all that comes from her.[13]

In this passage the Sons of Light are compared to the trees and the plants which come from the land, while the angelic hosts are compared to showers from heaven which are neither too light nor too heavy. As the showers of rain water the plants and make them strong, so God's angels will come in sufficient strength to assure victory to the Sons of Light with whom they will march shoulder to shoulder as they advance together against the Sons of Darkness and the hosts of Belial.

It is of the greatest importance that this divine intervention, whether it is in the pre-exilic, Maccabean, or Roman periods, does not preclude a spirit of intense activism among the sons of Israel who are the earthly warriors of the Lord. The Lord is in truth their commander-in-chief, and they receive battle orders through those whom he has chosen and consecrated for leadership in their Holy War.

We moderns may scoff at such primitive concepts. And we may doubt the ultimate truth of such crude theology. But our skepticism betrays us into the hands of untruth if we insist on believing that the Zealots did not share with the Qumran Covenanters of their day and with the Maccabees before them these ancient religious beliefs which go back to the pre-exilic history of Israel.

ZEALOTS AND OTHER PATRIOTIC JEWS

The only crucial difference between the Zealot groups and other patriotic Jews who stood outside the collaborating circle of tax collectors, Sadducees, and High-Priestly families was over the question, "When shall our policy of noncollaboration with the occupying powers and of non-

[13] 1QM 12:8–10, as translated by Lawrence Toombs.

fraternization with Jewish collaborators as well as Roman officials and soldiers be changed into the warlike policy of active resistance?" On this question there was room for practical difference of opinion. No doubt there were some groups of patriotic Jews who insisted on waiting for some clear sign from God before committing themselves to the battle. Some of the so called "apocalyptical" groups would probably have fallen into this category. But that does not mean that Jews belonging to these somewhat "reluctant" or "wait-and-see" groups would have been necessarily more religious than those who, like Phineas and the early Maccabees, consumed by zeal for God, his Law, and his temple, were eager to respond in zealous action against *any* flagrant affront to God's holiness. These "zealots" no doubt appeared to some of their compatriots to be "overly zealous," and we may readily believe that they were sometimes regarded as a bit "trigger-happy" by the more moderate groups. But we should not think that these more moderate Jews were any less patriotic than the Zealots. The Zealots certainly had no monopoly on patriotism.

When the showdown came, the whole nation would be caught up in the life-and-death struggle between God's people and their enemies. Every patriotic Jew, whether he be Pharisee, Essene, or Zealot, would be called upon to give his full measure of service in that Holy War. This war would be characterized by unimaginable bloodshed and suffering.[14] Furthermore, the blood shed in this Holy War was not all to be that of God's enemies. It was fully expected that the Sons of Light would suffer terrible casualties and unprecedented distress and anguish before the final deliverance came. This means that in any war believed by the Jewish participants to be the Holy War, heavy casualties, and disastrous defeat in battle would only serve

---

[14] Dan. 12:1; *War of Sons of Light against the Sons of Darkness,* Col. I, Lines 9–12.

to spur the believing warrior on to greater heights of self-sacrifice and valor. Even when as a result of adversity in war the Sons of Light were called upon to suffer horrible deprivations, as happened to the besieged Jews inside Jerusalem in the final phase of the war with Rome, even then they would fight madly on, because these casualties and sufferings were but certain signs of ultimate victory if only Israel would remain faithful to the end. This eschatological framework for the war of the Jews against Rome is precisely what is demanded in order to make sense out of what we know took place in Jerusalem in the closing days of the conflict.

In the final phase of the siege the Romans had broken through the last wall between them and the Temple of Zion. The Jewish defenders were conducting a last-ditch stand, fighting passionately in the narrow streets and from the housetops. Finally the Romans are able to set fire to the temple buildings. Jewish resistance continues with a new burst of fury as the news of the temple's peril spreads. Then, of a sudden, once the temple itself starts to go up in flames, the mad resistance comes to a dramatic end. And when at last the Romans with impunity commit the abomination of desolation by sacrificing to their standards in the very courtyard of the temple, there is only one thing to do. The Sons of Light must abandon Zion, because the Lord of hosts has abandoned his temple. There is no point in retiring to the impregnable towers of the upper city still in their possession, there to continue indefinitely their resistance to the Romans. Their covenant God had abandoned his temple, but he would never abandon his people Israel. He would tabernacle with them as he had long before the temple in Jerusalem had been built. They must return to the wilderness. There to prepare a way for the Lord of Hosts who would yet come and redeem his people from the hands of their enemies. So they treated with Titus to go with their wives and their children out of the city and down into the wilderness. This request was turned down, as of course it had to be by any military power which had a rudimentary understanding of the roots of the Jewish resistance. There in the wilderness these people would constitute a continued threat to Roman rule. Yet to the wilderness they must return! So with the same fury with which they once attempted to keep the Romans out of the city, the Jews now expended themselves in suicidal attempts to break through the Roman walls of circumvallation that they might get out of the place which had been abandoned by their God, and return to the place where he would return to them.

Theirs had been to them a Holy War. All their factional differences had been overcome by their unified belief that their covenant God would come with his hosts of angels to turn back the Roman legions before they reached his temple. This unity of belief had accounted for the solidarity of their incredible last-ditch defence of the temple. But the heavenly hosts had not come. At least not in sufficient strength to ward off the onslaught of the Sons of Darkness and the hosts of Belial. The Lord of Hosts had abandoned Zion, and in so doing he had left his people leaderless. Like troops without a general, the Jews frittered away their energies in fruitless efforts to escape or hide from the hands of the enemy, until at last they were being exterminated like rates in their holes. With their hopes crushed, and with the yoke of the Romans still about their necks, we may well believe that some began to wonder if there had been anything holy about the war. Certainly Josephus, who was an eyewitness to the whole tragic event we have been describing, was able to write about the war as if from its very beginning, so far from being a Holy War, it had indeed been contrary to the will of God. Nevertheless, we must make every effort to get behind this interpretation

Josephus places upon the war, to the facts he records as he describes the development of the conflict. So to do is to see a people caught up in a war which, however mistaken they might have been, was believed by them to be a Holy War—no doubt for some the war of the Sons of Light against the Sons of Darkness.

Relevance to New Testament Studies

It may be asked, what is the relevance of all this to New Testament studies? Granting that Jewish nationalism in both the Seleucid and Roman periods was religiously motivated, in fact rooted in the Holy-War tradition of pre-exilic Judaism, what then? Does this cast any new light on old problems? The answer to this question is definitely in the affirmative.

QUEST FOR THE HISTORICAL JESUS

The faith of the early Christian community in Jesus of Nazareth as the Messiah of God, through whom salvation had been brought to his people (though they knew it not), and through whom salvation was now being offered to all men, Jew and Gentile alike, cannot be properly understood when the New Testament meaning of "Christ" is centered merely in the teachings of Jesus, or even in these plus his life and death. For the New Testament as for the Old, it is God who has the final word, and he raised Jesus from the dead. One needs to take into account the resurrection of Jesus together with his death, life, and teaching in order to begin to comprehend the full meaning of "Christ" in the New Testament.

But to center attention on the Risen Christ to the exclusion of the earthly Jesus, a tendency among some Christian theologians, is to move in the same disastrous direction as the Docetists in the early Church. New Testament interpreters must make every effort to work back through the "picture" of Jesus Christ in the Gospels, which present Jesus as he was seen through the eyes of those who had come to know him as their Risen Lord, to the "picture" of Jesus as he was seen through the eyes of those who had seen his healing works, heard his earthly voice, responded to his message about the Kingdom of God, and been witnesses to and participants in his earthly ministry. This "picture" of Jesus of Nazareth will never by itself constitute an adequate object of faith for Christians. But we must have at least its main outlines and major details in order to possess that more complete picture of Jesus the Christ which is required for Christian faith. This "picture" of the historical Jesus is essential for the simple reason that the Risen Christ can never become real to the Christian unless the believer knows who it is that God Almighty has raised from the dead. What did he teach? How did he live? How did he die?

But it will be asked, what can we know about this Jesus of Nazareth aside from the fact that he was baptized in the river Jordan at the hands of John the Baptist, had a brief ministry in Galilee, and was crucified outside Jerusalem in the days of Pontius Pilate? The answer is that we can know a great deal, and we must continually strive to know more. We learn more through our study and restudy of the Gospel records. And we learn more as we are better able to understand the world in which Jesus lived.

We must keep in mind that most of the teachings of Jesus have been abstracted from their original historical setting and that at best our Gospel authors have only approximated the actual circumstances under which Jesus uttered them. No doubt in many cases we are brought very close indeed to the original setting for certain sayings of Jesus. But in other cases, as for example in Matthew with the so called Sermon on the Mount, no attempt has been made to give a picture of what each saying meant to those who first heard it. In interpreting these sayings of Jesus we are obliged in every case to find the proper historical setting. Not to do so is to do violence to the Christian faith, as well as to the original intent of Jesus. For Jesus was neither a holy angelic being who spoke directly out of eternity, nor was he a Greek philosopher who went about uttering universal truths and attracting students who formed around him some new school of thought.

Rather was Jesus a true son of Israel who wrestled with and agonized over the crucial political, economic, social, and religious issues of his own particular people in his own particular day. If there is anything universally true in his teachings, it is because there was something universal in the down-to-earth, day-to-day issues with which he truly came to grips in his teaching and in his life. His death and resurrection have given to his teachings and his life an ultimate and eternal dimension. But the Christian Church can never loosen its grasp on the central fact of the faith, namely that the Son of God was in the world; lived, taught, ministered, was crucified, dead, and buried as Jesus of Nazareth in a concrete historical time and place. Because when the Church loosens its grasp on that central fact, it ceases to be the Church. This means that some kind of quest for the historical Jesus must be carried on by the Church as a necessary enterprise of faith, binding upon the Church as Church.

OCCUPATION AND RESISTANCE

The world in which Jesus lived was the world of the Jews in Palestine in the last decades of the Second Temple. It was a strife-ridden world. And in Jesus' day Palestine was an occupied country. Roman garrisons were stationed in the land, and the High Priest held his office at the pleasure of Caesar. We must learn all we can about this occupation by imperial Rome of the land of Palestine and what it meant to the people of that country. That means that we must learn all we can about the Roman Empire and about the Hellenism whose cultural standards Rome continued to carry in the East.

But even more important we must learn all we can about the Sadducees, Pharisees, Essenes, and Zealots. Because, although the historical roots of these parties reached back into the pre-Roman period, in Jesus' day these groups represented in their essential nature the major distinctive religio-political responses on the part of postexilic Judaism to the religious, political, economic, social, and cultural problems created by the Roman occupation and to the resultant continued threat of Hellenization.

The Sadducees were the party of collaboration which like the Hellenizing party in the days of the Maccabees believed that Israel's separation from the heathen was the main source of her national distresses.[15] The Pharisees, Essenes, and Zealots in varying degrees and in different ways acted as parties of resistance to the forces of occupation and to the agents of collaboration. They all agreed that Israel should be a separate people, holy unto God. The heathen occupation of that land which had been promised by God to his people meant a contamination both of his people and his land. Those Israelites who collaborated or fraternized with the heathen only spread the infection. The nation would continue in distress so long as the heathen remained in the land.

As the Sadducees had their spiritual roots in the extreme Hellenizing influences of the early Maccabean period, so the Pharisees, Essenes, and Zealots had their spiritual roots in the conservative reaction against those same influences in the same period. Since each of these parties has a history which reaches back into the pre-Roman period, we must

[15] I Macc. 1:11.

be thoroughly acquainted with the history and literature of Judaism of the Hasmonean and Maccabean periods as preparatory to a full understanding of what was going on in the Roman period.

Among the Pharisees, Essenes, and Zealots there was substantial agreement on many if not most major points of doctrine. They differed sharply on many matters of practice, but taken together these three groups constituted the mainstream of the national resistance movement. If there were such a thing as "normative Judaism" in the first century A.D., we would have to define it in terms of this national resistance movement, which as we have seen placed so very great importance upon the Land, the Law, and the Temple. Certainly the popular theology of Jesus' day had its roots in this nationalistic theology which reached back through the Maccabean period into the pre-exilic history of Israel.

In the postexilic period the doctrine of the resurrection of the body was developed to the point where it became a mark of orthodoxy among those parties which constituted the mainstream of the national resistance movement. It is this belief in the resurrection of the body which largely accounts for the astounding phenomenon of mass martyrdom as well as mass military heroism on the part of Jews in the Greco-Roman period.

Jesus cannot be identified with any one of the three parties, Pharisees, Essenes, or Zealots. Yet there is no doubt that he shared more with each one of these three groups than he did with the Sadducees. His love for Israel was so great that he was willing to die for his people. He came, not to destroy the Law, but to fulfill it. He was consumed with zeal for the temple. He affirmed the resurrection of the body, and held the books of the Prophets and other later Jewish writings as authoritative as well as the five books of Moses. This is all to say that Jesus stood within the mainstream of orthodox first-century Judaism as we see that main stream reflected in the major parties of the national resistance movement. We must, therefore, learn all we can about this national resistance movement if we are to see Jesus within the historical setting most native to him.

Truly Jesus transcended the national resistance movement of his day. But that is something quite different from saying that he detached himself from it. To say that Jesus was detached from Jewish nationalism in his day is to say that he was out of touch with what was really going on among his people. The Zealots spearheaded the resistance against Rome. If we are to understand Jesus and his message fully, we need to know how and why he transcended the Zealot movement. This means that we must know who the Zealots were. What was their relationship to the Maccabees? What was it that motivated them to throw themselves as living sacrifices into the face of the Roman legions and lead their nation into a suicidal war? Upon the answers we give to these crucial questions will depend, in large part, our understanding of the original meaning of much that is of importance in the ministry and teachings of Jesus.

BACKGROUND OF JESUS

There is a prevailing tendency among New Testament writers to set Jesus against either one or the other of two false backgrounds. On the one hand we have had the background of secular, this-worldly nationalism, and on the other hand we have had the background of religious, other-worldly apocalypticism. We have imagined the Zealots to be this-worldly and activistic, and the apocalypticists to be other-worldly and passive.[16] The gospel portraits of Jesus have never really come alive against either of these back-

[16] The tendency to regard these two backgrounds as separate from one another and mutually exclusive received clear-cut expression as late as December, 1955, when a paper was read to the Society of Biblical Literature and Exegesis in New York City which had as its thesis, "That the Early Church's Conception of Messianic Fulfillment Was Related to Jewish Nationalism rather than to Jewish Apocalyptic."

grounds. The reason for this is plain to see. The Jesus of the Gospels is a real figure.[17] However, neither of the backgrounds against which we have tried to place him is real. A real person does not come alive against an unreal background. We must find for Jesus a real background, his true background, if we ever expect him to "come alive" as an historical person.

Those who have attempted to set Jesus against the background of this-worldly secular Jewish nationalism have inevitably made him into a semipolitical leader who was primarily concerned with establishing some sort of idealistic brotherhood of man.[18] Jesus in this role usually ends up as a pathetic or tragic failure for whom the cross symbolizes his cruel defeat at the hands of unregenerate humanity. Or he may become the great pacifist of antiquity, whose cross points defiantly forward toward Gandhi and others who have learned the power of "nonviolence."[19] There has been an instinctive rejection of all such interpretations of the historical Jesus by the great majority of New Testament scholars, most of whom regard these interpretations as bizarre examples of extreme modernizing.

On the other hand, the attempt to set Jesus against the background of other-worldly apocalypticism has had a similarly distorting effect upon our understanding of his historical role. Jesus appears as a strange contradiction. At one moment he seems to pour himself out in an active life of

[17] Some may feel that he does not always fit perfectly the intellectual framework or the historical perspective of those to whom we are indebted for our Gospel accounts. But all New Testament students, whether they be secular, Christian, or Jewish, agree that Jesus was an authentic first-century Jew.

[18] See Vladimir G. Simkhovich, whose brilliant essay, *Toward the Understanding of Jesus* (New York, 1921), does considerable justice to the background of Jewish nationalism but is vitiated by a complete disregard of apocalypticism, p. 73.

[19] So Robert Eisler, *The Messiah Jesus and John the Baptist* (New York, 1931), p. 568. The original and unabridged German edition was published under a Greek title, ΙΗΣΟΤΣ ΒΑΣΙΛΕΤΣ ΟΤ ΒΑΣΙΛΕΤΣΑΣ (Heidelberg, 1929).

self-giving service, while in the next he is completely passive and stands gazing up into the sky awaiting some heavenly Son of Man to come floating down on a cloud. It is all very unreal for the simple reason that there is no convincing connection between the active life of service and the passive life of waiting for some apocalyptic figure to usher in the Kingdom of God. The end result of this attempt is a profound skepticism with regard to the ultimate or even provisional success of any effort made to recover the historical Jesus.[20]

These two radically divergent interpretations of Jesus have failed to convince the general body of New Testament scholars, not because they do not contain very real elements of truth, but rather because the final results just do not seem to ring true to the Jesus of the Gospels. Neither of these interpretations by itself does full justice to the truth which is contained in the other. The truth is that the Gospel records have preserved quite clearly the fact that both nationalism and apocalypticism are important elements in the background of Jesus. We have failed in our modern quest for the historical Jesus in large part because of our failure to see him against the background of his real world, namely a world in which both nationalism and apocalypticism are important elements.

We have known for a long time that first-century Judaism contained both nationalistic and apocalyptic elements. But we have mistakenly labored under the illusion that there has been no connection between these important elements. This illusion grows out of the nature of our literary sources. On the one hand we have the histories of Josephus, which empasize in dramatic fashion that na-

---

[20] Cf. Albert Schweitzer, whose extreme skepticism really grows out of his own failure to achieve a convincing reconstruction of the inner history of the Passion narrative, which demands not only the eschatological framework, which Schweitzer gives it, but a background of zealous nationalism, which he completely neglects. *The Quest of the Historical Jesus*, pp. 389–401.

tionalism was extremely important in the first century. But for Josephus apocalypticism is of minor importance, and certainly he does not bring it into any creative and clear-cut relationship to the national resistance to Rome. On the other hand, in contrast to the historical works of Josephus, the religious literature of the Jews which can be definitely dated as coming from this period is strongly influenced by apocalypticism. Because Josephus has depicted the revolt against Rome as being largely secularly motivated, it has been difficult to see any connection between this war and Jewish apocalypticism. However, to think of Jewish nationalism in this period as something completely separate from Jewish apocalypticism, or vice versa, is to be guilty of false abstraction. We are not in a position to identify Zealotism as such with Apocalypticism as such. But as the newly discovered Dead Sea scroll, *The War of the Sons of Light against the Sons of Darkness*, definitely proves, Jewish apocalyptists sometimes shared in a remarkable way the militant spirit which breathed through the Maccabees and Zealots.[21] And as we have indicated in the first part of this chapter, the eschatological and apocalyptic overtones of the behavior of the last defenders of Jerusalem are quite clear to those who have ears to hear and eyes to see. In brief, the dichotomy between Zealotism and apocalypticism in the Roman period is a false dichotomy.

The apocalyptical belief in the intervention of hosts of angels to fight on the side of the Sons of Light provides us with a direct and interesting point of contact between Jewish nationalism and the Gospels. As we have seen, the Maccabees shared with pre-exilic Judaism this belief in the co-operative activity of the heavenly and earthly armies of the Lord. We have furthermore noted that the behavior of the Zealots in the war against the Romans can sometimes best be understood in terms of a belief in the intervention of

21 Cf. Millar Burrows, *The Dead Sea Scrolls*, p. 292.

angelic warriors to assist the Israelites in their battle against the heathen forces.

But it is to the *War of the Sons of Light against the Sons of Darkness* that we must look to get the most clear-cut evidence that at least certain groups of first-century Jews could believe strongly that the angelic hosts would march shoulder to shoulder with the Israelite warriors. This document assumes throughout that God will send his angels to assist the Sons of Light in their war against the Sons of Darkness and the hosts of Belial. Recognizing that this scroll has strong liturgical motives, and that the war envisioned in it is the final war at the end of time, some interpreters have fallen into the trap of thinking that the author conceives this eschatological war in "purely" apocalyptical terms. In other words, that it is not going to be a real conflict of blood, sweat, and tears. It is going to be a completely spiritual battle between the angelic hosts of the Lord and those of Belial. But such an interpretation cannot stand for the simple fact that this document makes it quite clear that though it will be the last war of this age, it will none the less be a real war in which there will be active fighting on a grand scale, with terrible losses on both sides. This much is very clear. But what above all needs to be pointed out is that along with the militant spirit to which attention has been drawn the reader finds a deep piety very much akin to that which breathes through many of our canonical Psalms. Thus after victory in battle the Sons of Light joyfully exalt the name of the God of Israel:

> Blessed be the God of Israel,
>> who keeps steadfast love for his covenant
>> and testimonies of salvation for the people of his redemption.
> He called men who were staggering to come forth from the prison house;
> But he gathered the assembly of the nations to bring them to an end without a remnant,

to establish by justice the heart of the faint,
to open the mouth of the dumb that he might declare
    aloud his mighty acts,
to teach feeble hands to make war.
He gives the trembling knees a firm standing place,
    and muscular power to the shoulder of those who strike.
By the poor in spirit (he brings low) the stubborn heart
And by those whose way is perfect they have brought an end
    to every wicked nation.[22]

In this document we have an expression of intense Jewish nationalism which is thoroughly religious, highly activistic in its ethic, eschatological in its concept of history,
and apocalyptic in its thought form. All of these elements
are united in one organic self-consistent whole. It is some
such background as this which is demanded by the Gospels
if ever Jesus is to step forth as a real figure of his own time.

JESUS REINTERPRETED

Jesus, in the night in which he was betrayed into the
hands of the Sons of Darkness, was remembered to have
said to one of his disciples, who had drawn his sword to
ward off those who had come to arrest Jesus: "Put up thy
sword. . . . Thinkest thou that I cannot now pray to my
father, and he shall presently give me more than twelve
legions of angels?"[23] This passage, which has always been a
puzzling one, definitely begins to take on new meaning
once it is seen against the background of "apocalyptic Zealotism." Not that Jesus fits perfectly the pattern of this
Zealotism. (The passage just cited is an example where in a
vital respect he contradicts the pattern.) But it is this pattern against which he was constantly being measured by his
disciples as well as by the multitudes who flocked to hear
and see him.
We are told that on one occasion, while preaching in the

22 1QM 14:4–7. Translation by Lawrence Toombs.
23 Matt. 26:52–53.

hill country east of the Sea of Galilee, Jesus had to make a quick withdrawal because he perceived that the multitudes had come "to make him king by force."[24] Against this background of Maccabean-Zealot nationalism, Jesus, however much he may have been misunderstood, comes alive and steps forth as a real "flesh-and-blood Jewish patriot who loved his people and his country."[25]

Jesus steps forth from the pages of our Gospels as one who loves his people and his land as deeply as Jeremiah or any of the other great prophetic figures. But he is also a patriot whose self-sacrificial love is not to be surpassed by any Judas Maccabaeus who had laid down his life to save his people. When Judas was killed in battle all Israel lamented him greatly and mourned for a long time, saying, "What a hero is fallen, the Saviour of Israel."[26] Jesus could never have commanded the loyalty of his disciples had he been less courageous and devoted than other Jewish patriots of his own day. The Gospels make it quite clear that Jesus was executed on the charge of a political crime. The authorities were afraid of his political power. He had been acclaimed "King of the Jews." This title he never denied, and he bore it nobly to the end. Jesus not only matched the zeal of a Zealot, he was crucified "as a Zealot."[27] "Greater love hath no man than this, that he lay down his life for his friends." "He gave his life a ransom for many." "He died for all."

It was not the crucifixion of Jesus which scattered the disciples, it was his arrest. The cross began to draw the disciples back together again. The Church may have been

24 John 6:15.
25 Cf. Amos Wilder, *Otherworldliness and the New Testament* (New York, 1954), pp. 67, 84, 93.
26 I Macc. 9:21. Cf. I Macc. 13:4.
27 See Oscar Cullmann, *The State in the New Testament* (New York, 1956), pp. 6, 11–12, 22. Cullmann does not regard Jesus as a Zealot. But he rightly insists that Jesus was regarded as a Zealot by the State, and that he had to come to terms with the Zealot movement (p. 12).

born on Easter morn, but it was conceived on Good Friday. "And I, if I be lifted up, shall draw all men unto me."

Jesus made his final break with the Zealot-apocalyptic pattern of expectation at the moment he allowed himself to be taken into custody by the forces of collaboration. By this voluntary act he disassociated himself in an unmistakable way from the Zealots. His entry into Jerusalem only a few days before had been ambiguous. The prophecy of Zechariah, with which Jesus apparently associated himself by riding into Jerusalem on the back of an humble ass, was capable of different interpretations. In the oracle of Zechariah the entry of the King of Zion is pictured as a triumphant entry of one who has already achieved victory over the nations and now rules from sea to sea. But the oracle goes on to give a description of how this victory over the nations is to be achieved. And in this description we have the picture of the eschatological war between the Sons of Zion and the Sons of Greece. The battle is described in apocalyptical terms not essentially different from those of the *War of the Sons of Light against the Sons of Darkness,* in which as we have seen there is a strong note of Zealotic activism.

As Jesus rode by and the crowds hailed him as King of the Jews, what was in their minds? Had this final battle already taken place, or was it about to take place, or did it still lie out in the indefinite future? And dare we ask, What was in the mind of Jesus? Had he so completely spiritualized the eschatological war that in casting out the daemons he had established in principle the victory of the Sons of Light over the powers of Darkness? Had Belial already been brought low? Or was the final conflict to come? If there was to be a final conflict, what form would it take? What was the King of the Jews to do? What was it that the Lord of Hosts would have his people do?

The eyes of the people are upon their king. Now they

will know what to do, because the Lord of Hosts will lead them through his anointed Son of David, as he had led them of old in the days of the Philistines. As the Lord had saved Israel from the Philistines through the consecrated sword of David, so in the days of Antiochus Epiphanes he had saved Israel from the Sons of Greece through the consecrated sword of the Maccabees. Could this be another saviour like the great Judas Maccabeaus? Who could blame them for hoping against hope? Had not Judas and Simon made similar triumphal entries into Zion? They had been waved on their victorious way by palm branches and celebrated with hymns. Why not sing wild hosannas to this Jesus of Nazareth and defiantly hold high branches of the palm tree, recognized even by Rome as a national symbol of Israel?[28]

That Jesus was entering the city unarmed only served to heighten the fact that he had not placed his confidence in the horse and the battle bow, but rather like David and the Maccabees his trust was in the Lord of Hosts who had promised through his prophet Zechariah that he would raise up the sons of Zion to do battle against the heathen forces. Like the boy David these sons of Zion would devour and subdue their enemies with whatever weapons were at hand, because the might of the heathen was to be of no more avail than the sword of Goliath.

On the one hand, this symbolic act of riding into Jerusalem on the back of an humble ass, placed Jesus in position to be hailed as the conquering king of the Jews whose dominions would stretch from sea to sea. On the other hand, this king was to be humble, and he was to declare peace among the nations. Thus there was in this act of Jesus real justification for the cries of hosanna from the crowds, and for their acclaiming him King of Israel and

[28] See W. R. Farmer, "The Palm Branches in John 12:13," *The Journal of Theological Studies*, Vol. III, Part 1 (April, 1952), pp. 62–66.

Son of David. But the jubilant throngs no doubt read into this act something more of the Maccabean-Zealot meaning than Jesus ever intended, and apparently they took little note of that which is truly distinctive about Zechariah's king, namely his humility and his concern for peace. According to one of the evangelists, not even the disciples of Jesus understood what had happened at first.

At any event, the multitudes soon caught on to the fact that though this man was following in the footsteps of the Maccabees in his triumphant entry into Jerusalem, and in his forthright act in cleansing the temple ("Zeal for thy house will consume me"), still his parabolic teaching was sometimes hard to understand, and his answers to crucial questions like the one about tribute money to Caesar were not those of a Judas Maccabeaus.

The multitudes who had crowded into Jerusalem that Passover, like the two disciples of Jesus on the road to Emmaus, "had hoped that he was the one to redeem Israel."[29] Then came news of his arrest. It must have spread through the city like wildfire.

Anticipation frustrated, like love scorned, sometimes issues forth in violent reactions. There is no need to be amazed at the fickleness of the impassioned throngs of excited pilgrims. They knew well that in daring to come to Jerusalem during Passover they were risking their lives. Some had seen, and others had heard of the terrible massacre of Jewish worshipers at previous festivals. They knew well that the Roman procurator always strengthened the armed guard over the city on occasions like this in order to be able to handle any emergency. The deep disappointment of the hopeful multitudes made them easy prey for the beguiling tactics of the agents for collaboration. If only Jesus had resisted arrest—if only there had been one drop of blood spilled! All that was needed was one small spark to set the conflagration going. But he allowed himself

29 Luke 24:21. Cf. I Macc. 16:2.

to be taken. He had not even lifted his hand—moreover he had not allowed his armed bodyguard to lift theirs. The Roman yoke would not be lifted this Passover!

The prospect of freeing Barabbas was perhaps more than they had a right to hope for. If the death of an impostor meant freedom for an imprisoned leader of revolt, then there was little choice for a patriotic Jew. "Crucify him, crucify him!" But it was precisely in his crucifixion that Jesus triumphed over Barabbas, the Zealots, and the Maccabean spirit. On the cross Jesus matched and surpassed the zeal of the Maccabees and Zealots. Not that these patriots had no stomach for martyrdom. They too had tasted death at the hands of their enemies—even death by torture at the hands of hardened executioners. But compare the compassion, the tenderness and forgiving spirit of Jesus on the cross with the bitterness and hatred in these climactic dying words of the seventh martyred son in II Maccabees:

You impious man, the vilest of all men, do not foolishly buoy yourself up in your insolence with uncertain hopes, when you raise your hand against the children of heaven; for you have not yet escaped the judgement of the almighty all-seeing God. For our brothers after enduring a brief suffering have drunk everlasting life under the covenant of God. But you, by the judgments of God, will receive the rightful penalty of your arrogance.[30]

Making full allowance for editorial phrasing, we still have substantially a different spirit animating these Maccabean martyrs from that which moved Jesus to cry, "Father, forgive them; for they know not what they do." He had said to those who had come to hear him:

You have heard it said, "Love your neighbor and hate your enemy." But I say to you, Love your enemies and pray for those who persecute you, so that you may be truly children of heaven; for your Father in heaven makes his sun rise on the evil and on the good, and sends rain on the just and on the unjust. For

[30] II Macc. 7:34-36.

if you love only those who love you, what credit is that to you? Do not even your enemies the tax-collectors do the same? And if you have regard only for your brethren, what more are you doing than others? Do not even your enemies the Romans do the same? The circle of your love must include your enemies, even as the love of your heavenly father includes his enemies.

This passage, which comes from the fifth chapter of the Gospel of Matthew, has been rendered freely in the light of its original historical background, in order to bring out the meaning it would have had to those who heard Jesus' earthly voice. This is a preliminary task of all sound exegesis. Not until we are in a position to know what it meant to those who first heard his teaching are we in a position to translate its meaning into terms which penetrate and illumine our own situations. This is no easy task. Let us admit the great gulf which separates the twentieth century from the first. But is it an unbridgeable gulf? Are we forever shut out of the first century so that we can never recapture its values, its manners, its ideals, its customs, its economics, its politics, its history, its art, its architecture, its theology, its world view? Each man must answer this question for himself. It is a profound question. It is not merely an historical question. It is a metaphysical question. It ultimately resolves itself into the question whether the past can ever be relived, in any meaningful sense.

Woe be to us if it cannot! For without a past the present is unreal and the future meaningless. Without a first century there is no twentieth century. Without Jesus of Nazareth there is no Jesus Christ the Risen Lord and there is no Christian hope in a Second Coming. The scholarly quest for the historical Jesus must continue, not as a pseudo-objective attempt to recreate Jesus in our own image, but rather as an enterprise of orthodox faith through which we strive ever more perfectly to see Jesus through the eyes of those who first heard his message and first confessed him to be the Christ.

SUMMARY CONCLUSIONS

On the basis of the evidence and arguments presented in Chapters IV and V we concluded that the Maccabees were the nearest historical counterparts to the Jewish nationalists of the Roman period.

On the basis of evidence and arguments presented in Chapter VI we concluded that the Maccabees were remembered by the Jews in Palestine during the first century A.D., and the evidence of *Megillath Taanith* corroborated this conclusion.

If the Maccabees were historical counterparts to the Jewish nationalists of the Roman period, and if they were remembered, they were not only counterparts but remembered counterparts. This means that they were conscious prototypes of the later nationalists. It follows, therefore, that the example and teaching of the Maccabees probably exerted a much greater influence on Jews during the New Testament period than is generally recognized.

It is suggested that the way is now open for a rewriting of Jewish history during the Roman period in which full justice may be done to the continuity between the Jewish nationalism of the Roman period with that of the Maccabean period. It is also suggested that the way is now open for a more serious study of the Maccabean uprising with a view to discovering how the continuing influence of the example and teaching of the Maccabees may have affected the life and thought of the Jews during the New Testament period. Finally, it is humbly suggested that the history and literature of the Qumran community, the ministry of John the Baptist and of Jesus, and the history and literature of the primitive Palestinian church will all find their proper setting against the background of that mainstream of Jewish Nationalism which it has been the purpose of this book to illumine.

APPENDIX: THE DATING OF
MEGILLATH TAANITH

The following considerations are among those which bear on the question of dating *Megillath Taanith*.

1. *Date of earliest known editions of the text*.[1] Already by the beginning of the nineteenth century there had been at least eleven separate editions of the text. The earliest of these were edited in the following places at the dates listed: Amsterdam, 1659; Basel, 1580; Venice, 1545. The very first edition of *Megillath Taanith* seems to have been edited in Mantua by Samuel Latif in 1513.

2. *Date of earliest known manuscript*. Lichtenstein gives descriptions of ten manuscripts, one of which he dates as early as 1509. The very earliest known manuscript of *Megillath Taanith* seems to be the De Rossi mansucript, dated 1344. Lichtenstein has compared the manuscripts and arranged them according to their relationships to one another. He proposes that they all go back to two main families of manuscripts which in turn are derived from a common "Urtext." When such an "Urtext" should be dated it is not possible to say with any degree of precision. But obviously it would go back considerably earlier than our earliest known manuscripts—and thus, presumably, would carry us well back into the Middle Ages. In any event, even if we were to date such an "Urtext," we should only have determined the latest possible date which we could give to *Megillath Taanith* including the Hebrew scholia. And even if

---

[1] I am dependent at this and at following points on Hans Lichtenstein, who has made a thorough study of the "Ausgaben und Handschriften" and presents a summary of his findings in "Die Fastenrolle: Eine Untersuchung zur jüdisch-hellenistischen Geschichte," *Hebrew Union College Annual*, VIII–IX (1931–1932), 260–64.

we could find and date the autograph of the scholiast himself, we would still have to look further back in time for the origin of the Aramaic calendar upon which he wrote down his comments. What we can learn from a study of the earliest editions and manuscripts of *Megillath Taanith* is that in dealing with this document we have not to do with something which has suddenly appeared on the modern scene and may any day now be proved to be a clever forgery of some ingenious Semitist.[2]

3. *Parallels of the Aramaic text of* Megillath Taanith *in Rabbinic literature.* Dalman lists the following Rabinnic references as passages in which fragments of *Megillath Taanith* are found: Mishnah, *Tann.* 2.8; *J. Taan.* 66ad, *J. Meg.* 70c; *Taan.* 12a, 15b, 17b, 18ab, *Meg.* 5b, 6a, *Men.* 65a, *R. Sh.* 18b, 19a, *B.B.* 115b.[3] These parallel passages are, needless to say, in Aramaic, and generally correspond so closely to the Aramaic of our *Megillath Taanith* that there seems to be no question but that there exists some very close literary kinship between the two. These parallels are sometimes introduced by the Rabbis without explicit reference to *Megillath Taanith*. But several of the passages are prefaced by some such expression as, "It is written in *Megillath Taanith*"; then follows a citation which parallels closely our *Megillath Taanith*. For example, in *Megillath* 5b we read: "It is written in *Megillath Taanith* 'The fourteenth day and the fifteenth day are the days of Purim on which there is no mourning.'" This is a very close parallel to one of the entries we have in our *Megillath Taanith*. Those who are experts in Aramaic and have made a close study of these parallels seem to be of the opinion that the Rabbis were quoting from the same text which also lies behind the manuscript tradition of our *Megillath Taanith*. In fact, those who have attempted to provide us with a reconstructed text on the basis of all the available evidence not infrequently have recourse to these Talmudic passages in determining the more original text.[4]

---

[2] It would not be necessary to make this kind of statement if it were not for the fact that many New Testament students are rightfully suspicious of relatively unknown Jewish literature about which they know nothing and have previously heard very little.

[3] Gustav Dalman, *Grammatik des jüdisch-palästinischen Aramäisch*, p. 9.

[4] So J. Derenbourg, *Essai sur l'histoire et la géographie de la Palestine d'après les Talmuds et les autres sources rabbiniques* (Paris, 1867), I, 442–44; Dalman, *Aramäische Dialektproben* (Leipzig, 1896), pp. 1–3; Zeitlin, *Megillat Taanit as a Source for Jewish Chronology and History in the Hellenistic and Roman Periods* (Philadelphia, 1922) pp. 65–68; Lichtenstein, "Die Fastenrolle," pp. 261, 318–22.

The citation from the Scroll of Fasting in the Mishnah is very brief, but there seems to be no reason to doubt that it refers to our *Megillath Taanith* or one very much like it. In discussing this Mishnaic passage the Rabbis asked, "Has it not been taught: R. Simeon b. Gamaliel said: Why does the text repeat the word בהון twice?"[5] This is not a reference to the text of the Mishnah, but to the text from which the Rabbis assumed the Mishnah was quoting. In that text there must have been an apparently unnecessary repetition of בהון. This is precisely what we have in the introductory sentence of the Aramaic text of our *Megillath Taanith:*

אלין יומיא דילא לאתענאה בהון ומקצתהון דילא למספד בהון:

This would seem to indicate that the Rabbis understood the parallel passage in the Mishnah to refer to a scroll known to them which at least *began* in very much the same language as does our *Megillath Taanith.*

Because these parallels from Rabbinic literature are so close to our *Megillath Taanith,* and because no other Fasting Scroll has come down to us, and none of the Rabbinic references to *Megillath Taanith* suggests that there was more than one such authoritative calendar, it seems reasonable to assume that, allowing for a certain amount of textual variation, our *Megillath Taanith* is the one referred to in the Mishnah, or at least that the one referred to in the Mishnah was very much like ours. A passage which strongly suggests that there was only one such well recognized and authoritative calendar is found in *Erubim* 62b:

R. Jacob b. Abba asked Abaye: Is it permitted to a disciple in a district under his master's jurisdiction to give a ruling that was as authoritative as those contained in the Scroll of Fast Days, which is a written and generally accepted document [literally, "that is written and lying"]?

It is true that no one of these passages in which the Rabbis refer to a Fasting Scroll, when taken by itself, proves necessarily that the Fasting Scroll which has come down to us is the one they were citing. Nonetheless, when taken as a whole, they do

[5] *Taan.* 18a. This question is asked to make a particular point in a controversy. If Rabbis could appeal to the text of something written other than the Scriptures or the Mishnah, it must have been a document of recognized and long-standing authority—so it would seem at least. The Mishnaic passage concerned is *Taan.* 2.8.

seem to indicate the early existence of not just any Fasting Scroll but one which must have been very much like the one which has come down to us. Thus the evidence of these Aramaic parallels in Rabbinic literature to our *Megillath Tannith* does seem to support the view that in dealing with our Fasting Scroll we have to do with a quite early document.

4. *The date of* Megillath Taanith *according to Jewish tradition.* The scholiast writes at the end of his commentary that Eleazar ben Hananiah of the family of Garon compiled *Megillath Taanith.* This Eleazar is generally identified with the Eleazar who played a leading role in the revolt against the Romans in A.D. 66–70.[6] This statement of the scholiast is more or less substantiated by a Talmudic passage which speaks of *Megillath Taanith* as having been compiled by Hananiah b. Hezekiah of the Garon family and by his followers.[7] Lauterbach holds that "the account in the Talmud and that in the scholium may both be accepted, since not only Hananiah the father, but also Eleazar the son, contributed to the compilation of the work."[8] It would seem that the evidence to be drawn from the traditional views on the origin of *Megillath Taanith* would point to an early date for our document. It is worth mentioning that there is no dissenting voice among the Rabbis. No one of the Rabbis ever seems to question the early origin of *Megillath Taanith.*

5. *The Aramaic of* Megillath Taanith. Dalman places our document at the very beginning of his published selections from Palestinian Aramaic specimens, regarding it as an authentic first-century writing.[9] Nine years later in his *Grammatik des jüdisch-palästinischen Aramäisch,* in which he discussed the grammatical characteristics of *Megillath Taanith,* Dalman could still, without making specific reference to its date, refer to it as an important document for Palestinian Aramaic.[10]

---

[6] So Derenbourg, *Essai,* I, 439; Lauterbach, "Megillat Taanit," in *The Jewish Encyclopedia* (New York, 1904), VIII, 427; Zeitlin, *Megillat Taanit,* p. 3; Lichtenstein, "Die Fastenrolle," p. 257.

[7] *Shab.* 13b.

[8] "Megillat Taanit," p. 428. Derenbourg, Lauterbach, and Zeitlin also refer to a passage in *Halakot Gedolot, Hilkot Soferim* (ed. Vienna, p. 104; ed. Zolkiev, p. 82c; ed. Hildesheimer, p. 615), which says that the eldest pupils of Shammai and Hillel helped in the compilation of *Megillath Taanith.* This led Lauterbach to conclude (p. 427) that "Megillat Taanit must have been composed, therefore, about the year seven of the common era."

[9] *Aramäische Dialektproben,* p. 32.

[10] Page 9.

Lichtenstein has made a close study of the Aramaic text and reports three Greek loan words which are in fact *termini technici*. He concludes that the presence of three such words in so short a work speaks for the antiquity and authenticity of the text.[11]

6. *The date of the events referred to in* Megillath Taanith. The latest events included in the calendar seem to date from the time of Hadrian. Thus the calendar seems to have been open for additions until at least that time.[12] The general view seems to be that the calendar as such existed long before the time of Hadrian, but that special days were added as time went on—that is, until the time of Hadrian, after which no further entries were made. There is a passage in Judith which presupposes some such list of days on which it was inappropriate to fast because those days called for rejoicing: "And she fasted all the days of her widowhood, save the eves of the sabbaths, and the sabbaths, and the eves of the new moons, and the new moons, and the feasts and joyful days in the house of Israel."[13] On the basis of this passage most authors seem to have an open mind to the possibility that such a calendar as our *Megillath Taanith* may have served a practical function within the Jewish community as early as the first century B.C.

Many, if not all, of the above-discussed considerations which bear on the question of dating *Megillath Taanith* must have played some part in weighing scholarly opinion in favor of dating this document as early as the latter half of the first or the beginning of the second century A.D. But in the final analysis, it is the self-consistent character of the internal evidence of the document itself which is decisive in determining the age and authenticity of *Megillath Taanith*.

A considerable portion of the ancient manuscript remains coming out of the wilderness of Judea in recent years is Aramaic. Once this material is published, we will have much additional information on which to base our judgment as to the age of the Aramaic of *Megillath Taanith*.

---

11 "Die Fastenrolle," p. 265. The three words are: חקרא for ἄκρα, דימוסנאי for δημοσιῶνι, and סימואתא for σημαῖαι; ἄκρα stands for the citadel in Jerusalem, δημοσιῶνι for the Roman tax-farmer, and σημαῖαι for the ensigns of the Roman legions.
12 Zeitlin argues that the last event chronicled in our document took place in A.D. 66. *Megillat Taanit*, p. 3.
13 Judith 8:6.

BIBLIOGRAPHY

SOURCES

OLD TESTAMENT. Biblia Hebraica. Edidit Rud. Kittel, textum masoreticum curavit P. Kahle. 4th ed. New York: American Bible Society, 1949.

I MACCABEES. Septuaginta Vetus Testamentum Graecum, Societatis Literarum Gottingensis. Vol. IX: Massabaeorum libri I–IV; fasc. 1: Maccabaeorum Liber. I. Edidit Werner Kappler. Göttingen: Vandenhoeck und Ruprecht, 1936.

II MACCABEES. The Old Testament in Greek, According to the Septuagint. Edited by Henry Barclay Swete. 4th ed. Vol. III. Cambridge: Cambridge University Press, 1912.

PHILO JUDAEUS. Philonis Alexandrini Opera quae supersunt. Ediderunt Leopoldus Cohn et Paulus Wendland. 7 vols. Berlin: Georg Reimer, 1896–1930.

JOSEPHUS. Flavii Iosephi Opera. Edidit, et apparatu critico instruxit Benedictus Niese. 6 vols. Berlin: Weidmann, 1887–1895.

MEGILLATH TAANITH. "Die Fastenrolle: Eine Untersuchung zur jüdisch-hellenistischen Geschichte." Aramaic text edited with critical apparatus, introduction, and explanatory notes by Hans Lichtenstein, in Hebrew Union College Annual, VIII–IX (1931–1932), 257–351.

GREEK NEW TESTAMENT. Edited with critical apparatus by Eberhard Nestle, newly revised by Erwin Nestle. 16th ed. New York: American Bible Society, 1936.

NOTE ON ENGLISH TRANSLATIONS CITED

In general we have followed the policy of quoting, where possible and advisable, from authorized or standard translations.

All quotations of I and II Maccabees, unless otherwise specified in a footnote, have been taken from *The Apocrypha, Revised Version* (New York: Thomas Nelson, 1894). The single quotation from the Book of Judith was taken from the same translation. Of Philo's *Legatio ad Gaium* we have in English only the translation by C. D. Yonge. This is found in Vol. IV, pp. 99–180 of *The Works of Philo Judaeus* (London: Bohn Classical Library, 1854–1855). Herbert Box, in his *Philonis Alexandrini In Flaccum* (London: Oxford University Press, 1939), has provided us with an excellent introduction and commentary as well as with a translation of *In Flaccum,* which has been used when citing this work.

Wherever possible we have used the translations of the works of Josephus made by H. St. John Thackeray and Ralph Marcus in the Loeb Classical Library, *Josephus* (G. P. Putnam's Sons, New York: 1928—; Vol. VII is, at present, the last to have been published). Where this library is incomplete, we have used D. S. Margoliouth's revised edition of W. Whiston's translation. This convenient one-volume translation has been collated with, and revised according to, the critical edition of the Greek text by B. Niese and contains an important introduction to the works of Josephus. The title is *The Works of Flavius Josephus* (New York: E. P. Dutton, n.d.).

The occasional quotations from the Old Testament have been made from *The Holy Bible,* newly edited by the American Revision Committee (New York: Thomas Nelson and Sons, 1901). New Testament quotations were taken from the *Revised Standard Version* (New York: Thomas Nelson and Sons, 1946).

For quotations from the Babylonian Talmud we have relied on the translations made under the general editorship of I. Epstein, *The Babylonian Talmud* London, the Soncino Press, 1948. In citing the *Mishnah* we have been dependent on Herbert Danby's *The Mishnah,* translated from the Hebrew with introduction and brief explanatory notes (London: Oxford University Press, 1933).

All other translations from which quotations have been taken have been identified by individual footnotes or can be found listed in the general bibliography under the name of the author of the original work.

OTHER WORKS

Abel, M. Les Livres des Maccabées. 2d ed. Paris: Librairie Lecoffre, 1949.

Ackroyd, Peter R. "The Problem of Maccabaean Psalms, with Special Reference to the Psalms of Solomon." Cambridge University Ph.D. dissertation, c.1947. Unpublished.

Alexander, Archibald. A History of the Israelitish Nation. Philadelphia: William S. Martein, 1853.

Allen, Joseph Henry. Hebrew Men and Times. Boston: Walker, Wise and Co., 1861.

Angus, J. "Zealots," in James Hastings, ed., Encyclopedia of Religion and Ethics. New York: Scribner's, 1922.

Aptowitzer, V. Parteipolitik der Hasmonäerzeit im rabbinischen und pseudoepigraphischen Schrifttum. Vienna: Verlag der Kohut-Foundation, 1927.

Avi-Yonah, M. "The 'War of the Sons of Light and the Sons of Darkness' and Maccabean Warfare," Israel Exploration Journal, Vol. II, No. 1 (1952).

Baron, Salo Wittmayer. A Social and Religious History of the Jews. New York: Columbia University Press, 1937.

Barton, George A. A History of the Hebrew People. New York: The Century Co., 1930.

Bentwich, Norman. Josephus. Philadelphia: The Jewish Publication Society of America, 1914.

Bernstein, Leon. Flavius Josephus: His Time and His Critics. New York: Liveright, 1938.

Bertholet, Alfred. Die Stellung der Israeliten und der Juden zu den Fremden. Freiburg: Paul Siebeck, 1896.

Bevan, Edwyn Robert. The House of Seleucus. London: E. Arnold, 1902.

Bevan, Edwyn Robert, and Charles Singer. The Legacy of Israel. Oxford: The Clarendon Press, 1927.

Bickerman, Elias. Der Gott der Makkabäer: Untersuchungen über Sinn und Ursprung der makkabäischen Erhebung. Berlin: Schocken, 1937.

———— The Maccabees. New York: Schocken Books, 1947.

Bonsirven, Joseph. Le Judaïsme Palestinien au temps de Jésus-Christ. Abridged ed. Paris: Beauchesne, 1950.

Box, Herbert. Philonis Alexandrini In Flaccum. London: Oxford University Press, 1939.

Braley, Edith Ross. A Neglected Era: From the Old Testament to the New. New York: E. P. Dutton, 1922.

Brandon, S. G. F. The Fall of Jerusalem and the Christian Church. London: S. P. C. K., 1951.

Burkitt, F. Crawford. Jewish and Christian Apocalypses. London: Oxford University Press, 1914. The Schweich Lectures for 1913.

Burrows, Millar. The Dead Sea Scrolls. New York: Viking Press, 1955.

Bury, J. B. The Ancient Greek Historians. New York: Macmillan, 1909.

Cassius, Dio Cocceianus. Dio's Roman History. Translated by Earnest Cary. 9 vols. New York: G. P. Putnam's Sons, 1914–1927. Loeb Classical Library.

Cullmann, Oscar. The State in the New Testament. New York: Scribner's, 1956.

Dalman, Gustaf. Aramäische Dialektproben. Leipzig: J. C. Hinrichs'sche Buchhandlung, 1896.

——— Grammatik des jüdisch-palästinischen Aramäisch. 2d ed. Leipzig: Hinrichs'sche Buchhandlung, 1905.

Danby, Herbert. The Mishnah. Translated from the Hebrew with introduction and brief explanatory notes. London: Oxford University Press, 1933.

Dancy, J. C. A Commentary on I Maccabees. Oxford: Basil Blackwell, 1954.

Derenbourg, J. Essai sur l'histoire et la géographie de la Palestine d'après les Talmuds et les autres sources rabbiniques. Paris: Imprimerie impériale, 1867.

Diodorus of Sicily. Diodorus Siculus. Vols. I–VI. Translated by C. H. Oldfather. New York: G. P. Putnam's Sons, 1933. Loeb Classical Library.

Dionysius of Halicarnassus. Roman Antiquities. Translated by Earnest Cary. Cambridge: Harvard University Press, 1937. Loeb Classical Library.

Dubnow, Simon. Die alte Geschichte des jüdischen Volkes. Authorized translation from the Russian by A. Steinberg. Berlin: Jüdischer Verlag, 1925.

Echard, Laurence. A General Ecclesiastical History. London: Jacob Tonson, 1702.

Edersheim, Alfred. The Life and Times of Jesus the Messiah. 8th ed., rev. New York: Longmans Green, 1903.

Eisler, Robert. The Messiah Jesus and John the Baptist. New York: Lincoln Macveagh, 1931.

—— ΙΗΣΟΥΣ ΒΑΣΙΛΕΥΣ ΟΥ ΒΑΣΙΛΕΥΣΑΣ. Heidelberg: Carl Winters, 1929.

Epstein, I., ed. The Babylonian Talmud. London: The Soncino Press, 1948.

Ewald, Heinrich. Geschichte des Volkes Israel. 3d ed. Göttingen: Dieterich'sche Buchhandlung, 1867.

Fairweather, W., and J. Southerland Black. Commentary on First Maccabees. Cambridge: Cambridge University Press, 1897.

Geiger, Abraham. Judaism and Its History. Translated from the German by Maurice Mayer. New York: Thalmessinger and Cohn, 1866.

Graetz, Heinrich. Geschichte der Juden. 2d ed. Leipzig: Oskar Leiner, 1863.

—— History of the Jews. Philadelphia: Jewish Publishing Society of America, 1893.

Grayzel, Solomon. A History of the Jews: From the Babylonian Exile to the End of World War II. Philadelphia: The Jewish Publication Society of America, 1947.

Guignebert, Charles. The Jewish World in the Time of Jesus. Translated from the French by S. H. Hooke. London: Kegan Paul, 1939.

Guthe, Hermann. Geschichte des Volkes Israel. 3d ed. Tübingen: Paul Siebeck, 1914.

Hadas, Moses. A History of Greek Literature. New York: Columbia University Press, 1950.

Hausrath, A. A History of the New Testament Times. Translated from the 3d German ed. by Charles T. Poynting and Philip Quenzer. London: Williams and Norgate, 1880.

—— Neutestamentliche Zeitgeschichte. 2d ed. Heidelberg: Bassermann, 1873.

Herford, R. Travers. Judaism in the New Testament Period. London: The Lindsey Press, 1928.

Hitzig, Ferdinand. Geschichte des Volkes Israel. Leipzig: S. Hirzel, 1869.

Holbergs, Ludwig. Jüdische Geschichte. Translated from the Danish into German by Auguste Detharding. Altona and Flensburg: Im Verlag der Gebrüder Korte, 1747.

Hölscher, Gustav. Geschichte der israelitischen und jüdischen Religion. Giessen: Alfred Töpelmann, 1922.

—— Die Quellen des Josephus für die Zeit vom Exil bis zum jüdischen Kriege. Leipzig: B. G. Teubner, 1904.

Holtzmann, Oskar. Neutestamentliche Zeitgeschichte. Tübingen: Paul Siebeck, 1906.

Home, James. The Scripture History of the Jews and Their Republick. London: Alexander Cruden and Joseph Davidson, 1787.

Jahn, John. A History of the Hebrew Commonwealth. Translated from the German by Calvin E. Stowe. Andover: G. and C. Carvill, 1828.

Jones, A. H. M. The Herods of Judaea. Oxford: The Clarendon Press, 1938.

Klausner, Joseph. Jesus of Nazareth: His Life, Times and Teaching. Translated from the Hebrew by Herbert Danby. New York: Macmillan, 1949.

Kohler, Kaufman. "Zealot," in The Jewish Encyclopedia. New York: Funk and Wagnalls, 1906.

Kuenen, A. The Religion of Israel to the Fall of the Jewish State. Translated from the Dutch by Alfred Heath May. London: Williams and Norgate, 1874.

Lagrange, M. J. Le Judaïsme avant Jésus-Christ. 3d ed. Paris: J. Cabalda et fils, 1931.

Laqueur, Richard. Der jüdische Historiker Flavius Josephus. Giessen: Münchow'sche, 1920.

Latimer, Elizabeth Wormeley. Judea from Cyrus to Titus. 2d ed. Chicago: A. C. McClurg and Co., 1900.

Lauterbach, J. Z. "Megillat Taanit," in The Jewish Encyclopedia. New York: Funk and Wagnalls, 1904.

Ledrain, Eugène. Histoire d'Israël. Paris: Alphonse Lemerre, 1882.

Lehmann-Haupt, C. F. Israel: Seine Entwicklung im Rahmen der Weltgeschichte. Tübingen: Paul Siebeck, 1911.

Lichtenstein, Hans. "Die Fastenrolle: Eine Untersuchung zur jüdisch-hellenistischen Geschichte," Hebrew Union College Annual, VIII–IX (1931–1932), 257–351.

Lightley, John W. Jewish Sects and Parties in the Time of Jesus. London: Epworth Press, 1925.

Magnus, Katie. Outlines of Jewish History. 2d ed., rev. by M. Friedlander. Philadelphia: The Jewish Publication Society of America, 1890.

Margolis, Max L., and Marx Alexander. A History of the Jewish People. Philadelphia: The Jewish Publication Society of America, 1927.

Mathews, Shailer. New Testament Times in Palestine. New and rev. ed. New York: Macmillan, 1933.

Mercer, Samuel A. B. The Life and Growth of Israel. Milwaukee: Morehouse, 1921.

Meyer, Eduard. Ursprung und Anfänge des Christentums. Stuttgart: Cotta, 1921.

Milman, Henry Hart. The History of the Jews. Reprinted from the newly revised and corrected London edition. New York: W. J. Widdleton, 1875.

Momigliano, A. "Roman Government of Palestine," "The Jewish Rebellion," "The Campaigns of Vespasian," "The Siege and Fall of Jerusalem," in The Cambridge Ancient History, X (New York: Macmillan, 1934), 849 ff.

Moore, George Foot. Judaism in the First Centuries of the Christian Era: The Age of the Tannaim. Cambridge, Mass.: Harvard University Press, 1927.

Morgenstern, Julian. "The Chanukkah Festival and the Calendar of Ancient Israel," Hebrew Union Annual, XX (1947), 1–136.

Morrison, W. D. The Jews under Roman Rule. New York: G. P. Putnam's Sons, 1902.

Niese, Benedictus. "Josephus," in James Hastings, ed., Encyclopedia of Religion and Ethics. New York: Scribner's, 1915.

Noth, Martin. Geschichte Israels. Göttingen: Vandenhoeck und Ruprecht, 1950.

Oesterley, W. O. E. A History of Israel. Vol. II. Oxford: The Clarendon Press, 1932.

Palmer, E. H. A History of the Jewish Nation. London: S. P. C. K., 1874.

Pfeiffer, Robert H. History of New Testament Times, with an Introduction to the Apocrypha. New York: Harper, 1949.

Plutarch. The Parallel Lives. Translated by Bernadotte Perrin. 11 vols. New York: G. P. Putnam's Sons, 1914–1926. Loeb Classical Library.

Polybius. The Histories. Translated by W. R. Paton. 6 vols. New York: G. P. Putnam's Sons, 1922–1927. Loeb Classical Library.

Porter, Frank Chamberlin. The Messages of the Apocalyptical Writers. New York: Scribner's, 1918.

Rad, Gerhard von. Deuteronomium-Studien. Göttingen: Vandenhoeck und Ruprecht, 1947.

Rankin, O. S. The Origins of the Festival of Hannukkah, the Jewish New Age Festival. Edinburgh: T. and T. Clark, 1930.

Raphall, Morris J. Post-Biblical History of the Jews. Philadelphia: Mass and Brother, 1855.

Reifenberg, A. Ancient Jewish Coins. 2d and rev. ed. Jerusalem: Ruben Mass, 1947.

Ricciotti, Giuseppe. Histoire d'Israël. French translation of the Italian 3d ed. by Paul Auvray; new ed. rev. and corrected. Paris: A. and J. Picard, 1948.

———— The Life of Christ. Translated from the Italian by Alba Zizzamia. Milwaukee: Bruce Publishing Co., 1947.

Riggs, James Stevenson. A History of the Jewish People during the Maccabean and Roman Periods. New York: Scribner's, 1900.

Robinson, H. Wheeler. The History of Israel. London: Duckworth, 1938.

Romanoff, Paul. Jewish Symbols on Ancient Jewish Coins. Philadelphia: Louis S. Werner, 1944.

Sanders, Frank Knight. History of the Hebrews. New York: Scribner's 1914.

Schlatter, A. Geschichte Israels von Alexander dem Grossen bis Hadrian. Stuttgart: Verlag der Vereinsbuchhandlung, 1906.

Schunk, K. D. Die Quellen des I and II Makkabäerbuches. Halle: Neimeyer, 1954.

Schürer, Emil. Geschichte des jüdischen Volkes im Zeitalter Jesu Christi. 3d and 4th eds. 3 vols. Leipzig: J. C. Hinrichs'sche Buchhandlung, 1901–1911.

———— A History of the Jewish People in the Time of Jesus Christ. 5 vols. New York: Charles Scribner's Sons, n.d. (A reprint of the authorized English translation published first in Edinburgh, 1886–1890.)

———— Lehrbuch der neutestamentlichen Zeitgeschichte. Leipzig: J. C. Hinrichs'sche Buchhandlung, 1874.

Schweitzer, Albert. The Quest of the Historical Jesus. 2d English ed. London: A. C. Black, 1922.

Seinecke, L. Geschichte des Volkes Israel. Göttingen: Vandenhoeck und Ruprecht, 1884.

Shotwell, James Thomson. The History of History. New York: Columbia University Press, 1939.

Simkhovitch, Vladimir G. Toward the Understanding of Jesus. New York: Macmillan, 1921.

Singer, Simeon. The Standard Prayer Book. New York: Bloch Publishing Co., 1949.

Stade, Bernhard, ed. Geschichte des Volkes Israel. Vol. II, Part 2: "Das Ende des jüdischen Staatswesens und die Entstehung des Christenthums," by Oskar Holtzmann. Berlin: G. Grote'-sche Verlagsbuchhandlung, 1888.

Stanley, Arthur Penrhyn. Lectures on the History of the Jewish Church. New ed. New York: Scribner's, 1893.

Strack, Hermann L. Introduction to the Talmud and Midrash. Authorized translation on the basis of the author's revised copy of the 5th German ed. Philadelphia: The Jewish Publication Society of America, 1945.

Sukenik, Eleazar L. The Dead Sea Scrolls of the Hebrew University. Jerusalem: The Magnes Press, 1955.

Tarn, W. W. Hellenistic Civilization. 2d ed. London: Eduard Arnold, 1930.

Tedesche, Sidney. The First Book of Maccabees. Translated by S. Tedesche, introduction and commentary by Solomon Zeitlin. New York: Harper, 1950.

———— The Second Book of Maccabees. Translated by S. Tedesche, introduction and commentary by Solomon Zeitlin. New York: Harper, 1954.

Thackeray, H. St. John. Josephus, the Man and the Historian. New York: Jewish Institute of Religion Press, 1929.

Thomas, C. Geschichte des alten Bundes. Magdeburg: S. Bühling, 1897.

Torrey, C. C. Documents of the Primitive Church. New York: Harper, 1941.

Toynbee, Arnold Joseph. Greek Historical Thought. New York: E. P. Dutton and Co., 1924.

Wellhausen, Julius. Israelitische und jüdische Geschichte. ed. Berlin: Georg Reimer, 1897.

———— Prolegomena to the History of Israel. Translated by J. Southerland Black and Allan Menzies. Edinburgh: Adam and Charles Black, 1885.

———— Sketch of the History of Israel and Judah. 3d ed. London and Edinburgh: Adam and Charles Black, 1891.

Wilder, Amos. Otherworldliness and the New Testament. New York: Harper, 1954.

Willett, Herbert L. The Jew through the Centuries. Chicago: Willett, Clark and Co., 1932.

Winter, Paul. "Magnificat and Benedictus—Maccabaean Psalms?" *Bulletin of the John Rylands Library* (Manchester: University Press), Vol. XXXVII, No. 1 (September, 1954), pp. 328–47.

Yadin, Yigael. The Scroll of the War of the Sons of Light against the Sons of Darkness. Ed. with an introduction, emendations, and a commentary. Jerusalem (Israel): The Bialik Institute, 1955.

Zeitlin, Solomon. "Hanukkah, Its Origin and Its Significance," *Jewish Quarterly Review*, new ser. XXIX (1938–1939), 1–36.

———— The History of the Second Jewish Commonwealth: Prolegomena. Philadelphia: Dropsie College, 1933.

———— Megillat Taanit as a Source for Jewish Chronology and History in the Hellenistic and Roman Periods. Philadelphia: Printed at the Oxford University Press, 1922.

———— See also under Tedesche, Sidney.

INDEX

ward, 18; true, 18, 19; chief city of, 19; nonbelligerent, imperial privileges to, 19; rebellious, of Palestine, defeat of, 19; of Asia and Africa, 19n; scriptures of, 19, 104n; apologist for, 20; led by pious men, 20; praiseworthy, pious, 21; revolt of, against Rome, 21; history of, in Greco-Roman period, 23; ancient history of, 24; national character of, in the Roman period, 25; of the Roman period, 26; victory of, over the Seleucids, 26; war of, against the Romans, 26, 29, 99; popular histories of, 37; seditiousness of, 40; nationalism of, 40, 41: patriotic, 41, 182-186; histories of, 43, 47; later, 43n, 148; mass revolt of, 48n; zealous, religious fanaticism of, 53, 54; persecution of, 54; Hellenizing, 56; Torah-loving, 58, 81; response of, 59, 60, 94, 113; willingness of, to die, 60; undaunted constancy of, 61; resistance of, 62 f.; laws of, 63; an apology for, 64; religion of, 64, 69; fanaticism of, 64, 79; tortures of, 65 f.; courageous, 68; great multitudes of, 68; three thousand, slaughtered, 68; father of, 69; leader of, 69; besieged, 69, 101, 102, 103, 104, 105, 106, 107, 110, 115, 118, 184; devoted, 70; extremist, 72; attitude of, 72; moderate, 72, 182; fighting on the Sabbath, 75; military weakness of, 76; zealous for the Torah, 77, 88, 123; confidence of, 79; passionate fighting of, 79; religious zeal of, 79; rushed to arms, 79; victory of, over Sennacherib, 79; in Babylon, 80; pious, 81, 82, 92, 96, 117, 181; piety of, 84; grieved, 89; national life of, 92; many ten thousand of, 94, 95; an appeal to, 101, 113; use of arms by, 102; in exile, 103; zealous, 108, 109, 11, 116, 119, 120, 126; abuse from, 110; motivated by religious beliefs, 115;

leaders of, 117; faithful, 117n; fanatical, 121; multitudes of, 123; literature of, 127; nationalistic, 129; in Palestine, 129 f., 132, 137, 142, 188; victories of, 130, 157; in Egypt, 137; in Jerusalem, 137; nation of, 137; annual observances of, 139; festivals of, 140, 142; historically minded, 144; religious meaning for, 150; Hellenized, 155; groups of, 171; religious literature of, 194; first-century, 195; King of, 197, 198, 199 —— war of the, 3; against Rome, 13, 14, 16, 55; origin of, 12; *Jew through the Centuries, The* (Willett), 29n
Joazar, high priest, 12
Johanan, high priest, 133
Johanan ben Zakkar, 128
John, 28n
John (book), 141; quoted, 118, 197
John of Gischala, 65
John the Baptist, 118n, 121n, 127, 187; movement of, 161; birth of, 172n; followers of, 172n
Jonathan, quoted, 179
Jordan, 163
Jordan, river, 117, 187
Josephus, 9n, 14, 17, 19, 34n, 35n, 82, 104n, 121, 122, 138, 139, 140, 150n; quoted, 3, 13, 14, 31, 49, 52 f., 53n, 55, 56 f., 58-60, 61, 62 f., 66, 68, 69 f., 71, 72, 75, 76, 78, 79, 88 ff., 93-95, 101 f., 103, 105-7, 110, 112 f., 114, 115, 117, 118, 123, 124n, 131, 149; account of the Judaeo-Seleucid war by, 4; care ⸌and industry of, 4; history of the Judaeo-Roman war, 4; references of, to Jesus Christ, 4 f.; works of, popular among Christians, 4; works of, 4, 5, 36, 114n; writings of, 4, 7n, 8, 9, 10, 11, 35, 60, 62-65, 86, 129, 142, 154; distortion by, 5; indiscriminate disparagement of, 5; lack of objectivity in, 5; modern criticism of the works of, 5; neglect of the works of, 5; nineteenth-century critics of, 5;

Stand, last-ditch, 110, 111-114
Standard Prayer Book, The, quoted, 132 f.
Stanley, Arthur Penrhyn, 27, 29, 34, 41; quoted, 28; *Lectures on the History of the Jewish Church,* 25n
Steinberg, A., 43n
Stowe, Calvin E., 24n
Strabo, 4n, 88n; the spontaneous evidence of, 39
Strack, Hermann L., *Introduction to the Talmud and Midrash,* 153n
Strife, civil, 21
Struggle, desperate, 112
Suicide, 69
Sulpicius Severus, 114n
Supplication, universal, 93
Support, popular, a wild and spontaneous manifestation of, 21
Surrender terms, 118
Swine, the flesh of, 36, 65
Swine's flesh, the enforced eating of, 54-56
Sword: the holy, 98, 99; use of, 150
Syria, 18n; a fiscal census of, 12; government of, 88; host of, 146
Syrian festival, 134n
Syrians, the 134n, 157; yoke of, 157
Syrian tongue, 148

Tabernacles, 138n; feast of, 136
Tacitus, writings of, 114n
Talmudic literature, 132
Tannaitic Rabbinical teachers, 127
Tarn, W. W., *Hellenic Civilization,* 51n, 55n; quoted, 10n
Tax collectors, 182
Teacher of Righteousness, 161, 170
"Teacher of Righteousness . . . , The" (Grieg), 170n
Tedesche, Sidney, 133n, 180n; *The First Book of the Maccabees,* 97n; quoted, 138n
Temple, the 84; in Jerusalem, 19; trophies from, 53; power of, 85; worship, 86; attitude toward, 87; defilement of, 87, 134n; money in, 88; desecrated, 88-93; treasury, 89; illegal entry and plundering

of, 90; destruction of, 91; inviolability of, 95; centrality of, 98, 124; courts of, 108; firing of, 111; fall of, 112; buildings, 114; set afire, 114; burns, while the, 114-16; rededication of, 133, 138; restoration of, 138; zealous for His, 150; defense of, 185
Temples, 58n
Tendenz, a problem of, 65
Thackery, H. St. John, 3n, 6n, 114n
Theaters, 58n
Theodicy, Deuteronomic, 9
Theological grounds, 20
Theology, 171; fundamental, 87; crude, 182; nationalistic, 190
Theudas, 117
Thomas, C., 34; *Geschichte des Alten Bundes,* 43n
Thucydides, 4n; speeches of, 100
Tiberias, 95; men of, 59
Tide of war, 112
Titus, 15, 17, 48, 53, 82, 90, 107, 108, 110, 113, 114, 116, 118, 184; quoted, 49; time of, 8, 59, 87, 105n; Arch of, 16; siege of Jerusalem by, 78; armies of, 91, 112; hailed as imperator, 115
Toleration, religious, 55
Toombs, Lawrence, 162n, 163n, 180n, 182n, 196n
Torah, the, 48, 49, 50, 52, 54, 69, 71, 84, 111, 120, 137, 139, 120n, 142n; quoted, 119; zeal for, 49, 51, 60, 68, 175; challenge to, 50; particularly of, 50; Scrolls, 52n, burning of, 52-54; a party zealous for, 56; loyalty to, 60, 62; willingness to fight and kill for, 60-65; defense of, 65; obedience to, 65, 68; willingness to suffer and die for, 65-68; institution of, 72; death struggle with the enemies of, 76; compromise, 76, 77; Jews zealous for, 77; preservation of, 77, 78; fighting on the sabbath and, 81; transgression of, 82; zealous for, 82; attitude toward, 83, 124; the power of, 85; and the temple, 85; supremacy of, 86, 92; na-

DATE DUE

FE 7'78			
FE13'79			
MR3 '80			
OC 19'82			
FE 6'84			
NOV 13 '84			
NO 27'84			
OCT F4 '86			

GAYLORD